OUT OF MIND

COGNITIVE APPROACHES TO CULTURE
Frederick Luis Aldama, Patrick Colm Hogan, Lalita
Pandit Hogan, and Sue J. Kim, Series Editors

OUT OF MIND

MODE, MEDIATION, AND COGNITION IN TWENTY-FIRST-CENTURY NARRATIVE

Torsa Ghosal

THE OHIO STATE UNIVERSITY PRESS
COLUMBUS

Copyright © 2021 by The Ohio State University.
All rights reserved.

Library of Congress Cataloging-in-Publication Data
Names: Ghosal, Torsa, author.
Title: Out of mind : mode, mediation, and cognition in twenty-first-century narrative / Torsa Ghosal.
Other titles: Cognitive approaches to culture.
Description: Columbus : The Ohio State University Press, [2021] | Series: Cognitive approaches to culture | Includes bibliographical references and index. | Summary: "Offers new readings of the works of Kamila Shamsie, Aleksandar Hemon, Mark Haddon, Lance Olsen, Steve Tomasula, Jonathan Safran Foer, and others to examine how twenty-first-century multimodal fiction both reflects historical beliefs about how minds work and participates in their reappraisal, offering insights into literary imagination's influence on how we think and perceive amid twenty-first-century social, technological, and environmental changes"—Provided by publisher.
Identifiers: LCCN 2021019821 | ISBN 9780814214824 (cloth) | ISBN 0814214827 (cloth) | ISBN 9780814281659 (ebook) | ISBN 0814281656 (ebook)
Subjects: LCSH: Modality (Linguistics) | Fiction—History and criticism—21st century. | Cognition in literature. | Semiotics and literature. | Fiction—Psychological aspects.
Classification: LCC P99.4.M6 G48 2021 | DDC 415/.6—dc23
LC record available at https://lccn.loc.gov/2021019821

Other identifiers: ISBN 9780814258101 (paperback) | ISBN 0814258107 (paperback)

Cover design by Alexa Love
Text design by Juliet Williams
Type set in Adobe Minion Pro

To my parents, Apurba and Kornika

CONTENTS

List of Illustrations   ix

Acknowledgments   xi

INTRODUCTION   Multimodality and Cognitive Literary Studies   1

CHAPTER 1   Typographic Minds: Cognitive Disabilities and Explanatory Pluralism   24

CHAPTER 2   Selfieing Minds: Picturing and Sharing Subjectivities   64

CHAPTER 3   Cartographic Minds: Spatial Thinking, Spatial Reading   106

CHAPTER 4   Anti-Archival Minds: Collecting, Deleting, and Scaling Memories   145

CODA   Binge Reading versus Picnoleptic Reading   182

Works Cited   197

Index   217

ILLUSTRATIONS

FIGURE 1.1	Christopher's perceptions at the London train station	41
FIGURE 1.2	An "idea-fish" surfacing on a page of *The Raw Shark Texts*	47
FIGURE 2.1	Digitally edited *Las Meninas* in *Book of Portraiture,* showing both Velazquez (extreme left) and the unnamed Japanese photographer (center) in place of the Infanta Margaret Theresa. Image courtesy Steve Tomasula.	74
FIGURE 2.2	Initial ToM framework (left), predictive processing (middle), enactive approaches (right)	79
FIGURE 2.3	Archival photo of Lazarus reproduced in *The Lazarus Project*. Original negative in Chicago History Museum.	81
FIGURE 2.4	Layout of a page from chapter 4 of *Book of Portraiture* showing a pixelated photo of U__ alongside generic instructions for selecting a model. Image courtesy Steve Tomasula.	96
FIGURE 2.5	Blurred photo illustrating Brik-Rora's experience of journeying through Eastern Europe	101
FIGURE 3.1	Caldeira's map within the print narrative of Straka's *Ship of Theseus*	125

FIGURE 3.2	Eric's and Jen's commentaries in the margins of *Ship of Theseus*	132
FIGURE 3.3	Map of Karachi that Karim draws on his way to the airport in 1987	135
FIGURE 3.4	The annotated map of Karachi that Karim sends Raheen from London in 1990	140–41
FIGURE 4.1	Opening page of *Woman's World*	157
FIGURE 4.2	Photograph of the *Spiral Jetty* enclosed within Alana's scrapbook. Image courtesy Lance Olsen.	175
FIGURE 4.3	Photograph of a bird enclosed within Alana's scrapbook. Image courtesy Lance Olsen.	179
FIGURE 5.1	*Tree of Codes* without a white sheet placed between pages (left). Reading *Tree of Codes* with a white sheet placed between pages (right).	190–91

ACKNOWLEDGMENTS

I owe much to friends, family, peers, and mentors who appear, if they appear at all in this book, in brackets, footnotes, and margins. This note is the aside where I get to step forward and admit that what is presented as my own thinking over the next several pages is but a result of my encounters with others. Yet, I must also acknowledge that I do not map the sites of my gratitude with any authority, for my mind changes in ways I do not always know. What follows is a provisional attempt at charting and ordering the numerous gifts of insight I have received.

This book's origin insofar as I can recognize it lies in a personal experience. I was an undergraduate student and a freelance feature writer in Calcutta. Just as the first decade of the twenty-first century was ending, the newspaper supplements for which I frequently wrote started to migrate from print to online platforms. With the shift in platforms, the desired length of articles and the nature of headlines changed. As my editors referred to the shortening attention span of readers while giving me more restrictive word counts, I wondered sometimes with annoyance, sometimes with fascination, what digital media were doing to our minds. Moreover, I became curious about the ways in which the new media culture would permanently transform the way we tell stories. It would be a few years before I got to systematically reflect on these issues. As I learned more about narrative form, media, and cognitive habits, my questions ramified and multiplied. Some of those questions and accompanying answers make up *Out of Mind*.

In the years I wrote this book, Brian McHale's sound critical thinking and his flair for expressing complex ideas with lucidity inspired me. Working with Brian, I learned to appreciate aesthetics and narrative, in new, meaningful ways. Frederick Luis Aldama's cognitive approaches to art and his commitment to community outreach model for me the ideal scholar-teacher-citizen. Jared Gardner's scholarship on films, comics, and electronic literature taught me to historicize media-objects. Jesse Schotter's enthusiasm for avant-garde writings, especially from the first half of the twentieth century, motivated me to develop a more contextually attuned understanding of my example texts. Jared's and Jesse's work push me to articulate what is new or different about the relationship of literature with other media in the twenty-first century. Danuta Fjellestad remained a supportive mentor throughout the process. Our conversations in Chicago and Uppsala have left a deep impression on my scholarship, and I learned a lot from our correspondences about multimodality.

Over the course of this book's composition, the meaning of home has changed for me more than once. Nandini Saha introduced me to contemporary experimental literature during my time in Jadavpur University, Calcutta, and paved the way for my continued interest in hybrid and genre-bending writing. Rimi Nandy, Sourya Chowdhury, and Arijit Das tolerated my exuberance about experimental literature when I was applying to graduate school and have remained steadfast friends despite my prolonged periods of absence from our shared hometown. After I moved to Columbus, the intellectual environment provided by The Ohio State University's Project Narrative—the affiliated faculty, students, and visiting researchers—allowed me to grow as a student of literature and media. David Herman introduced me to "postclassical" narrative theory. Jim Phelan and Robyn Warhol enriched my thinking about the social and cultural purposes of narratives. My friend Corey Efron remains an integral part of how this book came to be. Our exchanges about contemporary literature and films as well as the panels we collaboratively organized gave me the freedom to test nascent ideas and envision future possibilities. Conferences of the International Society for the Study of Narrative and Association for the Study of the Arts of the Present acquainted me with many scholars and friends whose brilliance I treasure.

At the California State University, Sacramento, where I am based at present, I thank my department head David Toise for building a culture of care and generosity; my friends Christine Montgomery and Rosa Martínez for helping me fine-tune portions of this book. Christy's and Rosa's text messages also sustained me as I finalized this manuscript during a period of social distancing. My senior colleagues, especially Nancy Sweet and Doug Rice, continue to advise me on how to balance research and writing with teaching and administrative responsibilities. I thank College of Arts and Letters' Scholarly and Creative Activity (SCA) and the university's Research and Creative Activity (RCA) awards for granting me the time and resources for completing this book.

Parts of *Out of Mind* were also written when I was away from whatever was 'home' to me at various points. The time I spent in the Literature and Media Innovation program of the University of Leuven, Belgium, with Jan Baetens as guide, and in the company of Laura Smith and Amelia Chu accounts for many ideas that found their way into this project. Studying "Genealogies of Memory and Perception" with Eduardo Cadava at the School of Criticism and Theory was illuminating. I met an extraordinary group of peers through SCT; Jill Frank and Emily Brennan Moran among them. Chapter 2 of this book reflects the understanding of photography I developed that summer in Ithaca in their company. During my research trip to Yale University's Robert B. Haas Family Arts Library and Beinecke Library, curator Molly Dotson was generous with her time. I was able to study *The Emblem of My Work,* the limited-edition catalogue in which artists respond to *Tristram Shandy*'s marbled page, discussed in *Out of Mind*'s introductory chapter, at the Beinecke. The artists' books to which I refer in chapter 4 (such as Tatana Kellner's *71125, Fifty Years of Silence: Eva Kellner's Story* (1992)) are housed in the Hass Family Arts Library.

I learn to be a more attentive reader of stories by not only insistently studying them but also writing them. Mentors, friends, and editors I have met through creative writing projects leave indelible marks on my critical thinking. Colleen Morrissey's voice in particular runs through my head every time I read and write stories.

This book is dedicated to my parents for being voracious readers, lovers of art, and skilled storytellers. Throughout my childhood, my mother read me stories that were not intended for children—I only recognize this in retrospect—and my father infused an appreciation for popular culture in me. For many years they also faithfully printed out and filed my features, fiction, and poems published across various online platforms to share with others, not trusting the internet to disseminate and archive my work. Now they have discovered the magic of WhatsApp forwards. Nonetheless, I concede that their effort of printing out was not as counterproductive as it initially seemed to me. Digital magazines and supplements turned out to be more ephemeral (for various economic and technological reasons) than I would have guessed.

In my family, my sister Trisha and my partner Rajat model open-mindedness for me. Their contributions to my research and writing are numerous. Trisha is an eager and thoughtful reader. I am astonished by her ability to see the same passage, the same moment, from multiple perspectives. Rajat cared for our home when I spent hours writing. He also listened with patience to me speak at length on subjects and stories unfamiliar to him.

The Ohio State University Press has been a delight to work with. Editor Kristen Elias Rowley's enthusiasm for my project and her suggestions helped shape this book. I am also very grateful to the peer reviewers of my manuscript for their insightful feedback.

Certain segments constituting chapter 1 appeared as "Shapes of Cognition in Typographical Fictions" in *Studies in the Novel* 51.2 (Johns Hopkins University Press); and an earlier version of my reading of *S.* presented in chapter 3 appeared as "At Hand—Handwriting as a Device for Spatial Orientation in J. J. Abrams and Doug Dorst's *S.*" in *Poetics Today* 40.2 (Duke University Press). I wish to thank the editors of these journals and the peer-reviewers of my articles. I am also thankful to authors Steve Tomasula and Lance Olsen for sharing page layouts from *Book of Portraiture* and *Theories of Forgetting* to reprint in *Out of Mind*.

I completed *Out of Mind* during the Covid-19 pandemic, when for several months the only way to encounter anyone was through digital screens. During this time, online access to books through university and public libraries allowed me to continue my research. I am indebted to the staff and editors at universities, university presses, and libraries who have worked (both during the pandemic and prior to it) to ensure the availability of humanities scholarship across platforms. Thank you!

INTRODUCTION

Multimodality and Cognitive Literary Studies

How do we think about thinking in the twenty-first century? How do narratives construct and mediate knowledge about cognition? What are the implications of the formal techniques authors use to represent cognition and mental pathologies in response to twenty-first-century social, technological, and environmental developments? *Out of Mind: Mode, Mediation, and Cognition in Twenty-First-Century Narrative* addresses these questions by analyzing contemporary British and American print fictions that combine a variety of semiotic modes (photographs, maps, different styles of inscription) to represent cognitive processes.

In order to produce knowledge about consciousness and cognition, philosophers and scientists have always relied on the latest modes and media: from Aristotle's "tabula rasa" and John Locke's "white paper" to Alan Turing's, John von Neumann's, and Jerry Fodor's versions of the "computational minds" there are numerous instances in which "mind" is modelled after what is "out[side] of mind" for heuristic purposes. Psychologist Douwe Draaisma observes that philosophical and psychological language describing memory has a "metaphorical cast" (2000, 3). Media technologies invented to store and reproduce information become the bases for generating novel models of memory. What Draaisma says about memory also rings true for other cognitive processes. Theories of cognition in general have a metaphorical cast. *Out of Mind* is concerned with literary narrative's engagement with this rich history and practice of analogical thinking about the mind. It maps how semiotic modes rendering characters' perception, comprehension, and memory in narratives are involved in the study of cognition across disciplines. While connecting cognitive-scientific and philosophical frameworks with the poetics of thought representation, this book reflects on the social, technological, and environmental conditions prompting widespread reappraisals of what it means to think in the twenty-first century.

The narratives examined in *Out of Mind* include Kamila Shamsie's *Kartography* (2002), Mark Haddon's *The Curious Incident of the Dog in the Night-Time* (2003), Graham Rawle's *Woman's World* (2005), Steve Tomasula's *The Book of Portraiture* (2006), Steven Hall's *The Raw Shark Texts* (2007), Aleksandar Hemon's *The Lazarus Project* (2008), Jonathan Safran Foer's *Tree of Codes* (2010), J. J. Abrams and Doug Dorst's *S.* (2013), and Lance Olsen's *Theories of Forgetting* (2014). These narratives were composed in an era dominated by classical computing, and the impact of computing technologies is palpable on their approaches to thought. Besides discussing this impact, *Out of Mind* considers how and why semiotic modes and media—including maps and pictures—that were troped on to interpret cognitive activities well before the emergence of classical computing come to be materially incorporated in them. That twenty-first-century narratives reproduce the modes and media in their material form rather than only allude to them through language is significant. The material presence of the dominant figures so frequently invoked in metaphors explicating thought defamiliarizes these figures, directing us—the readers—to recognize the technological and cultural forces behind widely accepted truisms about the mind. At the same time, literary narratives are not composed to simply communicate knowledge about cognition or convince readers of the validity of cognitive-scientific and philosophical theories, even when how minds work is a major thematic preoccupation of a narrative. Instead, narratives reframe extant and emerging knowledge in creative ways, incorporate and transform conventions of thought representation available in literary history, and playfully hint at unresolved issues and ideas. Without losing sight of the distinction in rhetorical goals of literary artifacts from scientific and philosophical disquisitions, *Out of Mind* charts the co-emergence of aesthetic and cognitive-scientific conceptualizations of normative and divergent thinking.

With its dual focus on innovations in cognitive models across disciplines and the aesthetic means of constructing thought in the same historical period, *Out of Mind* resists a recurring impulse in cognitive literary studies to treat narratives as data sets for inferring how we think in ahistorical and universalist ways. Contemporary cognitive literary criticism has embraced the idea that studying the narrative presentation of minds across historical periods can facilitate the understanding of how minds function in the actual world. David Herman's hypotheses related to how readers perceive represented entities and actions to configure "storyworlds" in their minds and Lisa Zunshine's argument that narratives train readers' cognitive faculties for social interactions in their actual world remain especially influential in this respect (Herman 2002; Zunshine 2006). Their studies depart from how narrative modes of presenting consciousness were understood in the structuralist vein, particularly by Dorrit Cohn (1978). Cohn emphasized the aesthetic complexities and conventions inherent in the presentation of thought in literary narratives and claimed that fictional presentations render characters' minds exceptionally transparent. However, as later narratologists became preoccupied with what seemed "universal," "objective," and "transferable" about consciousness represented in literature, issues of aesthetic complexity inherent in rendering consciousness became secondary to speculating about the nature of actual minds—the minds of readers—that engage with narratives.

For instance, Monika Fludernik (1996) delineates how we narrativize what we read based on our own experiences. She selects case-studies from various historical periods to show how the surface structures of texts rely on and reflect fundamental cognitive schemata. Although Fludernik adopts a diachronic and culturally situated perspective on narrative structures, she does not assume a similar stance in her remarks on cognition, experientiality, and interpretive frames. The mind of the reader constituted by the cognitive parameters imagined by Fludernik is decidedly universal.[1] Marco Caracciolo acknowledges that aesthetic experiences and non-literary narrative-driven experiences are not identical. Nevertheless, in *The Experientiality of Narrative*, he remains invested in pursuing the "structural similarity" between our interactions with the world and the experience of narratives since, he argues, "our engagement with fictional consciousnesses differs in degree, but not in kind, from our engagement with real ones" (Caracciolo 2014a, 51, 113). In extant cognitive literary criticism, I find a reflexive archive of how we—cognitive literary critics—think about thinking at present, influenced by theoreti-

---

1. Maria Mäkelä critiques the "interpretive default settings" attributed to the reader figure in Fludernik's *Toward a "Natural" Narratology* in particular and cognitive narratology in general (2018a, 273). Fludernik agrees with Mäkelä's assessment, observing that "Mäkelä is absolutely right to point out that the reader plays a central role in *TNN* and that this is a *synthetic* model (as she calls it) in which no empirically traceable reader is necessarily assumed," and Fludernik also concedes, "although as a literary scholar I am naturally interested in aesthetics, the research presented in *TNN is* not geared towards literary appreciation and the foregrounding of the aesthetic element in narrative texts" (2018, 336). See Christopher González (2017) for a reader construct within cognitive narratology that is not universalist and considers the material implications of the publishing market, among other factors (2017, 20–28).

cal positions in contemporary sciences of the mind. I consider the dialogue between literary criticism and contemporary sciences to be productive. However, current works in cognitive literary criticism, often implicitly or explicitly, convey the impression that the study of literary minds needs to share cognitive science's explanatory goals to be of value.[2] By contrast, I maintain that cognitive literary criticism can valuably exploit literary studies' long-standing interest in historical and cultural contingencies to reevaluate extradisciplinary debates about cognition. My book refers to prior scholarship in the field, including Caracciolo's enactive approach to narratives, especially where this approach illuminates psychological processes of fictional characters. At the same time, each chapter of *Out of Mind* takes aesthetic conventions of thought representation as points of departure, even when these conventional representations stray from the supposed shapes and functions of actual ones. I say supposed shapes and functions because, as my book stresses, it is not as if there is widespread consensus about every aspect of biological cognition in scientific and philosophical theories. Thus, instead of attempting to make sense of literary narratives through evolving cognitive-scientific frameworks, *Out of Mind* underlines that cognition, or contemporary knowledge of it at any rate, is dependent on historically and culturally contingent representational strategies.

Herman expresses the need to historicize knowledge about the mind in cognitive literary criticism, most notably in his introduction to *The Emergence of Mind* (2011), but the essays anthologized in the volume, including Herman's own essay,[3] do not hesitate to analyze consciousness representation in texts across historical periods using late twentieth- and early twenty-first-century cognitive theories. When the essays do not take recourse to contemporary cognitive-scientific frameworks, as Brian McHale points out, "the evidence of historical changes in consciousness is . . . adduced from the very same textual sources that are then explained *in terms of* those historical changes" (2012, 123). Some of these issues arise from positioning literature as straightforward reflection of "natural" evolutions in cognitive schema. However, as Maria Mäkelä notes, "the dialogic relation between the mental history of Western culture and the diachronies of literary form is—and has to be—a complex

---

2. Strong expressions of this idea come from David Herman. See for instance his claim that "narratology, like linguistics, can be recharacterized as a subdomain of cognitive-scientific research" in an essay titled "Narratology as Cognitive Science" (2000, n. pag.; also, see Herman 2002). Of course, not all cognitive literary critics agree with the precise terms of his thesis.

3. Herman's essay challenges "standard literary-historical accounts" that say that modernist poetics is directed "inwards." He shows how modernist minds subscribe to ecologically valid models of mind, such as those advanced by "postcognitivists" (the cognitive scientists I refer to as "second-generation" in *Out of Mind*) (2011, 264).

object of analysis, and it should not be reduced to a mere mirror relation" (2018b, 37). Instead of regarding the relationship of cognitive theories and methods with literary representations as one of reflection and imitation, it would be more productive to understand literary strategies and cognitive-scientific frameworks as *semiautonomously co-emerging*. What we mean by thought and the actions that we perceive as constituting thinking change over time. These changes become manifest in analogs and metaphors that co-emerge across domains of knowledge and aesthetic constructions. Concomitantly, various domains of knowledge and narrative structures also follow the logics of their own internal methods, biases, and histories. Literary criticism that factors in the logics of semiautonomous co-emergence when discussing narratives in relation to cognitive theories and heuristic models is still scant, and *Out of Mind* intends to fill the gap. Following sections of this introductory chapter identify the multiple players and factors involved in directing the course of convergences and divergences among cognitive models and aesthetic treatments of thought.

The aesthetic convention that serves as the springboard for *Out of Mind*'s exploration of cognition is the concurrence of semiotic modes or multimodality of twenty-first-century fictions. I reflect on the increasing use of multimodal features—typography, maps, pictures—for configuring characters' patterns of thinking and bring to the fore conceptualities issuant from the combining of particular semiotic modes. My book revisits the relations of cognitive sciences, media, and narrative previously traced by scholars such as Marie-Laure Ryan, N. Katherine Hayles, and David Ciccoricco, among others, in order to shed light on multimodal print literature. By drawing attention to the variegated shapes of consciousness represented in narratives, *Out of Mind* argues for the importance of recognizing imprecisions and inconsistencies in thinking about thought both in literature and in the sciences. It does so to question the enshrining of contingent explanatory models as "norms" that then become the basis for diagnosing and pathologizing seemingly divergent modes of thinking.

Why Multimodality?

My arguments in this book concentrate on narratives that use multimodal devices, because these both formally and thematically engage with the history of ideas around cognition. The publishing trajectory of such narratives offers insights into why they tend to combine a thematic interest in cognition with formal experiments in semiotic multiplicity. Historically, beliefs about readers' minds—the span of their attention, distraction, and memory—have played a part in guiding not only writers' but also publishers'[4] approaches to multimodality. For instance, when the London-based bookseller James Dodsley published the third volume of Laurence Sterne's novel *Tristram Shandy* in 1761, each copy of the book displayed a slightly different visual pattern on page 169. This was the multicolored marbled page, described by the narrator, Tristram as the "motley emblem of my work!" In order to achieve the desired texture, the central section of the page was manually daubed in marbled mixture and after the marbled impression dried on one side, the page was refolded for the other side to be impressed with the marbling. Every copy displayed a unique pattern. The potentially infinite variations were part of Sterne's design and as the curator of the Laurence Sterne Trust, Patrick Wildgust, observes, the page communicated "visually that his [Sterne's] work is endlessly variable, endlessly open to chance" (2013, n. pag.). However, as *Tristram Shandy* continued to be printed, black and white reproductions replaced the handmade multicolored page.[5] In the history of print literature, it is common to find multimodal features like illustrations and typographic idiosyncrasies present in the manuscript or the initial edition removed from later versions since whether these features engage or alienate readers remains a topic of contention.

Beatrice Warde, who was considered an expert on typography in the first half of the twentieth century, opined that "the most important thing about printing is that it conveys thoughts, ideas, images from one mind to other minds" (2009 [1930], 40). Its purpose is not the "delectation of senses" as "the mental eye focuses *through* type and not *upon* it" (2009 [1930], 41, 42). The American publisher Alfred Knopf would place a colophon on the last page of his books with information about the origin, name, and features of the type, but Knopf's friend and designer, William A. Dwiggins, considered the practice to be useless (see Gutjahar and Benton 2001, 1). Both Dwiggins and Warde advocated for concealing printed books' design features based on their beliefs about the experience of reading. Warde's observation that reading involves communication among minds rather than the gratification of senses is shared by many twentieth-century scholars of language and literature. Georges Poulet argues, along the lines of Warde, that reading causes actual objects around the reader to disappear and replaces them with "*congeries* of mental objects"

---

4. There is a distinction to be made between mainstream and smaller independent presses. Historically, smaller independent presses have been more open to idiosyncratic textual features. However, several narratives analyzed in *Out of Mind*, though not all, were published by bigger publishing houses such as the Penguin Group, Houghton Mifflin Harcourt, and so I speak of a broader cultural acceptance of multimodality in publishing.

5. For a detailed discussion of *Tristram Shandy*'s marbled page, see White (2005, 31–33).

(1969, 56). In literature, too, reading is sometimes represented as a transcendental experience,[6] which preserves the popular understanding of reading as a higher-order "mental" activity, distinguished from lower-order sensory perceptions.

John Bateman and Janina Wildfeuer (2014) observe that material aspects of literature are often undermined in popular and academic discussions because a conventional emphasis on the semantic content of language overrides concerns about the modes in which it is experienced. However, can any design feature be so thoroughly transparent as not to impact the readers' understanding of the language at all? The answer is "no" according to poet-typographer Robert Bringhurst, who remarks that typography—however simple—is always "an essential act of interpretation" (1996, 19). Long-standing debates about the sensory import of literary texts' design features have gained renewed urgency in the present-day media ecology wherein the transfer of a text from one set of modes and media to another is easily achieved.

In 2010, the London-based publishing house Visual Editions decided to celebrate *Tristram Shandy*'s visual features by designing and publishing it in a new format. Visual Editions' *Tristram Shandy* does not faithfully reproduce Sterne's multimodal aesthetic; rather, it reimagines the aesthetic. The new design recognizes that the experience of Sterne's novel was meant to be configured through readers' bodily and sensory contact with the text's material form. As the year 2011 marked the two-hundred-fiftieth anniversary of the publication of *Tristram Shandy*'s marbled page, the Laurence Sterne Trust invited several contemporary authors to create a multimodal page each that could stand as an "emblem" of their aesthetic. Graham Rawle, Susan Howe, Adam Thirlwell, Tom Phillips, and Robert Coover were among those who contributed to the project. Contemporary projects like these are informed by changing conditions of producing and disseminating literature, altering assumptions about what constitutes reading as an activity, along with broader shifts in the conceptualization of cognition.

The proliferation of digital platforms for designing, writing, and reading texts is a key impetus for forays in narrative multimodality. The multimodality of print narratives celebrates underutilized design possibilities afforded by the book as a media-platform. Mark Z. Danielewski's novel *House of Leaves* (2000), for instance, plays with layout and typography to remediate in book form the formal features associated with electronic storytelling, reminding us that footnotes are also "hyperlinks." Jonathan Safran Foer's *Tree of Codes*

---

6. Silverman (2012) explains that in nineteenth-century literature, reading books was associated with fantasies of communion.

(2010) proffers a more skeptical view of digital technologies than *House of Leaves*. Foer conveys his lack of enthusiasm for online reading by die-cutting pages of a twentieth-century book to compose a new narrative. *Tree of Codes* sheds light on how the material form of books impacts reading practices. Such experiments also prompt us—the readers—to recognize that the semiotic and medial composition of narratives influences our experience of them.

Contemporary multimodal narratives thus critically reflect on what is lost, gained, or transformed when a narrative comprises a particular set of semiotic modes and utilizes affordances of certain media platforms over others. For instance, J. J. Abrams and Doug Dorst's novel *S.* (2013) encloses objects such as letters and postcards within the printed book to construct a multilayered narrative, and a section of Steven Hall's novel *The Raw Shark Texts* (2007) unfolds like a flipbook in the print form. These features are sacrificed in the Audible audiobook and ebook formats. Danielewski has discussed how for the ebook edition of *Only Revolutions* (2006), he let go of the three-dimensionality of the bound book and reimagined the narrative in terms of a different structural metaphor (that of a two-lane highway) (Driscoll and Ven 2018). Similar to the print edition of *Only Revolutions,* Lance Olsen's *Theories of Forgetting* (2014) requires readers to turn the bound book 180 degrees to follow parallel narratives. *Theories* does not come in an ebook or audiobook format at all.

Narratives that do not rely on the plurality of semiotic systems and affordances of media-platforms unlike, say *S.* or *Raw Shark Texts,* can come across as "amodal": that is, similarly meaningful notwithstanding how they are experienced. Whether we read or hear these texts seems to be of no consequence. I am borrowing my usage of the term "amodal" from cognitive scientist Lawrence Barsalou. By amodal Barsalou means symbol systems whose "internal structures bear no correspondence to the perceptual states that produced them" (1999, 578). So, when I say that narratives can come across as amodal in the absence of semiotic plurality or interplay of media affordances, I mean that they can ostensibly support the assumption that our minds transduce texts into higher-order mental representations that do not rely on the specific sensory-motor systems involved in perception. By foregrounding the role of sensory channels and the body in reading at a formal (and often thematic) level, narratives with overt multimodal features challenge the very notion of amodality. They direct us to ask whether our experience of literature is ever *really* amodal. Or do affordances and constraints of perception shape comprehension of even those texts that seem transferable across modes and media without any loss in meaning? To what extent is meaning embodied and grounded in environmental conditions? Through their self-reflexive engagements with perceptual experiences, the multimodal design of contemporary narratives brings to the fore as well as challenges commonplace beliefs about cognition, which makes them especially suitable for my critical study.

My attention to print narratives is motivated by the understanding that considerable insight can be gained from focusing on how particular media platforms allow or restrict expression, in keeping with approaches such as platform studies developed by Nick Montfort and Ian Bogost (though Bogost and Montfort themselves maintain a focus on computational platforms and describe 'platform studies' as a family of approaches to digital media) (Bogost and Montfort 2009; Montfort and Bogost 2009). Since the narratives I discuss are interested in the idea of the book, my corpus overlaps with the texts Jessica Pressman (2009; 2020) identifies as literary instances of "bookishness" and that Alexander Starre (2015) understands as metamedial "book fictions," and Kiene Brillenburg Wurth, Kári Driscoll, along with Pressman (2018) examine to map the persistence and presence of books in the digital age. By delimiting my corpus, however, I am not trying to suggest that either the aesthetic treatment of thought or an interest in embodied, perceptual groundings of cognitive activities like reading are essentially tied to books. Electronic literature is also capable of generating the self-reflexive, metacognitive effects that are of interest to *Out of Mind*, albeit the aesthetic strategies for producing such effects may differ.

An ongoing interdisciplinary conversation about minds in the twenty-first century relates to attention becoming a scarce and fleeting resource. Artists and authors are constantly looking for ways to survive in the present "attention economy" (Bueno 2017).[7] Cognitive-scientific studies suggest that multimodal stimulation and feedback, at least in virtual environments, reduce an audience's response time and immerse them to a greater degree (see Cooper et al. 2018; Hecht, Reiner, and Halevy 2006). Even extremely simple digital texts combine multiple semiotic resources to elicit audience engagement. Such texts prepare readers for the fragmented and modular multimodal narratives in print. Ryan has observed that embodied interactivity is difficult to reconcile with narrativity, though narrativity or properties distinguishing narratives from non-narratives are in themselves challenging to categorize and continue to be debated (2015, 251). The present economy of attention, though, prompts us to ask whether it is possible to immerse readers in narratives without creating opportunities for interaction.[8]

---

7. See Bueno (2017) for discussion about the commodification of attention in the twenty-first century.

8. Though Ryan does not explicitly take up this question, she does pay attention to historically changing conditions and differences in conceptions of narrativity.

In the subsequent parts of this chapter I survey the theories—from multimodality studies, cognitive sciences, and philosophy of mind to cognitive literary criticism—that shape my research questions, direct my selection of research materials, and motivate this book's central claims.

Multimodality Studies

While some narratives analyzed in *Out of Mind,* such as Mark Haddon's *The Curious Incident of the Dog in the Night-Time,* have elicited critical responses for their multimodal representation of cognition, others like Kamila Shamsie's *Kartography* have not received attention for their multimodality. However, I maintain that any examination of the aesthetic treatment of thought in these narratives must begin with the semiotic multiplicity constituting their textual surface. Multimodality in fictions thematically concerned with the nature of thought paves the way for pondering whether thought is inherently multimodal. The possibility that cognition is multimodal at a fundamental level is explored in contemporary cognitive sciences, with some theories of grounded and situated cognition identifying multimodal simulations in the mind rather than amodal representations as constituting thinking (Barsalou 2020). It is thus crucial to examine the effects of semiotic multiplicity in the aesthetic depiction of cognition and, to do so, I draw upon insights from multimodality studies.

Multimodality studies examines how semiotic systems besides language enable meaning-making during communication. The notion of multimodality gained currency in the field of social semiotics, wherein Gunther Kress and Theo van Leeuwen observed that digital media have led to an exponential growth in communicative situations that involve more than one semiotic system; accordingly, they identified multimodality as an essential component of digital literacy (Kress 2010). By approaching the corpus of texts that I am analyzing in terms of their multimodality, I am also identifying the increasing use of digital technologies for writing, designing, and reading texts as a force behind their emergence.

Following Kress and van Leeuwen's account of multimodality in the late 1990s and the early 2000s, the notion became influential in a variety of fields, including rhetoric and composition studies, linguistics and stylistics, design, cognitive studies, and literary analysis. The concept's wide-ranging application has contributed to a lack of terminological clarity. For instance, Carey Jewitt identifies at least three different ways in which the term is used: "multimodal" can refer to theories of representation and communication, methods of analysis, or types of texts (2005; 2009).

Kress and van Leeuwen defined media as the material substrate or the "stuff" that supports communication and modes as regular, codified channels for configuring meaning. My use of the terms modes and media is built on this basic definition and distinction. Kress observed that a "multimodal approach to representation offers a choice of modes" (2010, 93). The definition of modes recalls an allied concept—that of the "sign." The key difference between mode and sign, however, arises from the fact that Kress and van Leeuwen are interested in not only the relationship between a signifier and a signified—the relationship that concerned Ferdinand Saussure—but also how an interpreter makes meaning from the given codes. Given the interpreter's dynamic role in communication, the relation between form and meaning is motivated rather than arbitrary, according to Kress and van Leeuwen. Kress observes, "The Saussurian account rules out individual action as a possible means for change" and argues that a "social account of meaning based on the significance of the agency of individuals is entirely at odds with a conception of arbitrary relation of form and meaning" (2010, 63).[9] The emphasis on agency rather than arbitrariness distinguishes modes from signs. It is worth pointing out here that though multimodal social communication (such as signage) indeed presents a choice of modes to the observer, multimodality in literature functions somewhat differently. Multimodal narratives do not always present a *choice* among multiple routes of communication to readers. Instead, they require readers to synthesize knowledge communicated through plural semiotic systems. In the narratives discussed in *Out of Mind,* multiple modes are instrumental rather than optional for the narrative's progression.

Beside Kress and van Leeuwen's definition of multimodality, Charles Forceville's study of multimodal metaphors also influences the uses and application of the concept in literary studies, and these two approaches are not entirely compatible. While most examples of multimodal communication that Kress analyzes involve more than one semiotic system, offering the interpreter more than one path for meaning-making, the metaphors Forceville considers "multimodal" appear in one perceptual domain while their targets remain in another domain of perception. Forceville builds his account from George P. Lakoff and Mark Johnson's (1980) theory of metaphors. For Forceville, as for Lakoff and Johnson, metaphors are structures of embod-

---

9. Kress and van Leeuwen find the figure of the interpreter in Charles Sanders Peirce's model of semiotics.

ied thought rather than signs, and are essentially multimodal since they are not created in language but expressed through language (or any other semiotic system) (Forceville 2009). Whereas Kress and van Leeuwen focus on semiotic multimodality, Forceville concentrates on perceptual multimodality. Semiotic multimodality results from the same text comprising more than one semiotic system, as is the case with graphic novels, whereas perceptual multimodality can be prompted by texts in which one semiotic system necessitates multiple sensory perceptions. Scholars writing about multimodality frequently combine these approaches (see Jewitt 2005, for instance). *Out of Mind,* too, remains responsive to the dynamics of both semiotic and perceptual multimodality.

An interest in conceptualizing the relationship of semiotic systems with perception and cognition runs through multimodality studies. Even Kress, who departs from Lakoff and Johnson's (and Forceville's) cognitive explanations of how sense is configured, preferring instead a social or constructivist understanding of semiosis, works with some fundamental assumptions about how the mind of the interpreter works and the plasticity of this mind (2010, 55). Similarly, in literary criticism, the framework of multimodality brings with it considerations about the kinds of minds and bodies texts are written for. In *New Perspectives on Narrative and Multimodality* (2009), Ruth Page suggests that readers understand narratives in embodied ways and so, multimodality can be an analytic framework that deciphers, examines, and decodes plural systems of choices presented by any literary text. She argues that "the distinct contribution of a multimodal analysis is to . . . reconceptualize all narrative communication as multimodal" (5). Alison Gibbons takes a more corpus-based approach to multimodality. Gibbons synthesizes several strands of commentary on multimodality, including those by Kress, van Leeuwen and Forceville, and combines these with cognitive stylistics and narratology to propound a model of cognitive poetics. Gibbons examines texts that functionalize one or more semiotic systems in order to activate more than one perception process as an essential component of narrative representation. Illustrated novels, for instance, contain both pictures and words, but Gibbons, and also other literary scholars such as Wolfgang Hallet, do not treat them as "multimodal literature" because the illustrations are neither part of the storyworld nor integrated into the narrative discourse (see Gibbons 2012b; Hallet 2009). Gibbons also constructs a corpus of "multimodal literature" that she observes "exists on a spectrum, from minimal to extensive in the level of incorporation of multimodality" (2012b, 420–21).

While both Page and Gibbons agree that multimodal communication orchestrates a range of perception processes and offers choices among semiotic systems, their approaches lead to different issues and outcomes. If all literature is multimodal, then there can be no distinct corpus of "multimodal literature." So, whereas the limitation of starting with a corpus is that it undermines the multimodal experiential potential of texts that ostensibly come across as amodal, the limitation of Page's more open approach is that it eschews the specific nature of experiences that result from the pointed juxtaposition or concurrence of semiotic modes in particular texts. My project is not committed to carving out a corpus of multimodal literature, though I examine texts that put together plural semiotic systems. The multimodal design of narratives by deviating from prevalent conventions of printing fulfills an expressive function. Overtly multimodal texts engage with the cognitive import of multimodality—for example, several of these narratives feature writer and reader figures juggling with a multimodal media ecology. The subjectivity of these characters is also produced via the assorted modes with which they engage. Even as I choose such texts, I accept Page's suggestion that the purpose of analyzing the multimodality of narratives is not to construct a corpus but to question the treatment of narrative as amodal.

Fiona Doloughan's *Contemporary Narrative: Textual Production, Multimodality and Multiliteracies* (2011) and Nina Nørgaard's *Multimodal Stylistics of the Novel: More Than Words* (2018) trace the impact of various social and technological developments on narrative forms. Nørgaard pays attention to the meaning-making functions of specific modal and material resources, such as typography and photographs. Nørgaard's isolation and treatment of specific multimodal features resonate with the structure of my book, though my project diverges in aim from hers. Whereas Nørgaard intends to "develop and explore a framework for stylistic analysis that incorporates multimodal semiosis," I am interested in the analogous portraits of minds multimodal devices develop (2018, 2).

The question guiding most of the pivotal work happening at the intersection of literary criticism and multimodality studies is how we—readers— infer meaning from multimodal textual design. The question that guides *Out of Mind* is how specific multimodal features succeed in evoking and modeling the idiosyncratic thought patterns of particular characters. In addition, my book explores how the multimodal configuration of characters' minds mediates beliefs and knowledge about how minds work in the twenty-first century.

Possible Minds

Social, technological, and environmental changes can activate novel ways of thinking and demand new theories of thought. The brain anatomy's capacity for change or plasticity at the neuronal level in response to various functional challenges was recognized in the twentieth century (see Zilles 1992). Possible changes include morphological alteration in brain areas and neuronal connectivity, generation of new neurons and other structural transformations (see Raisman 1969, Fuchs and Flügge 2014). Empirical research on attentional processes, memory, and social cognition, focusing on the impact of digital devices, suggests that "even simple interactions with the internet through the smartphone's touchscreen interface" can contribute to "sustained neurocognitive alterations due to neural changes in cortical regions associated with sensory and motor processing of the hand and thumb" (Firth et al. 2019). The digital media ecology[10] brings about behavioral changes—for instance, social media users frequently check these platforms to be rewarded with information and validation—that may lead to other functional alterations (see Small et al. 2009). The possibility of neurocognitive alterations so recognized need not be construed as an upgrade or loss by default. Changes in anatomy and behavior can simply be adaptive. But once we recognize cognitive faculties and resources to be adaptive, then it makes sense to accept that *what* we theorize as thinking as well as *how* we theorize thought also transform through social, technological, and environmental epochs.

The origins of contemporary cognitive-scientific theories can be traced to mid-twentieth-century cybernetics and computer sciences. The first-generation of cognitive sciences, popular until the 1980s, was dedicated to developing artificial intelligence. The guiding question of the field was "Can machines think?" and not "What is thought?" (see Turing 1950). The question later came to be interpreted as "Can machines do what we, as thinking systems, do?" (see Harnad 2009, 23–24).[11] Biological cognition thereby came

---

10. The concept of media ecology upholds the view that multiple media coexist, and the advent of new media does not mean that old media disappear. Older and newer media combine in different ways. Matthew Fuller observes that the term ecology "indicate[s] the massive and dynamic interrelation of processes and objects, beings and things, patterns and matter" (2005, 2). Also see Goddard (2014) and Ciccoricco (2015, 3–5) for elaborations on the concept and its implications for literary and media studies.

11. Harnad annotates Turing's paper and points out that "'think' will never be defined by Turing at all; it will be replaced by an operational definition to the effect that 'thinking is as thinking does.' This is fine, for thinking (cognition, intelligence) cannot be defined in advance of knowing how thinking systems do it, and we don't yet know how. But we do know that we thinkers do it, whatever it is, when we think; and we know when we are doing it (by

to both model and then be explained in terms of computation. Warren S. McCulloch and Walter H. Pitts (1990 [1943]) and Alan Turing (1950) lay down the central tenets for what has come to be known as the "computational theory of mind." John von Neumann, another influential figure in this intellectual history, argued that the biological brain has a *"prima facie* digital character" and compared the nervous system with logic gates (2000 [1958], 44). Von Neumann acknowledged that there are dissimilarities between his objects of comparison (i.e. natural and artificial intelligence) but maintained that computation proffers the most compelling explanation for brain functions. Jerry Fodor (1983) further expanded the computational model to explain cognitive processes as modular functions.

The computational model was subsequently refined and modified by its adopters. At a fundamental level, the model supposes that both natural and artificial intelligence convert inputs into symbols, then manipulate these abstract, arbitrary, amodal symbols following algorithmic rules, to produce desirable outputs. Even in its heyday, the model had its critics. Gerald Edelman rejected computationalism for its mind–body dualism, noting that it fails to account for the role of the body in cognition. Turning to William James's view of consciousness as a "process that emerges from interactions of the brain, the body, and the environment," Edelman explained experiences in terms of neuronal processes (2003, 5520). He argued that the brain is not a "computer" but a "selectional system" that generates and discriminates among neuronal circuits during experiences (1987, 56; 2003, 5521). John Searle (1992) questioned the cognitivist presupposition that if a machine carries out informational functions as human minds do, the machine can be said to be "thinking" or conscious in the same way. It is also worth mentioning here that even McCulloch, who (with Pitts) sought to define the logic of thought through a set of mathematical equations, did not abandon embodiment. He continued to look for the physiological substrate and anatomical configuration supporting the activity of his calculus of neurons.[12] In the twenty-first century, the computational model in its strongest form has relatively few champions given the growing recognition that it undermines issues of embodiment, perception, and action.

Alternatives to the computational model include "radical embodied cognition," which dismisses the idea that the brain requires intermediary symbols that are qualitatively and ontologically distinct from perceptual states to

---

introspection). So thinking, a form of consciousness, is already ostensibly defined, by just pointing to that experience we all have and know" (2009, 24).

12. See McCulloch (2016) for biological explanations and McCulloch's views on the embodiment of brain mechanisms.

process experiences (see Chemero 2009; Rowlands 2010). Francisco J. Varela, Eleanor Rosch, and Evan Thompson challenge the tendency of computationalist models to make rigid distinctions between higher-order (abstract reasoning) and lower-order (sensory) cognitive processes. While computationalist theories treat perception as an information processing problem, Varela, Rosch, and Thompson advance a pragmatic, action-oriented view of thinking. Their enactive framework intends to "determine the common principles or lawful linkages between sensory and motor systems that explain how action can be perceptually-guided in a perceiver-dependent world" (2016 [1991], 173). Philosopher Andy Clark treads the middle ground between theories of radical embodiment and computationalism. Clark's "extended mind" hypothesis does not completely get rid of the notion of internal mental representations (the idea that perceptions are symbolically encoded in the mind) found in computational models, but Clark argues that "explicit data storage and logical manipulation" are "at most, a secondary adjunct to the kinds of dynamics and complex response loops that couple real brain, bodies, and environments" (1998, 3). Mental representations, Clark maintains, constantly change based on a subject's history of interaction with the world. On the whole, embodied, embedded, enacted, and extended frameworks assume that cognitive tasks are distributed among agents and their environments, including technologies that constitute this environment. Therefore, natural and artificial intelligence need not replicate each other or perform the same functions. In place of replication, grounding and coupling figure prominently as metaphors for the dynamic relations among brain-body-world in more recent cognitive theories.

Changing approaches to cognition in the sciences and philosophy of mind also parallel those in the study of language. For instance, while Noam Chomsky proposed a syntactic theory to account for information-processing and language learning abilities, more contemporary linguists move away from the explanation of language and thought in terms of syntactic patterns. Lakoff and Johnson's theory of metaphors, to which I referred when discussing multimodality studies, explains linguistic cognition through mechanisms that are not specific to language comprehension. In keeping with embodied, embedded, enacted, and extended frameworks of cognition, recent research in linguistics also undermines the isolation of certain seemingly higher-order cognitive abilities from more global perceptual processes.

In its engagement with the sciences and philosophy of mind, my book attends to the intellectual history of cognitive models that resonate with the aesthetic treatment of thought in the multimodal narratives I study. Instead of borrowing tenets from the cognitive sciences to explain the successful construction of fictional minds, I show how contemporary authors configure fictional minds to stage myriad debates around cognition. In other words, *Out of Mind* is not going to demonstrate the validity of cognitive-scientific theories by finding their traces in narratives. Rather the book will illuminate how contemporary literary texts participate in speculations about how minds work. I adhere to the term "mind" throughout my book because it comes closer to connoting what the narratives represent. "Mind" and "brain" can have different meanings in cognitive sciences—computational approaches, for instance, maintain that the brain has the cognitive architecture of digital computers and the mind is what the brain computes. The narratives I discuss are not meditating on the neuronal architecture or brain anatomy of characters in the strictest sense, but evoking how characters think and feel about the world and themselves. The narratives' multimodal design calls attention to the involvement of multiple sensory channels in the experience of reading, and to that extent these narratives seem especially aligned with second-generation embodied, embedded, enacted, and extended approaches to cognition. My analyses thus lean more heavily on the second-generation theories.

To say that reading is embodied is not to simply reinforce the fact that we collect "data" through sensory channels from the narrative discourse, and then this data conjures higher-order representations elsewhere in the mind. Manuel Vega, Arthur M. Glenberg, and Arthur C. Graesser observe that our processing of symbols—such as language—can be said to be embodied if: "a) the meaning of the symbol to the agent depends on activity in systems used for perception, action, and emotion, and b) reasoning about meaning, including combinatorial processes of sentence understanding, requires use of those systems" (2008, 4). Thus, an embodied approach to reading would accept that it involves action, perception, and emotion. Evidence for the aesthetic experience's embodied nature comes from studies of mirror neurons. These neurons are known to be activated when a subject observes others performing an action or even when the subject encounters representations of such action through art.[13] The intensity of activation during vicarious experiences reflects (mirrors) the neuronal activation of the subject were she to participate in the action herself. These empirical studies offer insights into subjective perspective-taking, empathy, and intersubjectivity. However, despite confirming strong bodily and neural response to arts, the empirical studies in their current state are of limited use when studying aesthetic complexities. I do refer to some empirical studies in the following chapters, but, by and large, *Out of Mind* engages with theoretical positions.

---

13. See Iacoboni et al. (2005) for discussion of mirror neuron activation and Freedberg and Gallese (2007) for the impact of mirror neurons' discovery on the understanding of aesthetic experiences.

The cognitive-scientific debate between computational and more embodied approaches to thought that I sketched here in brief is developed at greater length in chapter 1. In the chapter, I study two multimodal novels to unravel the cultural implications of popularized ideas about cognition and mental pathologies. Chapters 2 and 3 are concerned with narratives that present the configuration of subjectivity as a process entangled with developments in technologies of self-representation (chapter 2) and intertwined with spatial cognition (chapter 3). In chapter 4, I discuss how depictions of amnesiac characters in multimodal narratives allude to as well as question storage-retrieval models of memory.

Emphasizing the conventionalized nature of fictional minds, Mäkelä has observed that in narratives "what we have is a set of possible worlds and possible minds that we cannot falsify (at least not without careful interpretation)—unlike in the real world, where we usually know a schizophrenic when we see one" (2006, 233). However, whether we "know a schizophrenic when we see one" in the actual world is debatable. What makes non-normative thinking legible are cognitive models and interpretive theories. These models and theories are plural, not always complementary, and also follow conventions.

While performing literary analysis, *Out of Mind* acknowledges the plurality of cognitive models and theories. This section's title "possible minds" invokes modal logic to suggest that beliefs, propositions, and findings about thought are grouped into tentative configurations during particular periods. The multiplicity of such configurations and unresolved debates around them results from the fact that many of these cognitive-scientific frameworks are neither entirely verifiable nor falsifiable. I am underscoring the hypothetical aspects of scientific models not to dismiss them or suggest that we dismiss the knowledge generated through them. My purpose is to contextualize the knowledge and stress that they manifest certain ideologies. Particular models help explain some aspects of thinking better than others and, as I will discuss in chapter 1, explanatory pluralism is now accepted as an essential feature of inquiry about complex phenomena in philosophy. *Out of Mind* aligns with such a philosophical position.

Cognitive Literary Criticism

The representation and construction of minds in narratives have long interested narratologists. The so-called "classical" studies in the field such as Cohn's *Transparent Minds: Narrative Modes of Presenting Consciousness in Fiction* (1978) and Ann Banfield's *Unspeakable Sentences: Narration and Representa-*

tion in the Language of Fiction (1982) take linguistic strategies of representation as their points of departure. These studies of consciousness representation precede the present "cognitive turn" in narratology. In the last three decades, scholars of narrative have increasingly turned to cognitive-scientific research to understand how stories engage readers as well as how readers engage with stories. "Cognitive narratology"—an umbrella term for the branch of postclassical narratology that draws upon contemporary sciences of the mind—has become an especially productive area of study. Fludernik, Herman, Zunshine, Caracciolo, Frederick Luis Aldama, and Alan Palmer, among many others, draw upon the cognitive sciences to explain the makings of fictional minds as well as how and why we—actual readers—engage with these minds.

Fludernik's *Towards a 'Natural' Narratology* (1996) argues that narratives can do without plot but not without human experience. Fludernik emphasizes embodiedness of the reading experience, suggesting that readers recuperate a text's semiotic structure in terms of their own experiences. Karin Kukkonen and Caracciolo identify her work as pioneering a "second generation" of cognitive literary studies, that they link to the "profound reorientation of thinking about the mind, the body, and their relationship to natural and cultural environments" in the cognitive sciences (2014, 268). Fludernik argued that "experientiality" is a dimension of narratives—she associates it with the presence of human protagonists in literary texts (1996, 30). In *The Experientiality of Narrative* (2014), Caracciolo revisits the concept of "experientiality" and contends that experientiality is not a property of narratives as such but is rather a dimension of reading, an outcome of readers' dynamic ways of responding to texts based on their past experiences. Caracciolo extrapolates from and creatively builds on enactive models of cognition to theorize readers' experientiality.

While Cohn treated characters' consciousnesses as the culmination of linguistic effects, contemporary cognitive narratologists often treat fictional minds as counterparts of human minds. However, H. Porter Abbott (2013) points out that literary texts can also configure "unreadable minds" to challenge readers in unique ways, resisting the practices readers may rely on in everyday social interactions. While readers may try to "naturalize" unreadable fictional minds by taking recourse to stereotypes, certain texts can defunctionalize such stereotyping. Moreover, Abbott argues for making the "ethical move" of accepting a specific character's "insistent unreadability," since "to penetrate the unknown can be hard to separate from the desire to appropriate and to tame—in effect, to spread knowability" (2013, 146). Knowability, Abbott recognizes, is akin to exercising power and can erase possibilities of differences. Abbott's argument serves as a caution against easily conflating fictional and actual minds. Like Abbott, Sue J. Kim (2013) also underscores the ideological, political, and ethical complexities that need to be considered while borrowing cognitive-scientific theories to study literature. Kim shows how cognitive psychology fails to account for the complexity of emotions like anger and outrage that can be collective, embodied, social, and phenomenological at once. Kim turns to cultural studies to offer correctives to the "clinical parameters" of cognitive studies of emotion, and her sustained engagement with cognitive psychology brings to the fore not only its insights but also its limitations (2013, 44). As I study the aesthetic treatment of thought and how such treatment mediates knowledge about cognition, I maintain that fictional minds can be relatively distinct and need not offer a holistic view of actual minds. This enables me to explore the inconsistent formulations of cognition as well as the plurality of analogs and metaphors rendering characters' minds in narratives.

Scholars working at the intersection of narrative, media, and cognitive theories, like Hayles, Ryan, and Ciccoricco, contemplate how shifting cultural and technological conditions impact thought and the aesthetic treatment of cognition in narratives. Hayles maintains that we think through and alongside media, and so humans have coevolved with technologies. Accordingly, she considers how experiments in contemporary print and electronic literature manifest cognitive and morphological changes in the brain. Ciccoricco similarly studies the presentation of thought across media and highlights how beliefs about cognition can be instrumentalized across media to configure complex aesthetic experiences. They seek to maintain a diachronic view of aesthetics and thinking that resonates with *Out of Mind*.

Overview of Chapters

Out of Mind strives to examine the dialogic relationships between semiotic multiplicity in twenty-first-century narratives and the plurality of scientific and philosophical models of mind. To that end, four critical chapters of the book concentrate on those works of contemporary Anglophone writers that treat the mind as their theme and at the same time employ multiple semiotic modes to represent thought.

Chapter 1, "Typographic Minds: Cognitive Disabilities and Explanatory Pluralism," considers how twenty-first-century narratives tackle early cognitive science's highly influential understanding of the mind as a digital computer. The chapter pays attention to narratives in which typographical designs significantly contribute to the representation of characters' thought processes.

Analyzing Mark Haddon's *The Curious Incident of the Dog in the Night-Time* (2003), I show that when fictions heavily lean on popular and scientific theories that equate biological cognition with computation, they also replicate early cognitive science's tendency of undermining the role of embodiment and perceptions in thinking. Haddon's novel models the mind of a character with cognitive differences (probably autism) after the information processing cycle of digital computers and corroborates the popular belief that autists are intelligent, as machines are, but lack "human" attributes, like empathy. However, *Curious Incident* also utilizes visual features of written language to portray the character's divergent—and seemingly abstract, formulaic—thinking. The novel's typography suggests the understanding that readers' sensory perceptions come into play when they read, and undercuts the conceptualization of cognitive functions, such as language comprehension, as amodal and disembodied to some degree.

Following my analysis of *Curious Incident*, I study Steven Hall's *The Raw Shark Texts* (2007). Here too typography remains instrumental in rendering thought, but rather than equating the protagonist's thinking with computation, Hall's novel plays with competing and contradictory explanations for how and why the protagonist lost his memories. In this light, I take *Raw Shark Texts* to be an instance of a literary narrative that refuses to commit to any one model of cognition. The narrative suggests that singular explanatory models are of limited value for understanding how minds work. My reflections on pluralism in *Raw Shark Texts* paves the way for examining the multiple analogs (besides computers) and semiotic modes used in twenty-first-century narratives to configure cognitive states.

Chapter 2, "Selfieing Minds: Picturing and Sharing Subjectivities," focuses on narratives that are concurrently interested in social cognition and the pictorial modeling of subjectivity in the sciences and philosophy of mind. Steve Tomasula's *The Book of Portraiture* (2006) and Aleksandar Hemon's *The Lazarus Project* (2008) incorporate pictures and trope on features of pictorial compositions to depict characters' emergent self-awareness during social interactions. The character narrator of *Lazarus Project* is an immigrant in post-9/11 America, a society swelling with xenophobic and anti-immigrant sentiments. He sets out to compose a multimodal, fictional narrative that dwells on the use of pictures in psychopathological studies at the turn of the twentieth century and braids this historical fiction with his own experiences of living in twenty-first-century Chicago. Tomasula's *Book of Portraiture* is more fragmented and historically expansive than Hemon's novel. *Book of Portraiture* is made up of five chapters, each featuring a distinct group of characters. The characters engage in self-representation in response to how they think others perceive them. While portraying his characters' attempts at self-representation, Tomasula charts the intersections of pictorial technologies and visual cultures with scientific accounts of subjectivity.

My analysis of the two novels delineates how they render subjectivation as an emergent and relational process, dependent on predictive and enactive connections with the world. *Lazarus Project* and *Book of Portraiture* challenge assumptions about the singularity and boundedness of the self. Whereas discussions about the interpersonal dimensions of selfhood in cognitive narratology typically turn to the "Theory of Mind," my study of *Lazarus Project* and *Book of Portraiture* shows that they destabilize the crude self–other distinctions on which Theory of Mind (with its notions such as "mindreading") hinges.

Chapter 3, "Cartographic Minds: Spatial Thinking, Spatial Reading" builds on the study of subjectivity representation in chapter 2. It concentrates on a pair of narratives—Kamila Shamsie's *Kartography* (2002) and J. J. Abrams and Doug Dorst's *S.* (2013)—that explore how our understanding of who we are integrates our experience of where we are. Shamsie, as well as Abrams and Dorst, plot their characters' sites of attention and their manners of interacting with their surroundings. Mapping operates at a conceptual level in both *Kartography* and *S.*, and serves to illustrate certain characters' ways of thinking about the world and themselves. The novels thus engage with notions like "cognitive map" and "mental mapping." Moreover, the artifactual maps included in them either elaborate on or challenge characters' "cognitive maps." The multiplicity of artifactual and cognitive maps overlaid in these narratives replicates for readers the compounding of spatial relations in digital ecologies.

In the depiction of mapping as a strategy characters use to find their bearings within their worlds, I find embedded the vital claim that readers, too, map textual topologies to orient themselves in relation to the represented objects and entities. By identifying mapping as an analog for how readers track their knowledge of storyworlds, *Kartography* and *S.*, I argue, prop up the spatial foundations of the reading experience and point to the complication of this experience in a media ecology where digital devices multiply the possible trajectories of attention and action.

Chapters 1–3 attend to the multifaceted relation of narrative strategies of consciousness representation and the cognitive-scientific culture that produces novel models to explain mental activities. Chapter 4, "Anti-Archival Minds: Collecting, Deleting, and Scaling Memories," focuses on the dismantling of an analogical relation in the intellectual history of cognitive theories. The model in question is that of the archive as an equivalent of memory. I consider alternatives to the archival model surfacing in two narratives—Graham Rawle's

Woman's World (2005) and Lance Olsen's *Theories of Forgetting* (2014)—that explore memory's limits through the construction and manipulation of personal media archives. Characters in Rawle's *Woman's World* and Olsen's *Theories of Forgetting* gather, extract, and piece together texts and images to record their experiences of the past and present. The space of the book that holds the appropriated and found content functions as an archive in its own right. Whereas commonsensical views and early cognitive-scientific theories associate archival or storage-and-retrieval mechanisms with biological memory, more recent research on false memory and imagination inflation question that association. These studies recognize memory as a process—constitutive of actions—instead of construing memory as data localized and deposited in some corner of the human brain. Rawle's and Olsen's narratives, I argue, participate in the questioning of the archival metaphor for memory. They offer a picture of the mind as "anti-archival" by highlighting the plasticity of both archives and biological memory.

I began this introduction by asking how we think about thinking in the twenty-first century. The book's coda, "Binge Reading versus Picnoleptic Reading," argues that our thoughts and beliefs about how we think cohere into theories of reading, and theories of reading are plural in the twenty-first century. At a time when we rapidly consume words, images, and other semiotic modes online every day, essays, studies, and thought pieces on reading abound. Many of these paint the contemporary reader's mind as distracted and tainted. In this context, I suggest that the narratives discussed in this book mediate the ideas and challenges we associate with reading in digital culture. The mishmash of semiotic systems constituting them exploit contemporary readers' media literacy, but the multimodal design can also impede readers' pace of consumption, forcing them to read slowly rather than binge. I use Jonathan Safran Foer's *Tree of Codes* (2010) to anchor my concluding remarks, identifying it as a narrative that stages the tension between binge reading and attentive perusal, between reading as forgetful consumption and reading as slow memory work.

In cognitive literary studies, major debates concern fictional minds' relation with actual minds. My position in that debate is founded on the group of narratives I analyze. As the following chapters will clarify, I maintain that narratives' configuration of characters' habits of mind nests and reflects assumptions about the minds that will read them, though the relation between actual and fictional minds cannot be reduced to a one-to-one correspondence. And even though fictional minds may not always illuminate how we—readers—actually think, the generic rise of multimodal strategies of thought representation is worth studying because these strategies archive sets of beliefs about cognition, how we think about thought, in the twenty-first century.

CHAPTER 1

Typographic Minds

Cognitive Disabilities and Explanatory Pluralism

"Our writing tools are also working on our thoughts," observed Friedrich Nietzsche after he used a typewriter in the 1880s, because his nearsightedness had made writing by hand for long stretches of time extremely strenuous (qtd. in Kittler 1999, 200). Unsatisfied with the machine, Nietzsche soon enlisted human aid to replace it. However, Martin Stingelin and Friedrich Kittler argue that Nietzsche's brief encounter with the typewriter transformed his writing as well as his philosophy of writing (Stingelin 1994; Kittler 1990). Their reflections on Nietzsche's relationship with the typewriter in the light of late twentieth-century media ecology drive home the idea that writing machines direct paradigms of thought. Kittler maintains that the interaction of computers—the contemporary mass medium of inscription—with our cognitive and sensory faculties cannot be explained from an anthropocentric point of view; rather it is imperative to consider how the technological media define "humans" (Kittler 2006). Indeed, the mid-twentieth-century information sciences and cybernetics, the bases for Kittler's "information-theoretical materialism," also spawned the first generation of cognitive science, in which technological media—computers in particular—served as analogical models for defining and understanding the human mind. The central claim of the first generation of cognitive scientists, who were strongly committed to developing artificial intelligence, was that the mind (or brain) is a computational device.

According to the computational model of cognition, the human mind converts lower-order sensory perceptions into higher-order abstract, arbitrary, and amodal (AAA) representations in order to "process" them. Thinking entails the manipulation of symbols (the AAA representations) following sets of rules and formal properties (see Fodor 1980, for example). The hypothesis about symbolic representations derives from the fact that though digital computers take multimodal inputs and produce multimodal outputs, the various semiotic modes (written language, numbers, sound, pictures), notwithstanding their differences and specificities, are all encoded as binary states during computation.[1] Thought is conflated with abstract information processing in this model of cognition, based on the assumption that when a computer program manages to simulate some functions of the brain, it is not performing a computational interpretation of mental processes but functioning *as* the "mind" itself. This supposition underlay Alan Turing's Turing Test as well as much of the early AI-research. When explaining biological cognition in terms of mechanical intelligence and arguing that the brain computes sensorimotor stimuli as symbolic representations, strong computationalist positions suggest that embodiment and grounding in broader environments are redundant for making sense of experiences or making meaning from language. In this way, computationalism keeps intact the mind–body dualism we come across in influential theories about thought since, at least, the time of René Descartes.

This chapter considers how the "computationalism" of early cognitive sciences and media theories affects the aesthetic treatment of thought in twenty-first-century literary narratives. I pay close attention to a subgroup of contemporary multimodal narratives in which typographical designs significantly impact the narrative's progression. Alison Gibbons has labelled this subgroup of multimodal literature "typographical fictions" (2012b). I turn to these narrative fictions to delineate how computing technologies inform thought representation in contemporary narratives because these texts not only draw on computational theories of the mind but also embrace the multimodal designing capacities of computers as writing interfaces. My argument is that the manner in which the proposition that the mind requires abstract, arbitrary, amodal representations for meaning-making has been absorbed in social and cultural spheres, as exemplified by thought representation in some of the typographical fictions, perpetuates stigmas about cognitive differences and disabilities. The description of cognition in computational terms proves incapable of accounting for potentially non-representational ways of sense-

---

1. With the advent of quantum computing though, present-day computation is no longer confined to binary states—quantum bits allow states to be superposed. All discussions of "computation" in this book, however, refer to classical computing.

making and leads to the pathologizing of divergent behavioral patterns. Analyzing Mark Haddon's novel, *The Curious Incident of the Dog in the Night-Time* (2003), I show that when fictions heavily draw on those popular and scientific theories that equate biological cognition with computation, they also replicate early cognitive science's tendency of undermining the role of embodiment and perceptions. Since the 1990s, a second generation of cognitive sciences has contested computationalism. Despite the emergence of these alternative explanatory frameworks though, computationalism continues to dominate our cultural imagination, and this dominance has far-reaching implications. *Curious Incident* has become the urtext among twenty-first-century autism narratives for its depiction of a child narrator who overcomes various odds to solve a "murder mystery" and reunite his parents (Murray 2008, 47).[2] Haddon models the thought processes of this character narrator with cognitive differences (probably autism) after the information processing cycles of digital computers; thereby, corroborating the popular notion that autists are intelligent (as computers are) but lack "human" attributes like empathy.

Following my analysis of Haddon's novel, I examine yet another instance of typographical fiction—Steven Hall's *The Raw Shark Texts* (2007). *Raw Shark Texts* blends elements of science fiction and experimental literature to chart the quest of a narrator who aspires to recover the memories he lost due to a traumatic experience. Hall, rather than structuring his character narrator's thought processes in terms of computation, presents competing and contradictory explanations for how and why the character lost his episodic memories. These competing hypotheses are articulated in the narrative—for instance, when the character narrator Eric compares his mind with a broken machine—but more often, the different cognitive models become manifested *as* other characters (Ludovician, Mycroft Ward et al.). Each character in Hall's novel is a speculative realization of some popular cognitive-scientific paradigm. Eric's cognition appears to be a sum of them all—not in the sense of being a "super-consciousness," but in the sense that Eric's amnesiac condition demands explanatory pluralism. No single paradigm can fully account for the nature and scope of his memory loss. Thus, *Raw Shark Texts* refuses to commit to any one model of cognition. It explores philosophical possibilities arising from the "mind is computer" hypothesis while also attending to the ways in which embodiment and materiality might configure thought. Through contradictions and hesitations, the narrative concedes that monolithic heuristic models may be of limited use for understanding how the mind works.

---

2. The bestselling novel has won several awards including the Whitbread Book Award, Commonwealth Writers' Prize, and was long listed for Man Booker. It has also been adapted to West End and Broadway shows.

N. Katherine Hayles and David Ciccoricco have considered the extent to which computing technologies influence thought representation in contemporary narratives across media. Both Hayles and Ciccoricco draw on second-generation cognitive sciences that refine or subvert the earlier computational models by suggesting that cognition is embodied, embedded, enacted, and extended. Second-generation research, spawning in neuroscience, psychology, philosophy, artificial intelligence, and linguistics, does not oppose the idea that technological media impact their users. However, these approaches developed across disciplines by researchers such as Patricia S. Churchland, Vilaynur S. Ramachandran, and Terrence Sejnowski (neuroscience), Lawrence Barsalou (psychology), George Lakoff and Mark Johnson (linguistics), and Andy Clark (philosophy of mind) argue against the reductive equation of mechanical and living beings. Instead of defining agents in terms of the machines they use or vice versa, the more recent theories suggest that cognition is embodied, grounded in agent–environment interactions, and action-based. In other words, while the first-generation approaches insist that the "mind is a computer," the second generation of sciences and philosophy of mind maintain that embodied subjects and computers interact, occasioning dynamic configurations but any one of these cannot be reduced to the other. Stronger formulations of the second-generation theses refute the need for symbolic representations in the mind altogether. For instance, Mark Rowlands observes that in non-Cartesian cognitive sciences, bodies, artifacts, and seemingly external processes do not simply scaffold the "brain," but that these "processes occurring in the environment—that is, outside the brain—can, in part, literally *constitute* cognitive processes" (2010, 22). These second-generation cognitive sciences provide the impetus for my critical position on computationalism in this chapter. However, the newer approaches are in themselves quite eclectic with several ongoing, unresolved debates among researchers. In fact, the existence of competing explanations for cognitive processes (and many other phenomena) accounts for the growing acceptance of "explanatory pluralism"[3] in the philosophy of sciences (see Dale et al. 2009; Mantzavinos 2016). Unitary models of explanation for complex phenomena tend to rely on simplification and methodological reduction. Such theoretical models account for only certain aspects of the phenomenon. Contrary to these epistemic frameworks, explanatory pluralism assumes that "*the best form and*

---

3. Mantzavinos (2016) observes that "explanatory games" rather than one way of "explication" may be the most productive approach to reconcile with the fact that explanatory activities often entail the distribution of labor across social spheres or (in the academic context) disciplines. Mantzavinos, thus, defends explanatory pluralism in place of unitary models of explanation in the sciences.

level of explanation depends on the kind of question one seeks to answer by the explanation and that one needs more than one form and level of explanation to answer all questions in the best way possible" (De Vreese et al. 2010, 372; emphasis original). In this light, I reflect on *Raw Shark Texts*' embracing of explanatory pluralism and contrast it with *Curious Incident,* after demonstrating the influence of the earlier epistemological model—that is, the computational theory of mind and computer metaphors—on the literary conventions shaping fictional minds.

While referring to tenets of computationalism (and also some of the second-generation theories), *Curious Incident* and *Raw Shark Texts* use experimental typography to materialize the character narrators' cognitive disabilities. In *Curious Incident,* these differences have to do with how the character narrator Christopher responds to sensory stimuli. He is not comfortable in the proximity of other people, especially strangers, and can even be hostile to the touch of his loved ones. His visual perceptions are also presented as disabling to some degree. He completes the tasks he sets out to perform—he travels alone from Swindon to London, brings his estranged parents closer to each other, solves a mystery around the murder of his neighbor's dog, and completes writing a book, but he has to distance himself from his immediate environmental surroundings to accomplish these tasks.[4] While the novel's experimental typography indicates to the reader that Christopher has a heightened sensory awareness of the environment around him, this augmented sensory interface is shown to prevent him from distilling meaningful information from the world. If Christopher cannot immediately make meaning from the different semiotic modes (like language, facial expressions, or touch), then his perception of these modes results in cognitive overload. It is this cognitive overload that Haddon's typographical variations, such as his use of bold face and Miscellaneous Symbols, signal. Finally, when Christopher's heightened sensory interface with his environment has landed him in crisis, Haddon has him devise unique programs, mustering the strength of his mind—the "central processing unit"—to resolve the crisis. Thus, meaning-making is presented as a higher-order process that requires Christopher to briefly withdraw into a hypothetical mind-space, distinguished from the multisensory stimuli-presenting environment in which his body is situated. The narrative discourse reinforces a hierarchic relation between mind and body, and this mind–body dualism can be traced to computationalism. At the same

---

4. While studying the writings and experiences of people with autism (not fictional characters), Silverman observes that their ability to privilege "sensate experience over sense making" can push us beyond meaning-fetishism (2016, 309). However, Haddon's novel is ill at ease with sensate experiences.

time, given that visual features of written language—the weight and face of type, font, layout, color—are of significance in the novel, the book also draws attention to how readers' verbal-pictorial sensory perceptions come into play and complicate the semantic field during reading. Thus, the typography manifests a contradiction. On the one hand, it facilitates the narrative presentation of thought as though it were a computational process and affirms the computational model's mind–body dualism. On the other hand, it calls attention to the multisensory nature of the reading experience, subverting to some extent the understanding of complex cognitive functions, including language comprehension, as disembodied and distanced from perceptual states.

As opposed to *Curious Incident,* Hall's *Raw Shark Texts* does not regard sensory interface with the material world as a problem for the protagonist Eric Sanderson to overcome. In fact, sensory perceptions and environmental grounding turn out to be vital for engendering Eric's sense of self and the recovery of his memories. Hall's typography demarcates multiple ontological levels constituting the narrative. These levels are supposed to vary in their material composition. The textual actual world—that is, the central "reality" the fiction projects—is saturated with objects, while abstract, arbitrary, amodal (AAA) representations dominate the textual alternate possible worlds, which are satellite worlds of the textual actual world. In possible worlds theory, which I am drawing on to discuss the layered ontology of Hall's fiction, textual alternate possible worlds can be thought of as alternate realities differing in status from the actual world. According to Nicholas Rescher (1979), the actual world has an autonomous existence whereas alternate possible worlds are outcomes of dreaming, imagination, storytelling, and so on. Fictions are "possible worlds" from the point of view of our world, but as Ryan (1991) argues, fictions project the textual actual world and reinscribe the distinction between actual and non-actual in their universe. Characters' hypothetical imaginings belong to the realm of the possible world within the textual universe. The actual and alternate possible worlds eventually bleed into one another in *Raw Shark Texts,* which becomes a source of crisis for the protagonist, Eric.[5] Eric has to position his body within networks of tangible media objects in order to temporarily stop the metalepsis—that is, the dissolution of actual and possible worlds. For instance, Eric surrounds himself with Dictaphones to prevent the attacks of a virus-like shark that preys on his memory. We can detect nostalgia for obsolete media objects in such scenes, and this nostalgia for older media also surfaces in other narratives this book discusses. However, Hall's

---

5. See Marie-Laure Ryan (1991) for additional discussion on textual actual and possible worlds.

treatment of Eric's condition also conforms to what Dwight Fee understands as late twentieth-century (and early twenty-first-century) discourses' "subtle but noticeable desire . . . to engage the complexity of human pathology in ways that recognize the contingency of psycho-scientific knowledge and its political, cultural, and technological embodiments" (2000, 2). *Raw Shark Texts* suggests that the materiality of technological platforms extend, anchor, and bolster Eric's embodied thinking. In Hayles's words, Hall's novel responds to the "growing power, pervasiveness, and *hiddenness* of databases" by exploring "what it would mean to transport (post)human subjectivity into a database, at the same time that it enacts the performative power of imaginative fiction conveyed through written language" (2011, 115). The hiddenness of databases engenders an apparent separation between content and form, which is analogous to the model of thought without a body evoked in *Curious Incident*. However, in *Raw Shark Texts,* it is the antagonists who are pure representations without bodies—one of them is even called "Nobody." The combination of materiality and embodiment—the interface of media and bodies—offer the sole promise of a happy ending to Hall's Eric.

Reverse engineering Haddon's and Hall's presentation of cognitive disabilities (autism and memory loss) allows us to study the dominant scientific and folk psychological assumptions about these conditions. Haddon's novel exerts a significant influence on popular culture and is frequently cited in academic studies of autism. Scholars in the field of cognitive narratology such as Lisa Zunshine, Elena Semino, and Marco Caracciolo, those in disability studies such as Stuart Murray and Ralph Savarese, and those interested in multimodality studies such as James Bucky Carter have analyzed Haddon's novel. Critical conversations about the novel across these fields make it ideally suited for an interdisciplinary study such as mine that not only connects cognitive literary criticism and multimodality studies but also reflects on how cognitive literary studies operates with those contested notions about cognitive norms and disabilities that Haddon's construction of a supposedly autist fictitious character brings to the forefront. *Raw Shark Texts*' debt to postmodernist fictions is more easily recognized[6] than its similarities with *Curious Incident.* This is perhaps because Haddon's novel is taken to be a

---

6. Haddon described Hall's novel as the "bastard love-child of *The Matrix, Jaws,* and *Da Vinci Code*" (Sweeney). Several narrators and characters from postmodernist fictions and films share the amnesiac condition of Hall's narrator. William Gibson's "Johnny Mnemonic" (1981) and Neal Stephenson's *Snow Crash* (1995) also dramatize memory retrieval and loss. In each case, the fiction betrays some degree of uneasiness about the status and function of the human mind within a digital media ecology. I return to the theme of amnesia in chapter 4 of this book.

mimetic portrayal of cognitive difference while *Raw Shark Texts*, with its use of techniques such as the mise-en-abyme and interior metalepsis, calls attention to its own synthetic nature (Phelan 2007) or "unnaturalness" (Alber et al. 2010). However, as I discuss, Haddon constructs his character narrator out of influential discourses about cognition, and formally, the novel employs typography to signal cognitive difference. In these respects, the novel is similar to *Raw Shark Texts*.

Constructing Cognitive Difference through Typography

To a greater or lesser degree, printed literature has always utilized the visual affordances of typography. It is easy to spot prose fictions that occasionally switch typographic weights, typefaces, or fonts. However, the group of texts that Gibbons labels "typographical fiction" and Brian McHale calls "concrete prose" move beyond the occasional use of bold face and italics to sketch icons or expressive designs out of typed letters (Gibbons 2012b; McHale 1987, 184–90). Alternately, these texts may also set up typographic systems where variations in the font, face, or weight of type significantly contribute to the narrative's progression.

The effect desired and achieved from manipulating typography frequently inflects these fictions' thematics. The origin of typographical literature does not coincide with the emergence of computers—novelists and poets have made idiosyncratic uses of typewriters as well. The distinctive feature of the typographical fictions produced in a culture dominated by computers is that the typographic design becomes frequently and conventionally associated with atypical consciousness. For instance, Johanna Drucker and Brad Freeman worked with the novel interfaces and applications of the time—Mac/Apple, Quark, and Adobe FreeHand—to produce *Otherspace: Martian Ty/opography* (1992), in which the typographic layout represented the emergence of an alien sentience. The sentience, identified as "Martian consciousness," reveals itself to the protagonist "Telepathic Jane" through the computer screen and printouts. In a similar vein, contemporary fictions with experimental typography often mediate the experiences of characters with perceptual or cognitive disabilities. Zampano, a narrator in Mark Z. Danielewski's typographical fiction, *House of Leaves* (2000), is blind. Danielewski's more recent series *The Familiar* (2015) follows Xanther, who sees alphabets "wiggle" and is epileptic, while Haddon's *Curious Incident* and Jonathan Safran Foer's *Extremely Loud and Incredibly Close* (2005) highlight the cognitive differences of child narrators who are diagnosed by literary critics and commentators as autistic,[7] and Hall's *Raw Shark Texts* features a narrator with dissociative fugue. This is not to say, however, that *all* contemporary typographical fictions are necessarily concerned with disabilities. Yet, there is a pattern whereby switches in typeface, font, or font color are associated with characters who have seemingly non-normative cognitive or perceptual faculties.[8]

In some respects, the convention of representing cognitive difference through typography seems especially counterintuitive in today's media ecology. After all, given that every computer-user (not just expert artists or designers) can manipulate layout and type with ease, using even the most ordinary of word processors, one would not expect typographic deviation to indicate cognitive difference. However, experimental typography has come to be an oft-used semiotic tool to flag atypical consciousness, perhaps because, as Jay Bolter observes, "the printed page has remained a conservative writing space . . . its letter forms stabilized between the 16th and 18th centuries and have since changed only a little" (1991, 65). So, when readers encounter expressive display fonts that contemporary writing interfaces easily afford as opposed to the standard book fonts, they might be able to "tell immediately that something was wrong" (1991, 65). The impulse to use experimental typography to represent some kind of atypicality is thus tied to the history of writing interfaces and printing.

That deviant typography in fictions produced within a digital media ecology frequently connotes *cognitive* difference specifically relates to computers being seen as "intelligent machines": computers are distinguished from earlier writing machines, such as typewriters, based on their ability to partake in cognitive tasks, like thinking and remembering. Early computers were developed not to replace typewriters—though they did that too—but to replace simpler calculators. Inventors such as Charles Babbage, Ada Lovelace, and Alan Turing, whose ideas led to the development of modern computers, turned to the mind as a prototype for outlining the functions that this machine accomplishes.[9] And then, taking this idea a step further, the first-generation cognitivists,

---

7. See Loftis (2015) for a comparative study of Foer's and Haddon's novels. I say "diagnosed" because the novels do not use the label of autism, but scholars (Semino 2014, Zunshine 2006) argue that the narrators are individuals with autism.

8. In a sense, these fictions realize the vision William Faulkner had when in an editorial piece he mentioned he would have liked to color-code the narrative of Benjy Compson—a character whose cognitive differences account for the fragmented style of his narration in *The Sound and The Fury* (1929). A limited-edition reprint of the novel in 2012 used fourteen colored typefaces in keeping with Faulkner's plan (Boyagoda 2012).

9. See Boden (2006) for an extensive history of the relations of cognitive sciences with theories of computation.

such as Fodor (1980), argued that since computers were modeled after the human mind, they could offer insights into mental processes, an argument which remains a foundational premise for computational models of the mind. As such, electronic text editors and word processors—both the early electronic machines called word processors and the later software applications—tend to be marketed as capable of participating in and inflecting the user's thoughts. For instance, a 1981 advertisement for a text editor called Mince boasted:

> Because our MINCE TEXT EDITOR gives you a full screen image of the text being edited... What you see on the screen is what you get. Period!
> ... Our SCRIBBLE FORMATTER lets you *think* in terms of the actual structure of the document . . . No longer will you have to worry about *remembering* margins, vertical spacing, etc . . . ("Advertisement" 1981, 123; italics mine)

"What you see is what you get," abbreviated to WYSIWYG, is the goal to which user-friendly computer interfaces aspire.[10] A complex, behind-the-screen process that involves the conversion of mechanical impact on the keyboard to electronic signals to illuminated pixels makes this capacity to see on screen what one is typing possible. To "*think* in terms of the actual structure of the document" includes the provision of letting the machine's working memory store the data—that is, "remember"—on the writer's behalf. As Hayles observes, "The more one works with digital technologies, the more one comes to appreciate the capacity of networked and programmable machines to carry out *sophisticated cognitive tasks,* and the more the keyboard comes to seem an *extension of one's thoughts rather than an external device on which one types*" (2012a, 3; emphasis added). Hence, typography becomes a visual analog for the nature of thought in fictions, and expressive display fonts come to signify atypical ways of thinking.

However, the visualization of cognitive differences through typography produces fictional texts that are "multimodal," necessitating that readers construe the narrative's meaning through a combination of verbal-pictorial perceptual channels. Literary narratives that use traditional typography can come across as amodal—that is, whether the narrative is read or heard may seem to be of no consequence for the reader's engagement with it, which is in keeping with the computationalist views of linguistic cognition as independent

---

10. Windows word processors have typically taken the WYSIWYG approach, assuring users what they see on screen while typing will correspond to the printed output. In practice this means that users do not need to mark up their text with commands and tags to determine the layout of the printed text.

of sensorimotor contact with the external world.[11] Contrary to the seeming amodality of traditional literature, then, typographical fictions, which explicitly require the interplay of the reader's senses, prompt readers to recognize the extent to which perceptual processes impact the experience of literature. In this way, even though typographical fictions such as *Curious Incident* and *Raw Shark Texts* align certain characters' minds with computing devices, their multimodal forms also throw light on the role of embodiment in reading and meaning-making.

Blueprint of the "Mind" in *The Curious Incident of the Dog in the Night-Time*

While introducing the claims of Simon Baron-Cohen's influential (and now controversial) monograph *Mindblindness: An Essay on Autism and Theory of Mind* (1995), John Tooby and Leda Cosmides explain, "our cognitive architecture resembles a confederation of hundreds or thousands of functionally dedicated computers (often called modules) designed to solve adaptive problems. . . . There is a 'theory of mind' module . . . and a multitude of other elegant machines" (xiii–xiv). Baron-Cohen distinguishes two kinds of people: the mindreaders (neurotypicals) and the mindblind (autists). Fundamental to this distinction is the idea that any sensory input leads to amodal, symbolic representations that either "naturally" or "artificially intelligent systems" can compute downstream (Baron-Cohen 1995, 85). The computational mind that Baron-Cohen outlines is also modular, in keeping with cognitive schemas advanced by other computationalists like Dan Sperber and Jerry Fodor: each module (i.e., the 'theory of mind' module) is informationally encapsulated and stands alone to some degree with limited access to information stored in other modules. The step-by-step description of cognitive processes is based on how information flows through computational systems. Mindreading in Baron-Cohen's terms is the ability to attribute mental states (such as intention) to the people with whom one interacts by, first, representing or encoding the sensory cues they offer, and then, decoding the representations. According to

---

11. Proponents of computationalism maintain that we understand word meanings by statistically considering properties of the family of other words that accompany them independent of perceptual experiences, environmental contexts, or surroundings. Meaning-making is not fully grounded in experience. Scientists and philosophers who take an "embodied" view of language contest this idea and many of them discard the hypothesis about symbolic representations. Taking into account recent empirical studies, Buccino et al. (2016) argue that language comprehension activates the same sensorimotor systems that would be involved in the experiences to which the words refer (also see Harnad 1990).

Baron-Cohen, autists (the "mindblind") have "Theory of Mind" deficit, which means that when they encounter other people and visually perceive others' body language, they fail to come up with appropriate mental representations and are, in turn, unable to deduce mental states. By suggesting that autists cannot make sense of what they perceive under particular circumstances, Baron-Cohen's notion of mindblindness sets up barriers between perception and comprehension, as though the former and the latter modules exist independent of each other. Baron-Cohen's sweeping claim, "It is probably impossible to imagine what it is to be mindblind, in the same way as it is impossible to imagine what it is to be a bat," misappropriates philosopher Thomas Nagel's anti-reductionist and therefore anti-computational stance on consciousness to dehumanize autists and accord them the status of separate organisms (Baron-Cohen 1995, 4; Nagel 1974). Following this logic, *Curious Incident* is celebrated as a feat of a mindreader's imagination. Oliver Sacks, for instance, commends Haddon for showing "great insight into the autistic mind" (hardcover edition's jacket).

Haddon's novel is framed as a narrative that Christopher Boone, a fifteen-year-old boy, is composing about his own experiences and, like Sacks, scholars such as Elena Semino, James Bucky Carter, Vivienne Muller, and Lisa Zunshine take Christopher to be autistic. His narration is supposed to offer neurotypical readers an entry into the world of someone who has difficulty "reading" other people's minds. Zunshine, who argues that mindreading is one of the reasons why we read fiction, observes that Christopher is mindblind as he has difficulty imagining things that did not happen to him (read "proper novels"),[12] and that the narrative he is writing "is mostly lacking in attribution of thoughts, feelings, and attitudes to its protagonists (we, the readers, supply those missing mental states)" (2006, 12).[13] In other words, according to Zunshine, it is not the mindblind Christopher who makes sense of what he encounters when he goes about his "detection," after he stumbles on the corpse of a dog one night, but "we," the presumably neurotypical readers, the mindreaders, who do so.

By differentiating the mindreaders from the mindblind, Baron-Cohen's theory perpetuates the stigma against autistic people. Melanie Yergeau observes that the acceptance of the Theory of Mind in disciplines from cognitive studies to narratology has contributed to the "dis*enmind*ment" of people with autism

---

12. In *Curious Incident*, Christopher reads Arthur Conan Doyle's novels but distinguishes those from "proper novels" like Virginia Woolf's.

13. Zunshine has since revised her position about the 'lack' of Theory of Mind. In a later article she notes that the failure in empathic imagination can be the neurotypical observers,' rather than the autists' (Savarese and Zunshine 2014).

(2013, n. pag.). I discuss Baron-Cohen's Theory of Mind and "mindblindess" here not to consolidate an ableist power dynamic, but rather to establish how Haddon's novel's portrayal of cognitive difference is in dialog with contemporary cognitive-scientific formulations. Accordingly, the critiques to which the narrative representation can be subjected also apply to those formulations and their ideologies.

Christopher Boone's Theories of Mind

Haddon maintains that he set out to write a novel about cognitive differences, not about autistic cognition (Haddon 2009, n. pag.). In fact, *Curious Incident* never mentions the condition. However, the novel plants clues to invite reflections on autism. While the ensuing portrayal of Christopher is empathetic to an extent, it does little to dispel stereotypes about autism; at its best, the novel stipulates that readers relate to Christopher despite his limitations.[14]

The novel opens with Christopher describing the corpse of a dog. He speculates about the scenario that led to the dog's murder: "There was a garden fork sticking out of the dog . . . *I decided* that the dog was probably killed with the fork because I could not see any other wounds in the dog and *I do not think you* would stick a garden fork into a dog after it had died for some other reason" (1; italics mine). This opening paragraph demonstrates Christopher's grasp of intentionality: he has an understanding of his own mind when he says, "I decided" and "I do not think"; further, he is able to speculate about other people's intentions when he reasons that no one would stick a garden fork into an already dead animal. The second person pronoun "you" assumes an audience and attributes intention to this mind. In other words, at the outset, Haddon constructs Christopher as a narrator who is self-aware and socially perceptive.

However, in the subsequent sections, Christopher remarks that he has difficulty communicating with people as he cannot decode their facial expressions. He mentions that with the help of his teacher Siobhan he has drawn and labelled faces, classifying them according to the emotions they signify, to train himself for social communication. We are presented with some of these pictorial icons, resembling emoticons, to illustrate his adaptive strategy. It is not as if Christopher does not visually perceive the differences in people's

---

14. Savarese observes that Haddon's novel reinforces the claim that "autists don't experience empathy" (Savarese and Zunshine 2014, 19). Murray, however, argues that notwithstanding Haddon's use of clichés about autism, the novel normalizes the disability and includes "an idea of pleasure" (2008, 49).

facial expressions—in fact, Christopher says he sees more than most people do. Rather Christopher thinks that he cannot satisfactorily encode and decode what he sees without a formula (the labelled pictorial icons) in place.

While Christopher asserts that he is more adept at mathematical reasoning than understanding visual or somatic cues, he seems to be using both the linguistic and pictorial modalities with equal ease while communicating with his readers. His narrative—the book he is supposedly writing—is replete with different kinds of images and typographic designs. Although many of these typographic designs and images are included to illustrate the difficulty they present for Christopher, Carter concludes that their very presence in the book contests the stigma around autists' problems with social communication. Carter reasons that "if we suspend our disbelief, we see that in and of itself the existence of said book and our reading of it means that Christopher is a rather skilled communicator . . ." (2007, n. pag.). Such a reading seeks to distinguish what Christopher as narrator says about himself from how Haddon portrays him, and I take this to be a productive distinction. At the same time, the assertion that the aesthetic choice of repeatedly emphasizing the character narrator's struggle in ways that are in line with stereotypical understandings of a cognitive disability are the character narrator's and do not reflect the narrative's attitude to the disability does not quite hold up to scrutiny, as I will show while examining the mindstyle Haddon develops for Christopher in the following section. For now, returning to the narrative's opening, we note that Christopher does what he claims to be difficult for him at the outset: attributing intentions to others. This is typical of *Curious Incident*. Christopher also says he has difficulty decoding metaphors, but, nonetheless, his first-person narrative uses metaphors, the most notable of them being the mind-is-computer metaphor.

What Christopher says about himself draws upon theories of mindreading and mindblindness. Early on in the narrative, he remarks, "I sometimes think of my mind as a machine . . ." (7). At this stage, he does not explain what kind of a machine his mind is. However, in a later section, he says, "When sometimes I am in a new place and there are lots of people there it is like a computer crashing and I have to close my eyes and put my hands over my ears and groan, which is like pressing CTRL + ALT + DEL and shutting down programs and turning the computer off and rebooting . . ." (143–44). Evidently, Christopher is making sense of his cognitive processes in terms of computation. This closely parallels the manner in which Oskar, the narrator in Foer's multimodal fiction, *Extremely Loud and Incredibly Close*, explains his cognitive processes to a stranger: "He asked me why I was talking like that. I told him, 'Oskar's CPU is a neural-net processor. A learning computer . . .'" (2005,

4–5). Both Haddon's and Foer's narrators' observations are in keeping with the present-day tendency of likening high-functioning autism to artificial intelligence. Majia Holmer Nadesan observes that individuals with extraordinary expertise in technology are often psychopathologized as autists, and people who are diagnosed as autists are often celebrated for their skills in science and technology. The result is that "although the [early] cognitive framework actually applies a computational model of cognition to all people, its application appears (on the surface) most strikingly appropriate for people with either high-functioning autism and/or who exhibit technical/scientific expertise, or both" (Nadesan 2005, 131). Autist savants are a popular character type in narratives across media: *Rain Man*'s Raymond (1988), *Big Bang Theory*'s Sheldon Cooper (2007–2019), and Sherlock in *Sherlock* (2010–2017) are some examples. Equating autistic minds with artificial intelligence undermines the materiality of machines, the embodiment of living beings, and the potential for complex assemblages among these entities.

Christopher's interaction with his personal computer is mentioned only a few times in the novel, when he plays *Minesweeper* and *The 11th Hour* on it. The most sustained discussion of computing technologies actually occurs when Christopher sums up what he has learned from the television show, *How the Mind Works*, named after cognitive scientist Steven Pinker's 1997 book. Pinker has been a proponent of computationalism and, following Pinker, Christopher concludes that the mind is "like computers," "just a complicated machine" (116). He elucidates:

> And when we look at things we think we're just looking out of our eyes like we're looking out of little windows and there's a person inside our head, but we're not. We're looking at a screen inside our heads, like a computer screen. (116)

The theory to which Christopher alludes says that embodied subjects simulate sensory stimuli on a mindscreen for the cortical homunculus (or a "little man" located in the brain) in order to read and process them. Cognitive scientist Daniel Dennett has critiqued this theory for promoting mind–body dualism, a "Cartesian Theater" (1991, 101–38). In the novel, Christopher also notes that this theory contributes to a model of infinite regress. He writes, "This homunculus is just another picture on the screen . . . And when the homunculus is on the screen . . . there is another bit of the brain watching the screen" (118). If sensory perceptions need to be represented or encoded for an area of the brain-within-the-brain to process, then this representation would further need to be meta-represented and so on. Despite posing questions about the homunculus model, however, Christopher continues to refer to the "computer screen" as an analog for his mind-space. While attempting to explain the continuity of visual perceptions, he observes that "you don't notice that you're blind during saccades because your brain fills in the screen in your head" (117). Subsequently, he argues that people's ability to mentally represent things they are not looking at in the moment distinguishes them from animals—these mental representations are the sources of imagination and reasoning. This proposition further reinforces the hierarchy between body and mind by privileging amodal representations over embodied perceptions. The persistence of the mindscreen and computer metaphors in Christopher's narration recalls theories that diagnose people who supposedly do not simulate accurate mental states as mindblind and position them as vastly inferior subjects to those who can. When the notion of mindblindness constructs autists as deficient compared to neurotypicals based on conjuring mental representations, the sentience of their bodies and sensory modes of meaning-making are undermined. In using computational analogies and privileging mental representations over sense perceptions, the depiction of Christopher conforms to the body of knowledge that discriminates against those who seem to be like him in the actual world.

Of course, Christopher is a fictional character. So, the contradictions and problems in his musings are worth noting not because they poorly explain minds in the actual world, but because, in bits and pieces, they betray assumptions integral to computational explanations of biological cognition. These assumptions critically inform the narrative's use of multimodal features, as I discuss in the next section. Reflecting on why computationalism became an ideology in the early cognitive sciences, John Searle remarks, "We wanted to know if there was not some sense in which brains were intrinsically digital computers in a way that green leaves intrinsically perform photosynthesis or hearts intrinsically pump blood. It is not a matter of us arbitrarily or 'conventionally' assigning the word 'pump' to hearts or 'photosynthesis' to leaves" (1992, 208–9). However, as second-generation cognitive theories with their emphasis on pragmatic couplings of agents and environments persuasively argue, brains are not intrinsically digital computers. Fodor, who used computational models himself and popularized the modularity of mind, criticized Pinker's widely popular and reductive *How the Mind Works* (see Fodor 2001). At the same time, the repudiation of computationalism in specialized branches of scientific and philosophical discourses has not lessened the fascination with it in a digital media ecology. *Curious Incident,* a popular twenty-first-century fiction, partakes in building up this fascination by suggesting a fundamental connection between computation and autistic cognition.

It perpetuates the belief that people with autism are akin to "computing machines," intelligent and adaptive but lacking in social skills and empathy.

Multimodal Mindstyle

Notwithstanding the prevalence of computer metaphors in how Christopher theorizes his own mind, the narrative never indicates that he is using the machine to compose his murder mystery novel. In the storyworld, his manuscript is handwritten, but *Curious Incident* uses typography that is quite specific to writing on a digital device. The typography engenders a tension in the novel because the resulting multimodal design of the text is meant, paradoxically, to illustrate Christopher's problems with multimodality. For instance, when Christopher explains what it feels like to be bombarded by a multitude of perceptual stimuli—a host of brand logos at the London train station—we are shown a block of characters that recall Unicode and ASCII art (170). Unicode allows for the combination and manipulation of alphanumeric and special characters in ways that can be used to obfuscate the semantic content of the visible signage, and this affordance helps simulate the dizzying effect the London station has on Christopher (see Figure 1.1). Haddon's schematic presentation of how the brand logos at the station actually look and how they begin to appear to Christopher demonstrates the flow of information through Christopher's modular mind: he sees the logos and attempts to mentally represent them for his brain-computer to make meaning downstream, but the representations go awry, blocking the process altogether. Stranded at the station with no help from the higher-order meaning-making modules of the mind, Christopher must shut his eyes and slowly count to fifty to stop the in-flow of impenetrable verbal-pictorial designs. As per the novel's premise, it is Christopher who successfully represents this crisis in the book for his readers to understand it—he even prefaces the illustration of the Miscellaneous Symbols with the phrase "they looked like this" to signal that he has created them (169). This is similar to other instances when Christopher presents maps and diagrams to demonstrate how he navigates his world, although there also are visual designs and typographic manipulations in the novel that are not attributable to him. Christopher's supposed agency in illustrating crises and his readiness to share the algorithmic rule sets he uses to navigate the world reinforce rather than dissolve the power dynamic between him and his neurotypical readers, who can make sense of the multimodal designs that put a strain on him in ways he cannot.

Sweet Pastries **Heathrow Airport Check-In Here** *Bagel Factory* EAT excellence and taste **YO!** sushi Stationlink Buses W H Smith MEZZANINE Heathrow Express Clinique First Class Lounge Fuller's London Pride Dixons Our Price Paddington Bear at Paddington Station Tickets Taxis ♀ ♂ Toilets First Aid Eastbourne Terrace ████████ington Way Out Praed Street The Lawn Q Here Please Upper Crust Sainsbury's Local ⓘInformation GREAT WESTERN FIRST ⓟ Position Closed Position Closed Position Closed Sock Shop Fast Ticket Point ⓢ Millie's Cookies Coffee AIRLINERS COLLIDE OVER INDONESIA: 350 FEARED DEAD Freshly Baked Cookies and Muffins Cold Drinks Penalty Fares Warning Savoury Pastries Platforms 9-14 Burger King Fresh Filled! the reef° café bar **business travel special edition** TOP 75 ALBUMS Evening Standard	Sweathr♀♂■ow☺ⒸAirpheckla*glory*EAenceandtaste**YO!**suusetHee sortCWHSmithEANE**N**Stat_{nH}✱ioead*Bho*athrnieFirlassLoULERnreHe BSeasyCar.com*TheM*p*a*nardBe_{sttf}Fu_Ller'sLonPr^{nde}idePaiesstrDzzix onsOuri*sP*PurdEboi▣▵*a*ceicHousP_{u⓪}©_{η⓪}neawatPoagtonTetsTa*d* Fac♂ToileddistsFirs←⦵·ta⚥B^{UNG}feFi5us✘✳HPDNLeTerrace█▪Ⓗ██ ingtonW♀astaySt◎atio✏■nlinkOutC⨁losed?&qed3iniBr1uow o[CliPraicxiskeIDdPointDrS⬛treetTheLyuawHea⦵■rCrustMufly B⬜aki6dE♀TonClose^H*♭*excelle^{to xpr}essnQinrePlek4shSaisesUp① ← ▲pensburiy'sLcidSo^{hl·T}◎_i*f*_{rm}ationREAT**M**➕✚ASTERCoINEokie sWESTEfinsCojRN2FningSTan1⓪RSTⓅP0allnforositioNCH✕⬘ⓧE nSTAYATS3hopFast⊙⊶Positd█Penie→♫sPloNIa8⓪▪④⊋✦tfoe9 sWef°cusCoffReosv_{eled}posi▢tnesskix①⓪edco resho*j*⊛〉ⓒ⓪5AL_{Bial edM⧈}iaf*ebarbee*an*CrKl*'geing☉F3illeFFTOUr⚥mEGIEs9TEDFrese ✱0█s*analty*FarmingSa⦵vou^{ry⦿a}stri14Burzd!the**℘**❺•resit✱⦿rh█⨁ aspecitionTOP7UMSEved*a*rd

FIGURE 1.1. Christopher's perceptions at the London train station

Caracciolo observes that the "unusualness" of Christopher's narrative perspective forces Haddon "to try out innovative stylistic techniques" including the typographic schema (2014b, 187). The stylistic techniques influence the novel's reception. Caracciolo suggests that Haddon's style defamiliarizes the reading experience and in turn, plays a pivotal role in regulating the readers' closeness and distance from the narrator, contributing to the readers' empathy and the novel's humor (2014b, 202). I agree with Caracciolo's assessment, though I am critical of the extent to which the empathy and humor also entrench problematic societal understandings of autism. Haddon's typography enforces notions of modular encapsulation and separation of cognitive processes—thereby confirming the hypothesis that bodily perceptions need to be mentally represented for the brain-computer to process them.

Through the typographic design, Haddon materializes Christopher's mind as a tangible space: the world projected onto his mindscreen is laid out on the book's pages. This aspect of Haddon's narration is realized in the Broadway production of *Curious Incident* (dir. Marianne Elliott, 2012) wherein letters and numbers that Christopher encounters are externally projected on the stage. Within the book, Haddon manipulates the typography, switching among typefaces (i.e., bold, italics, underline), to highlight the cognitive challenges and sensory overload multimodal communicative situations present to Christopher. For instance, apart from the section numbers (equivalent to chapter titles) which are always in bold, bold words are interspersed throughout the novel starting from its fifth page. We might want to take an imaginative leap and attribute these to Christopher, but unlike his other narrative choices, Christopher never reflects on or explains these. In such cases, while the words emptied of meaning are part of Christopher's narration (like the London station episode where the pictorial signs belong in Christopher's narration but whatever meaning readers make of them is unavailable to Christopher), the typographic design is Haddon's way of marking up Christopher's cognitive difficulties.

Through the novel, Haddon develops a "multimodal mindstyle" for Christopher. Stylisticians take mindstyle, a term coined by Roger Fowler, to imply a "distinctive linguistic presentation of an individual mental self" (1977, 103). The term has been used to discuss linguistic styles that can be associated with characters and narrators as well as implied authors. However, in recent years Gibbons, Nina Nørgaard, Beatrix Busse, and Rocío Montoro have analyzed texts that employ a "multimodal mindstyle." In their discussions, multimodality of mindstyle is understood to be working at the level of the cognitive processes involved in interpreting linguistic codes; for instance, they discuss the visual content inferred from verbal metaphor. What I call Haddon's "multimodal mindstyle" here also takes into account the visual design features used to construct the narrator's cognitive characteristics.

Three groups of words are in bold throughout Christopher's narration: a) titles of books, TV shows, and games such as *The Hound of the Baskervilles, Minesweeper,* and *How the Mind Works*; b) labels and instructional signs: for instance, the word Berghaus that Christopher encounters on his mother's jacket (19) and the "keep off the grass" sign (29); and c) words, ideas, or phrases which pose problems for Christopher to solve. Metaphors are listed in bold as Christopher mentions the difficulties those present for him (15). The first two categories of words and phrases in bold establish that Christopher absorbs certain kinds of written texts as visual icons — that is, devoid of the semantic content necessary for them to be processed as words. Visual icons then become vehicles of sensory bombardment. This is evident when, during the trip to London, the brand names and signs turn into Miscellaneous Symbols and Special Characters. At other times, words presented as visual icons chart Christopher's coping mechanisms. When Christopher encounters the statement "BEER / Helping ugly people / Have sex for 2000 years" on the T-shirt of his neighbor, the text is in bold and indented as it would have been on the shirt (36). The visual design drives home the point that Christopher finds it easier to focus on and reproduce a string of text he sees as though it were an image rather than mentally represent and decode his interlocutor's facial expressions, reminding readers that he is, in Baron-Cohen's term, mindblind. The indented presentation of the text underscores that Christopher did not even comprehend the language here—because he could not appropriately encode and decode what he took to be a visual icon under stressful conditions—which accounts for the humorous appeal this event has for readers who, unlike Christopher, "read" the text. The typography reinforces Haddon's characterization of Christopher as someone who tackles the world around him differently from neurotypical readers. This is why Caracciolo says that humor in the novel works when readers respond to the text in a way "closed to the character" (195). This observation is not far removed from Zunshine's assertion that neurotypical readers supply mental states for Christopher, except Caracciolo also argues that the humor exposes the absurdities of social conventions.

When Christopher tries to make sense of jokes, they become puzzles and are in bold, as is the case with Christopher's father's joke: "His face was drawn but the curtains were real" (8). Unlike the titles and labels which Christopher recalls as visual icons, the joke in bold face is a visual representation of information Christopher encounters aurally. In this way, Haddon's multimodal mindstyle illustrates what Christopher means when he remarks, "I can see what someone is saying written out like it is being printed on a computer screen" (113). By stressing that visualizations on a screen are necessary for Christopher to respond to aural stimuli, the narrative, once again, recalls the representational hypothesis of the computational model of cognition.

Notably, the scenarios that most puzzle Christopher require him to juggle among multiple modes of perception. Figurative language such as puns in jokes or metaphors require rapid oscillation among the linguistic, the visual, and the aural. Taken together the many uses of boldface in the novel serve as a signpost for cognitive challenge and this cognitive challenge involves multimodal processing. While Haddon's use of a multimodal mindstyle demands that neurotypical readers attend to the visual dimension of words, it stresses the difficulties Christopher has when tackling multimodal communication. Given that multimodal processing is a criterion used to test cognitive overload among neurotypicals and autists in contemporary empirical studies (see Chen et al. 2016; Sperduti et al. 2014; Magnée et al. 2011), Haddon's stylistic choices are especially charged with ethical and social significance.

Christopher's musings about cognition and the manner in which Haddon renders his thought processes channel a mishmash of popular and scientific discourses about autism, several of which stem from the dominance of computational analogies for the mind. The first generation of cognitive scientists maintained that akin to digital computational devices, which turn multimodal inputs into symbolic representations for processing them, the brain also converts inputs from all sensory channels into amodal representations. However, the impediments that certain sensory experiences pose for Christopher as he navigates the world around him ultimately betray the inadequacies of computationalism with its modular and disembodied understanding of mind.

At the same time, as I have already acknowledged, the other end of the scientific spectrum—the second-generation research on cognition—does not offer a uniform explanation for what "embodied" cognition means. Even the distinction between the first and the second generations is not as well defined as the generational terminology that other scholars and I use would seem to imply. And though the turn toward embodied cognition has prompted a series of studies on autism, thus far, these have come up with a range of findings, some of which contradict one another (see Sperduti et al. 2014). Yet recent studies also increasingly highlight the complex cognitive and perceptual networks that constitute consciousness. Andy Clark,[15] Anthony Chemero, Andrew Wilson, and Sabrina Golonka, among others, argue that compartmentalizing sensory faculties and decoupling thought from perceptions or agent–environment interactions is implausible. Wilson, a proponent of the "radical embodied cognition" hypothesis, observes that in orthodox computational models, mental representations are supposed to

> encode knowledge about the world that we use to make inferences to support perception, etc. But if we have such poor perceptual contact with the world that we need representations, how did we ever get access to the knowledge we needed to encode? This *grounding problem* is a disaster. Radical embodiment solves it by never creating it in the first place—we are in excellent perceptual contact with our environments, so there are no gaps for representations to fill . . . (Stafford 2015)

Christopher's mind, as depicted in *Curious Incident*, is atypical for struggling to appropriately represent perceived data on a metaphoric mindscreen. Within the storyworld this remains a source of trouble, given its fundamental assumption that perceptual experience is a lower-order process distinguished from the higher-order mental representations that lead to meaningful use of sensory data. However, for the embodied mind, perceptual experience would not be "data" and sense-making would not entail withdrawal from the stimuli-presenting environment. In Francisco J. Varela, Eleanor Rosch, and Evan

---

15. Clark's theories are associated with connectionism and predictive processing models that explain cognition in terms of emergent processes. Fodor, even though he critiques Pinker, considers connectionism to be inferior to computational explanations.

Thompson's enactive view, for example, common principles are supposed to link sensory and motor systems and cognition is understood as perceptually guided action (2016 [1991], 173). Hanne De Jaegher adopts a similar position and suggests, "An organism casts a web of significance on its world. It regulates its coupling with the environment because it maintains a self-sustaining identity or identities that initiate that very same regulation. This establishes a non-neutral perspective on the world" (2013, 6). In other words, embodied understandings of cognition disavow one normative and mentalistic way of accounting for thought processes.

Intertwining linguistic and pictorial modes of representation, Haddon's typographic design in *Curious Incident* necessitates that readers understand the narrative through a combination of perceptual processes. In that sense, the narrative layout acknowledges the sensory bases of cognition. Though this does not compensate for the problematic conflation of the autistic mind with computational mechanisms, the book's multimodal design does point out that the neat separation of seemingly lower-order perceptual processes and higher-order abstract reasoning in the first-generation cognitive theories on which the novel bases its representation of cognitive disability is flawed.

Curious Incident thus underlines the questionability of computational explanations for the intricate and divergent processes constituting cognition. The impossibility of a single explanatory model, including computationalism, to encapsulate cognition shapes Hall's *Raw Shark Texts*. *Raw Shark Texts* alludes to computationalist theories while also engaging critiques of both computationalism and the embodiment-oriented cognitive theories. Whereas there is a decisive emphasis on encoding perceptions as symbols for the mind to function in Haddon's presentation of Christopher, Hall's novel is built on the tension between representations and perception.

As a metafiction, *Raw Shark Texts*'s meditation on cognition directly concerns how narrative fictions are composed and experienced. Reading fiction, to use Clark's phrase, is a "representation-hungry" activity that seems to involve "off-line, abstract, and environmentally decoupled reason" (1999, 350). The computational approach to cognition would easily explain the readers' ability to experience vivid storyworlds as mental simulation or projection based on sensory input. Yet, *Raw Shark Texts* never resorts to pure computationalism when reflecting on reading. The novel suggests that reading is an embodied interaction with semiotic modes—words, pictures—that are both "real, external objects that we encounter and manipulate" and instruments for evoking seemingly abstract representations (Clark 1999, 350). Through the different fictional characters, Hall experiments with myriad models of thought. In the end, as I show, his novel highlights the inextricability of the body from the environment in which it is situated, challenging the theoretical possibility of simulating or mentally representing anything independent of perceptual processes.

Explanatory Pluralism in *The Raw Shark Texts*

Hall's *Raw Shark Texts,* like Haddon's *Curious Incident,* presents a character narrator who, at least at the outset, attempts to make sense of his own mental processes in terms of mechanical operations. After regaining consciousness in the novel's opening scene, the narrator Eric Sanderson observes, "the engines and drivers that keep the human machine functioning at a mechanical level have trip-switched" and flung him from his first life to his "second life" (3). What he is describing here is the experience of losing episodic memories—that is, memories of his past experiences.

Eric labels his condition "memory blindness" (6), while his doctor, Dr. Randle, calls it a "dissociative condition" (7), a form of amnesia. The novel's title puns on Rorschach tests meant to diagnose personality and psychological disorders. Though controversial as a method, Rorschach tests have had clinical and forensic applications.[16] During the tests, patients are asked to interpret ambiguous shapes of inkblots on the assumption that a person's inherent disposition impacts the manner in which they make meaning of signifiers. Some of the assessment methods focus on measuring the patient's degree of deviance from common responses.[17] In Hall's novel, Eric is not literally subjected to a Rorschach test but to a recurrent series of events that serves an analogous function. Eric often "sees" a fish form out of typed words. Images of this fish, identified as a shark called the Ludovician in the storyworld, are also presented to us, the readers (see Figure 1.2). A visual icon made of words, the image imitates the shape of actual-world fishes as well as represents an object which has an unstable ontological status within the storyworld. With the pun on the Rorschach test, the novel suggests that what Eric sees when looking at the visual icon is supposed to offer insights into his cognitive difference. However, Eric's narration also primes readers to "see" the fish, and extending

---

16. Named after the Swiss psychologist Hermann Rorschach, the test was in use since the 1920s and assessed cognition and personality. The Rorschach test is no longer held in high regard within the scientific community.

17. The test results have been used to pathologize a wide range of "differences" (including schizophrenia and, in the 1960s, homosexuality). In Rorschach tests there is little emphasis placed on how the signifier and its perception in a given context interact with the patients' experiential background.

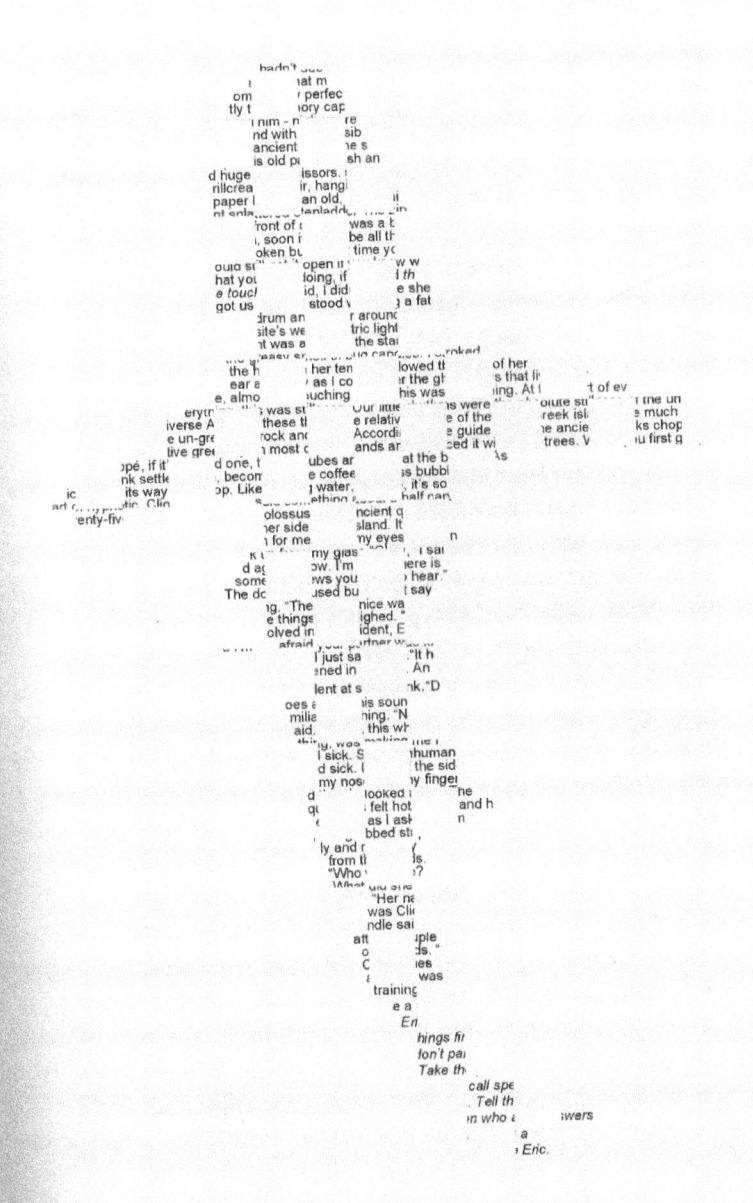

FIGURE 1.2. An "idea-fish" surfacing on a page of *The Raw Shark Texts*

the narrative logic, it would seem that readers share Eric's deviance. Eric can defend himself against the attacks of the "idea-fish" if he remains attentive to his own surroundings. By insinuating that objects in Eric's environment protect him from the predatory icon, *Raw Shark Texts* dwells on the relationship of environmental grounding with seemingly offline or abstract thought processes.

While putting Eric through a series of events that try his mind, Hall's narrative tests various hypotheses about cognition. Disagreements in cognitive-scientific studies about the extent to which meaning is grounded in the body and materiality of channels of communication (hardware) are dramatized in the novel. They contribute to conflicts and ontological uncertainties as *Raw Shark Texts* constructs several mises-en-abyme, or infinitely recurring sequences: the amnesiac narrator, Eric, is writing the book we are reading in order to defend himself and the memories he is gradually recovering over the course of the narration from the attacks of an "idea-fish" that has previously fed on his mind. Distinguishing his emergent subjectivity from his past self that the shark supposedly consumed, the narrator calls himself "Second Eric" and refers to his past iteration as "First Eric." The two Erics are reflections of one another, though the Second Eric is supposed to be an embodied presence in the textual actual world while the First Eric is a figment Second Eric imagines on the basis of the letters and postcards First Eric left behind. Despite Second Eric's efforts the "idea-fish" creeps into his book. Its flesh—typographically designed—is now made of words cut out of Second Eric's narration. Thus, Eric's avatars remain trapped in a recurring circuit of remembering and forgetting, and this is only one among many such loops constituting Hall's novel.

The opening sentence of the novel reappears at a much later point in the text. First Eric loses his memory to the "idea-fish" after an "actual" shark kills his girlfriend, Clio. The deceased Clio returns as Scout, a character who guides Second Eric in the quest to recover his memories (i.e. rescue the remains of First Eric). Characters have multiple avatars that surface in both spaces and the counterpart of spaces—"un-spaces." An academic Trey Fidorous,[18] who is trying to annihilate the shark, tells Eric that he must impersonate others—take on other peoples' identities—to protect himself. While Eric assumes others'

---

18. The names of characters in Hall's novel frequently allude to other literary characters, authors, or in some cases, computer programs. Trey Fidorous is a pun on Tryphidorus (also spelt Triphidorus), the third- or fourth-century Greek poet known for writing *The Taking of Ilios*. Fidorous in Hall's novel takes an interest in dead languages and spreads language viruses. Ludovician, the name of the shark, might be alluding to "ludic" and also Lutwidge from Charles Lutwidge Dodgson, which was Lewis Carroll's given name.

identities (one body taking on multiple personalities) as a defense mechanism, Eric's enemy (in addition to the shark) named Mycroft Ward is a self-replicating personality, poised to take over all human bodies. Thus, Eric's epiphany—"*the view becomes the reflection, and the reflection, the view*" (385; emphasis original)—sums up the world of the novel in which elements of the textual actual world and textual alternative possible worlds mirror one another. Eventually, though, which is the reflection (projected reality) and which the view (perceived reality) cannot be clearly distinguished. In other words, this is a narrative in which what appears to be the textual actual world standing apart from textual alternative possible worlds turns out to be its reflection, making it impossible to differentiate between "reality" and "representations."

Given that *Raw Shark Texts* is also self-reflexive about its own status as fiction, it highlights the status of the textual actual world as an alternative possible world from the vantage point of an actual reader. The narrative's suggestion is that the boundaries of the readers' perceived world and the projected or imagined world (the world of fiction) are porous. However, the degree, the processes, and the implications of this porosity are not easily determined, and this indeterminacy fuels the narrative. The characters and events are pieces of a larger puzzle designed to speculatively test the relation of cognitive processes that seemingly depend on abstractions (reasoning, imagination) with that of perceptions, grounded in the body and its material surroundings.

Several episodes in *Raw Shark Texts* question how we make meaning from language, ask whether there are embodied and sensory bases for language comprehension. For instance, during Second Eric's quest, Fidorous instructs him to swallow a piece of paper with the word "water" written on it in such a way that the seemingly amodal signifier (the word) turns into the tangible signified (actual water) and quenches his thirst. Second Eric's drinking of conceptual water and shark-hunting in a "conceptual boat" demonstrates the "link between the acts of imagination that enable a reader to construct an English drawing room or a raging ocean from words on the page [and] is, in *mise-en-abyme*, played out for us within the very fiction upon which our imaginations operate" (Hayles 2011, 120). In the textual actual world, representations infect Second Eric's perceptions when the verbal-pictorial shark—the "idea-fish"—surfaces as a quasi-sentient being, materialized as an icon on the page. Second Eric can thwart this process of contagion threatening his actual world by resorting to the materiality of media-objects like books, Dictaphones, and so on.

Raw Shark Texts ultimately exploits the indeterminate relationship of a narrative's semiotic composition and medial configuration with the meaning readers infer from it. The same tropes can be found in postmodernist concrete prose (see McHale 1987). However, the mise-en-abyme structure of Hall's novel also improvises upon cognitive-scientific hypotheses about how minds work. In approaches like radical embodied cognition, no abstractions are supposed to be involved in cognitive operations—no perception-independent world projected on a mindscreen (see Wilson and Golonka 2013; Chemero 2009). Enactivists like Varela, Rorsch, and Thompson (2016 [1991]) also challenge brain-body-world divisions in theories of consciousness. Along similar lines, as an advocate for the notion of grounded cognition, Lawrence Barsalou dismisses the idea that conceptualization is fundamentally different from perception. Rather, he explains, conceptualization partially reactivates the sensory motor areas that are involved in the perception of the object to which the concept refers. Though Barsalou does not fully repudiate the notion of mental representations, he asserts that these representations are not amodal, abstract, arbitrary, but recruit the same neural mechanisms as perception (Barsalou 1999; also see Barsalou et al. 2018). Hall's narrative presentation of consciousness plays with these plural viewpoints. The internal logic of the storyworld suggests that readers of fiction abstract and represent information at least to some extent. At the same time, since the protagonist's two opponents are disembodied replicants, the narrative is not quite aligned with strong computationalist positions either. *Raw Shark Texts* remains playfully uncertain about how minds work, even as it affirms the dependence of memory as well as imagination on semiotic systems, material groundings, and embodiment.

Eric's Thoughts and Things

Where does the material world end and abstractions begin? Indeed, what distinguishes thought from things (that impede the incursion of abstractions like the "idea-fish" in Hall's storyworld)? Hall's novel grapples with such questions related to the nature of consciousness, with special emphasis on how the "things" one perceives constitute one's subjectivity. William James had observed that "'thoughts' and 'things' are names for two sorts of objects, which common sense will always find contrasted and will always practically oppose to each other," although this binary between thought and things maybe false (1904, 477). James notes:

> ... the whole philosophy of perception from Democritus's time downwards has just been one long wrangle over the paradox that what is evidently one reality should be in two places at once, both in outer space and in a person's

mind. 'Representative' theories of perception avoid the logical paradox, but on the other hand they violate the reader's sense of life, which knows no intervening mental image but seems to see the room and the book immediately just as they physically exist. (1904, 481)

Contemporary cognitive-scientific theories (such as the computationalist models) that uphold the view that arbitrary, abstract, and amodal representations intervene between perception and thought follow the "representative" theories James cites. However, James himself maintained that though "things" seem to refer to what exist in the field of perception and "thoughts" to anything that is currently outside the perceptual field, they are inextricably entangled. He argued that both the thought of things and things thought of are "real" since every experience gets counted twice, as "object" in one context and "mental state" in another. Notwithstanding James's conclusions, the metaphysical quandary about the status of thought and things continues to fascinate twenty-first-century fiction authors as much as it intrigued James's contemporaries, though the historical conditions motivating the fascination and narrative strategies mediating it differ. In Virginia Woolf's *To the Lighthouse* (1927), for instance, Mr. Ramsay's son—Andrew—tells the artist Lily Briscoe that his father's books are about "subject and object and the nature of reality." When Lily says she does not follow Andrew, he explains, "Think of a kitchen table . . . when you are not there," which alludes to both James's and, if we go further back, Plato's chosen article (the table) for puzzling over the relation of objects with their mental representations. More recently, Tom McCarthy's *Remainder* (2005) sets up an elaborate and bizarre meditation on the same issue. In *Remainder* the unnamed amnesiac narrator commissions a host of characters to "reenact" in the textual actual world events he partly remembers and partly imagines to understand who he really is. Zadie Smith aptly describes McCarthy's novel as "a book about a man who builds in order to feel" and praises McCarthy for "empt[ying] out interiority entirely" (2008, n. pag.). Akin to McCarthy's narrator, Eric of *Raw Shark Texts* "makes [himself] an inside and an outside, an Eric and a not-Eric" to cope with memory loss and the death of the woman he loved (29). While reviewing *Raw Shark Texts*, McCarthy understands Eric's attempts at "shoring everything else up" and building an "inside and outside" as "a kind of three-dimensional embodiment of his psychological state" (2007, n. pag.). According to McCarthy, much of Hall's novel is "textbook post-traumatic theory" and "textbook literary alienation" (n. pag.).

In Eric's post-traumatic experiences thoughts and things, reality and representations continually swap places. Hall represents this psychological condition through the formal techniques of mise-en-abyme and metalepsis. The novel's multimodality triggers and augments the ontological confusions characteristic of mise-en-abyme and metalepsis in narratives. In general, both metalepsis and mise-en-abyme require at least two, if not more, narrative levels. Metalepsis implies the short-circuiting or transgression of the boundaries of these levels, while mise-en-abyme implies reflexivity and duplication.[19] In *Raw Shark Texts,* Eric's ramifying subjectivities (First Eric, Second Eric, Eric, not-Eric et al.) with their divergent material realities create necessary conditions for both the infinite regress of mise-en-abyme and the metaleptic jumps. In fact, through typographic manipulations the novel's mise-en-abyme structure gives way to moments of interior metalepsis.

Raw Shark Texts employs some commonplace idioms such as "voice in the head" and "mind's eye" to describe thought metaphorically and signal the domain of First Eric as ontologically separated from the domain of Second Eric. While First Eric Sanderson floats as a pure concept—ideas without a body—he attracts the Ludovician or the shark. Second Eric tries to hold on to an embodied presence by grounding himself among media objects. At the outset, the distinction between First Eric's world and Second Eric's world resembles, to use Daniel Dennett's term, a "Cartesian Theater," since it is founded on mind–body dualism: First Eric is an amodal representation in the Second Eric's mind, blocked out of his consciousness due to the latter's "memory blindness." However, the more the Second Eric recuperates the First Eric, the more he (Second Eric) turns into a reflection of First Eric, who is more vulnerable to the attacks of the "idea-fish." The boundaries between the textual actual world and the world of ideas are transgressed every time the shark appears before Second Eric and before us, the readers. The shark is a multimodal representation of Eric's ideas in the book and flags the onset of interior metalepsis, which Cohn defines as "metalepsis that occurs between two levels of the same story—that is to say, between a primary and secondary story, or between a secondary and tertiary story" (2012, 106).[20] The worlds of First and Second Eric, the domains of words and things, not only belong in the global structure of a larger storyworld that accommodates both but also bleed into each another.

---

19. See Pier (2016) and Cohn (2012) for differences and similarities between metalepsis and mise-en-abyme.

20. Cohn distinguishes interior metalepsis from exterior metalepsis, explaining that "I call *exterior* all metalepsis that occurs between the extradiegetic level and the diegetic level—that is to say, between the narrator's universe and that of his or her story (e.g., John Fowles's *The French Lieutenant's Woman*)" (2012, 106).

A threat to Eric's sanity throughout the narrative, the shark appears as a visual icon around seven times in the book (16, 57–58, 95, 126,[21] 155, 217, 328–79). Some of these depict the "actual" Ludovician that eats Eric's memories while others are representations that Eric and others create during their search for the Ludovician. As I previously mentioned, the image of the shark is also a distorted reflection of the typed text that makes up Eric's narration. When the shark's body is imaged as patches of text cut from Second Eric's narrative, the narrative conveys that the shark is made of the memories it devours (155). In this way, the text *visually* suggests a mise-en-abyme as Eric's narrative potentially appears twice—once as he narrates and a second time as fragments from which the shark is typographically constructed. The appearance of the shark anticipates the interior metalepsis during which Eric seemingly loses touch with things.

While the shark is a more eye-catching typographic figure, more ubiquitous instances of typographic play also limn the borders between thoughts and things. Italics serve three major functions in *Raw Shark Texts*: they channel epigraphs from other texts, they are used for emphasis, and they mediate Second Eric's thoughts at the moment of experience rather than at the moment of narration. Italicized sentences, often in the present tense, can be read as "self-quoted monologues," that is, as quotations of Second Eric's past thoughts (Cohn 1978, 161). For instance, when Second Eric is describing his quest to find Fidorous, he recalls, "my mind clanked and struggled to pass thoughts coherently from one area to another . . . *I'm just tired. I'm coming down with something*" (132). It is the experiencing Second Eric rather than the narrator Eric who is sick and exhausted. However, these visually signposted boundaries between represented thought and speech, the distinction between what Eric imagines and what he says, blur due to the presence of the First Eric, whose name is italicized at the outset (15). Given that First Eric—a past avatar—lurks in Second Eric's consciousness as a voice-in-his-head, the italics also contribute to a dual voice phenomenon. Second Eric starts recalling sections from First Eric's letters in italics, just as First Eric presents his own past journals in italics (this could be a remediation of handwriting; 79). For instance, Second Eric notes, "*Dr Randle can neither help nor protect you*" (61; another version of the same sentence occurs in 23), which is a quote from First Eric's letters. Thus, italics signal the potential for slippage among Second Eric's thought at the time of experience, Second Eric's narration, and First

---

21. The shark on pages 126–27 is made of sections from Charles Darwin's *Origin of Species*, which is reminiscent of Paul H. Barrett, Donald J. Weinshank, and Timothy T. Gottleber's (1981) concordance to Darwin's *Origin of Species*.

Eric's knowledge. This slippage is also a necessary condition for the appearance of the shark.

The shark's appearance is foreshadowed when Second Eric, while discussing his memory loss with Dr. Randle, observes, "*Little holes. Little bits missing. Things nibbled away here and there*" (14). The statement seems figurative since Second Eric, due to his amnesia, is supposed to know nothing of the shark at this point in the narrative discourse. First Eric's letters will later introduce him to the memory-devouring Ludovician. So, the italicized phrase here stages a possible slippage among Eric's multiple personae, each with different degrees of knowledge about his past, present, and future. It could be that Second Eric is creating what looks like a self-quoted monologue but is actually folding a retroactive reflection on his own condition. This could also be the First Eric voicing what he knows as Second Eric's voice-in-the-head. Alternately, it could be a metaphor that accidentally anticipates what the experiencing Second Eric does not yet know. We, as readers, can decide one way or another, but what is of note is that the italicized phrase simultaneously activates all these possibilities. Another instance of such slippage occurs when, during one of the first attacks of the Ludovician, Second Eric finds himself drowning in "conceptual water" and immediately shouts "*help. Shark. Help me*" (60). It is not clear whether Second Eric has read the First Eric's letter yet, which explains that the animal hunting him is a predator fish. In the narrative discourse, we come across the information about the shark later. So, Second Eric's cry for help and his ability to anticipate the shark's attack is inflected by First Eric's knowledge, even though Second Eric cannot be logically aware of it. As such, the italics become visual cues for readers to detect the layering of Eric's voluntary and involuntary thoughts with perceptions and experiences. That is to say, although Eric describes his mind as a clanking machine (in the vein of Christopher), the way Hall presents his thoughts highlights the impossibility of decoupling hypotheticals (imaginations, abstractions) from perceptual experiences.

The Ludovician, according to the logic of the storyworld, moves between the realms of Eric's imagination and perceptions, threatening to leak out of his thoughts and contaminate his environment. The typography visualizes instances when the leakage begins to occur: the typographic shark is at once Eric's thought and a thing that he can ostensibly see and touch. Narrating perception presents some challenges. Monika Fludernik observes that sensory perception is "one part of consciousness which may or may not be fully articulated in terms of verbalization" (1993, 299). Fludernik bases her observation on the assumption that perception is "non-reflective" and gives rise to thought processes, which she equates with the possibility of articulation—that is, she adheres to a distinction between higher-order cognitive processes and lower-order sensory modalities. Second-generation cognitive theories challenge such distinctions (see Barsalou 1999, 2008, 2009). Taking my cue from these theories, I am not enforcing distinctions between perception of sensory stimuli and seemingly higher-order processes like language comprehension in my narrative analysis. While I agree with Fludernik's observation that not all aspects of sensory experiences lend themselves to verbal articulation, I contend the notion that thought necessarily equals verbal articulation or is fundamentally distinct from sensory perception.

In *Raw Shark Texts*, the pictorial arrangement of typed characters (over and above verbal articulations) dramatizes perceptions. For instance, a rectangular box with the word "distance" typed in different font sizes visually reinforces the shark's emergence in Second Eric's field of vision mediated by a television screen. Eric moves toward the screen to get a closer glimpse of the shark and what he sees is framed in a rectangle with a huge O toward its one corner and the word "eye" written around it (58). Meanwhile, the "screen [throws] itself forward" and the room turns "pitch-black" but for a green light coming from the smoke detector. After being blinded by the turn of events, Second Eric attempts to draw upon other modes of perception, including haptic and auditory sensations. However, he manages to experience these sensations only at a conceptual level: "The idea of the floor, the carpet, the concept, feel, shape of the words in my head all broke apart on impact with a splash of sensations and textures and pattern memories and letters and phonetic sounds spraying out from my splashdown" (59). The entire sequence activates the transgression of ontological levels—the world of the moving images mediated by the television screen invades the textual actual world. The actual world of Second Eric becomes the domain of First Eric, the world of concepts. The emphasis on visual perception in the sequence is unmistakable: the sight of the shark forming on screen (its 3D illusion on 2D space) results in the first metaleptic jump, wherein the screen—the threshold separating Eric's actual world from the world of representations—is shattered and this, in turn, gives way to momentary blindness resulting in the multimodal sensations, which are experienced as "concepts" and indicate Second Eric's crossing-over to the world of "ideas." According to the logic of Hall's storyworld, the only way Eric can anchor himself in the world of things is through sight. He realizes as much when he recalls, "I screwed down my eyes again, trying to will myself back to the familiar world of solids and space" (60). Eric needs (visual) perception to thwart the interior metalepsis which lands him in the world of abstractions, but he transgressed the boundaries of his world in the first place because of the Ludovician, which infected him through the sense of sight. Thus, the narrative charts a loop in terms of what perceptions can do. Sight triggers the metaleptic jumps but also temporarily stops them.

Hayles observes that the novel presents Second Eric's case as an almost cautionary tale about the dangers as well as pleasures of immersion in an imagined (i.e., fictional) world. As my analysis shows, the novel also suggests that thinking is grounded in perception (especially visual in this particular instance), even as it involves abstractions. Conceptually the shark stands for a world of abstractions even though it is a visual icon on the book's pages. The concrete presentation of the shark shows readers what Eric sees. In the storyworld, the sight of the Ludovician is contagious. As per that logic, readers of this novel are as susceptible to the attacks of the shark as Eric. Like him, readers half see and half imagine this shark. When reading fictions, we interpolate and extrapolate from semiotic modes and medial substrate. The storyworld that fictions evoke is thus not made of pure abstractions but assembled through our perceptions and experientiality.[22] The multimodal design of *Raw Shark Texts* reminds us of the many ways in which the artifactual book or a similar media platform is necessary for experiencing fictional worlds (worlds of representation), just as the "plain stuff" in Second Eric's textual actual world is necessary for him to recollect the past without being consumed by the "idea-fish." The materiality of the book simultaneously mediates and mitigates the viral appearances of the Ludovician and the contagious touch of fiction. The seductions of print fiction are juxtaposed in the narrative with the threat posed by Mycroft Ward, a character who is a conglomeration of computational theories.

Eric's Allies and Others: Thinking Machines and Books with Bodies

Mycroft Ward and the Ludovician are Second Eric's antagonists and obstruct the quest to retrace his memories. Even Scout, Eric's guide in the quest, is not immune to their attacks. Trey Fidorous describes Ward and the Ludovician as each other's nemesis: "matter and anti-matter." In other words, Second Eric's two enemies can potentially destroy each other if Second Eric can orchestrate an encounter between them. Both Ward and the Ludovician are, at one level, concepts without bodies. They are self-propagating viruses that infect others' minds and memories, take over others' personalities. Hall contrasts

---

22. Fludernik considers the readers' experiential background as a key contributor to narrativity. See Caracciolo (2014a) for a discussion of how the reader may enact the consciousness and bodily-perceptual experiences of the different characters they encounter in fiction.

them with Second Eric, whose quest culminates in a growing recognition of the centrality of his body and the articles in his environment in configuring who he is. The characterization of Second Eric is in line with non-Cartesian approaches to cognition. Meanwhile, Ward and the Ludovician are manifestations of hypotheses that, one way or another, uphold the Cartesian distinction between mind and body.

Mycroft Ward is all data. He requires bodies to breed, though the specificity of the body is redundant for him. Whichever body he assumes functions as no more than a scaffolding for the data he uploads to them. The characterization of Ward as an enemy playfully reflects on and problematizes computational models, wherein the mind is understood to be an autonomous processor of encoded perceptual data. Scout, Second Eric's guide and accomplice, narrates Ward's history to him: Ward worked in the military in the late nineteenth century, but before his death he decided to "unshackle himself from the multitudinous failings of the corporeal harness and progress forward ad infinitum" (199). Ward designed a question-answer test to imprint his personality on others, so that he can exist in multiple bodies simultaneously. The question-answer template recalls the Turing test. Scout explains that through the process of replication, "what had once been a single human personality became a vastly intelligent mind machine" (204). Ward infects Scout while she plays an online game and subsequently takes over part of her personality.

Ward's name is a pun on the word processing program, Microsoft Word. And, as Jessica Pressman (2009) notes, it is also a pun on the name of Sherlock Holmes's brother "Mycroft," who works for the British government and is a "human computer." Ward's personality exists independent of any particular body, and the differences that emerge from being contained in multiple bodies are standardized by a character named "Nobody." Nobody is described as "concept wrapped in skin and chemicals" with no eyes (178). Even as Eric wonders whether Nobody can still be understood as a biological subject, Scout refutes such a possibility. Ultimately, Ward and Nobody are best understood as programs attempting to transmute natural intelligence.

Ward is characterized as a computer virus that manages to enter bodies through machines—Scout contracts him while playing an online game. Ward then overburdens the victim's memory in an attempt to replicate the subjectivity of a deceased nineteenth-century figure. Ward's spreading mechanism is similar to that of the virus Melissa alluded to in the narrative. The virus code is pictured as a mosquito. The insect's pictorial flesh is made by erasing fragments of the computer code that spread the virus. This code originated in the US and spread in other parts of the world through emails around 1999 (the novel dates it between 2000 and 2001) and placed a burden on mail servers.[23] The appearance of the virus as a parasitic insect is a visual analogy for what a computer virus does, but similar to the concrete presentation of the Ludovician, it also anticipates leakages between Eric's actual and possible worlds. Eric wonders whether the mosquito-like figure of the Melissa code belongs to Trey Fidorous, but the disk with the image of the mosquito has unsalvageable contents (96). With impaired or erased memory, the disk can be understood as a victim of the parasite imprinted on it. The material substrate—the disk— remains though meaningful content has been wiped from it. The disk functions as a red herring in Eric's quest. Similar to Nobody, it seems to be leading Eric toward Fidorous but directs him toward Ward instead.

While Ward breeds across bodies, the Ludovician is first and foremost an entity that breeds in conceptual domains that have lost material and bodily groundings. Being an "idea-fish," it is a representation that contaminates minds in the absence of things. Whereas Ward takes over bodies to overwrite their memories, the Ludovician consumes memories and leaves the body as though it were an empty shell. In this sense, both Ward and Ludovician are constant reminders of the fragility of a hypothetical mind without body or a body without mind.

Despite being presented as a conceptual entity in the textual actual world, however, the Ludovician's body is typographically materialized on the pages of the book. Its form—that of a shark—is based on the image of a predatory fish that, Hall's narrative suggests, is popularly and collectively conjured since Steven Spielberg's film *Jaws*. Hall's novel even remediates the film's climax. This "idea-fish" is also a perceptible stimulus in the textual actual world. It enters Second Eric's consciousness through sight. The two-fold nature of the shark as "thought" and "thing" recalls James's observation that any conceivable experience gets counted twice over, as an object as well as a mental state. In Hall's storyworld, the Ludovician, while being simultaneously thought and thing, is also inhibited by the materiality of other things.

My present discussion of the various characters (Eric, Ward, Nobody, Ludovician) from *Raw Shark Texts* strives to show how the novel juxtaposes several first- and second-generation, Cartesian and non-Cartesian approaches to cognition. Characters such as Ward and Nobody are aligned with particular Cartesian cognitive models. However, Eric and the Ludovician are, rela-

---

23. The Melissa virus is a particularly pertinent reference given the nature and thematics of *Raw Shark Texts*. Just as the novel alludes to several popular films and books, the handle of the programmer who created the virus was KWYJIBO, which came from an episode of *Simpsons*. The virus was lodged in language games. One of the payloads of the virus was the game Scrabble. The word game would bombard machines with loads of texts.

tively speaking, more complicated. There are computational undertones to the Ludovician, given that contemporary iterations of computationalism take materiality into account, accepting an "explanatory pluralism." As Marcin Miłkowski points out,

> Computationalism is here to stay—but [. . .] it does not rely on a Cartesian gulf between either software and hardware or mind and brain. The computational method of describing the ways information is processed is usually abstract—but cognition is possible only when computation is realized physically and the physical realization is not the same thing as its description. (2013, ix)

Miłkowski is suggesting that computational explanations must incorporate accounts of how abstract representations are physically implemented. To explain implementation, one cannot refer to the computation idiom itself but instead come up with other "acceptable causal explanations" (2013, x).[24] Such a premise can account for the Ludovician's peculiar materiality in the textual actual world. It is a representation that needs a material substrate, but this substrate is simply a framework, not fundamentally constitutive of what the Ludovician is.

Computationalist theories, though referenced extensively throughout *Raw Shark Texts,* are also challenged by the alternative models of cognition Eric seems to embody. When Second Eric uses Dictaphones and other mediaobjects to thwart the attacks of the shark, he is embedding and extending himself in a network. Cognitive scientists such as Clark and Edwin Hutchins have argued that the brain turns to the environment and external aids to supplement the limitations of memory (Clark 1998, 272; Hutchins 1995). Clark observes that these external resources or things in the world are "alien but *complementary* to the brain's style of storage and computation. The brain need not waste its time *replicating* such capacities. Rather, it must learn to interface with the external media in ways that maximally exploit their peculiar virtues" (1998, 220). In other words, Clark suggests that for maximum efficiency, the human mind does not need to imitate the functions of external media but learn to interact with as well as manipulate them. This is Second Eric's strat-

---

24. While introducing Baron-Cohen's *Mindblindness* (1995), Tooby and Cosmides acknowledge that a "physical system" is required to implement "computational relationships" in the psychological architecture (1995, xv). Proponents of non-Cartesian accounts of cognition such as Rowlands and Chemero, however, consider these sorts of admittance of physicality to be insufficient. Saying that computation is physically implemented means that the physical (bodily or environmental process) is simply a shell or scaffold for high-order information processing.

egy of coping with the shark. Consequently, Dictaphones, books, typewriters, and diaries help him create a closed loop as a defense against the Ludovician's attacks.

Given that Ward stands for Word Processor and is described as an "intelligent mind machine," the character links writing technologies with particular cognitive models. Ward's antagonistic status in the novel channels an anxiety about the digital media ecology's impact on minds and memories (81). The narrative identifies typewriting and handwriting as antidotes to Ward: Second Eric is supposedly using a typewriter to write the novel, and Scout uses keys from the typewriter as letter bombs to thwart the attack of the Ludovician on one occasion. So, older writing technologies are supposed to avert dissolving into the world of pure concepts identified with Microsoft Word in Hall's novel. The world of pure concepts is a world in which thought is disembodied and is, therefore, the world of "Nobody" as well as Ward. Handwriting presents an even safer haven compared to the typewriter. When Second Eric goes looking for Fidorous, Scout takes him through a tunnel that Second Eric also calls the "Biro-world." Biro stands for ballpoint pen and biro-world is a paper tunnel inscribed with Fidorous's handwriting (221). Unlike *S.*, a novel I discuss in Chapter 3, *Raw Shark Texts* does not reproduce handwritten material except when Second Eric and Scout map their way to orient themselves within the paper tunnel (227, 232). The papers constituting Fidorous's tunnel are of myriad kinds: "newspapers, chip wrappers, glossy magazines, great strips of wallpaper," and so on, but "every scrap [is] covered, smothered, buried in lines and squares and triangles and swirls of blue and black and green and red biro words" (222). So, if Ward represents mind without body, Fidorous's handwritten paper tunnel emphasizes the irreducibility of the body. Due to its indexical associations, handwriting becomes the symbolic expression of embodied consciousness in the narrative and leads Second Eric and Scout to Fidorous. Fidorous is thus located on the opposing end of the spectrum from Ward, who takes over the consciousness of those who come in touch with him while remaining an elusive entity himself.

In *Raw Shark Texts* the presence of books and other things as reliable means to extend and distribute cognition suggests the untenability or limitations of Cartesian dualism, a disembodied mind without material grounding. Books and other artifacts are supposed to pause the vertiginous feeling *Raw Shark Texts*' mise-en-abyme structure triggers. First Eric writes, "*Books of Fact/Books of Fiction*: Books of fact provide solid channels of information in many directions. Library books are best because they link the book itself to every previous reader . . ." (68). While the materiality of books prevents the idea-fish in the narrative from devouring the information contained in them, digital computers are cast as unsafe spaces for storing information. First Eric, for instance, says "there is *no* safe procedure for electronic information" (81). The narrative for the most part seems to take data to be untethered to hardware, lacking in materiality. In the climactic episode though, Fidorous builds a conceptual loop made of four computers and uses them to print out Second Eric's narrative. In that episode, Fidorous affirms that computers form stronger loops for distributing information than technologies such as the Dictaphone that Second Eric uses. Contrary to the preceding events in the novel, where electronic information is understood to have no particular form, this scene describes and underscores the tangled hardwire loops of computers. Instead of simply casting computers as "thinking machines" or a metaphor for human thought without a body, Fidorous recognizes that computers and electronic data can complement embodied cognition. Though computers are still disparaged as technologies of standardization, contrasted with the idiosyncratic properties of handwriting and typewriters in the narrative, through Fidorous the narrative also concedes that computing technologies can couple with embodied subjects in effective ways, and artificial intelligence need not supplant natural intelligence.

Why Make Up Minds?

In sum, Haddon's and Hall's narratives, *Curious Incident* and *Raw Shark Texts,* foreground both the aesthetic possibilities and the problematic implications of taking computers as medium and analog for thought representation. As I mentioned in my introductory chapter, there are, at least, two influential strands of commentary on the value of studying the fictional representation of consciousness. On the one hand, Cohn argues that fictional minds are unique because they are made accessible to us through literary strategies. Actual minds are never revealed to us in the same way. According to her, "the special life-likeness of narrative fiction . . . depends on what writers and readers know least in life: how another mind thinks, another body feels. In depicting the inner life, the novelist is truly a fabricator" (1978, 5–6). Cohn further argues that language patterns used to conventionally fabricate consciousness—she variously calls this mimesis, a fantasy, an invention, imaginary psychology—are important for understanding the history of the novel (Cohn 1978, 9). On the other hand, David Herman (2011) calls Cohn's position the "exceptionality thesis" in order to refute said thesis. Herman reasons that fictional minds are configured and understood with reference to actual minds we encounter in everyday life, and hence, fictional minds can, in fact, illuminate actual minds. My present study stresses the constructedness of literary minds without claiming that this construction has no basis in a novelist's perceptual life world. For instance, twenty-first-century authors would not turn to computers and computation as analogs so frequently while rendering consciousness had they not been inhabiting digital ecologies. At the same time, I do not think that insights from present-day cognitive sciences are unequivocally applicable or useful for studying fictional minds since fictional minds are no different from actual minds. Instead, I maintain that literary minds are historical artifacts that can be studied to understand how thought is conceptualized in a given era and the implications of such a conceptualization. Since literary minds are constructed, scientific models and cultural attitudes engendered in specific media ecologies inform them to a greater degree than cognitive literary studies that refute the so-called exceptionality thesis seem to acknowledge.

Computational principles have influenced multiple branches of knowledge production throughout the twentieth and twenty-first centuries. The manner in which digital computers convert inputs concerning actual world problems into symbols, process them, and present results applicable to actual world phenomena has had a profound effect on theories of cognition. While early studies on computation drew on human cognitive faculties as models for intelligent machines, in a rather circular turn, the first generation of cognitive scientists also used computational concepts to explain thought. My analysis of the two novels has shed light on some of the limitations of likening mental processes to computation.

The narrator of *Curious Incident* explicitly endorses the early cognitive theories that rely on the computer metaphor and computationalism, as he likens his cognition to computation, but Haddon also renders the narrator's atypical consciousness through experimental typographic design. The experimental typography demands a degree of modal and media literacy from the readers—a multisensory engagement with language that the novel denies to its narrator, given that typographic experiments typically illustrate the narrator's cognitive overload in multimodal communicative situations.

Hall's fiction, on the other hand, partly mirrors the insights of second-generation cognitive theories that do not place amodal representations hierarchically above sensory perceptions. Perceptions and the relationship of thought with things emerge as fundamental for constituting the protagonist's sense of self. Through characters such as Nobody and Ward, Hall's novel, unlike Haddon's, also parodies the assumptions implicit in computationalism.

When examined together *Curious Incident* and *Raw Shark Texts* exhibit the far-reaching impact of computers on both literary aesthetics and how we think about thinking in the twenty-first century. With an allegiance to computationalism, Haddon's novel constructs a model of thought that needs mental representations, stripped of sensory grounding; but, on the other hand—orchestrating the visual affordances of digital writing interfaces—the novel also invites readers to approach the text in multisensory ways. For its part, *Raw Shark Texts* adopts an explanatory pluralism that encapsulates the current state of knowledge production about cognition across disciplines. The coexistence of multiple analogs for mental phenomena in both popular and scientific discourses today stresses the speculative bases for much of what we think we know about thinking. Accordingly, the next few chapters of this book explore how pictures, maps, and archives inform thought representation in narratives, while also acknowledging that neither the fictions nor the alternate analogs used to explain habits of mind remain untouched by the computing technologies that dominate the present media ecology.

CHAPTER 2

Selfieing Minds

Picturing and Sharing Subjectivities

Toward the end of their influential essay "The Extended Mind," philosophers Andy Clark and David J. Chalmers ask, "What, finally, of the self? Does the extended mind imply an extended self?" and answer the question with a tentative, "It seems so. Most of us already accept that the self outstrips the boundaries of consciousness; my dispositional beliefs, for example, constitute in some deep sense part of who I am. If so, then these boundaries may also fall beyond the skin" (1998, 18). Their hesitant articulation betrays the contentiousness of selfhood and subjectivity as notions.[2] Cognitive philosophers and scientists sometimes put forward self-concepts as by-products of particular cognitive schemata, as is evident in Clark and Chalmer's formulation of an extended self to go with their extended mind hypothesis; at other times, they raise metaphysical questions about whether or not the self is "real,"[3] has neural

---

1. The extended mind hypothesis to which I also refer in the introductory chapter and chapter 1 maintains that brain-body-world combine to form cognitive systems.

2. In cognitive sciences and philosophy, selfhood and identity are sometimes understood as social concepts while subjectivity is considered experiential. Since I am studying narrative modes of thought representation, the form of 'me-ness' I discuss is at the nexus of the experiential and the social, and I use subjectivity and selfhood interchangeably.

3. Thomas Metzinger argues that "nobody ever was or had a self. All that ever existed were conscious self-models that could not be recognized as models" (2003, 1). The assertion has gained some notoriety—Zahavi (2014) notes that Metzinger represents contemporary philosophy's skepticism about studying selfhood. Metzinger's polemical phrasing underplays the

correlates, whether subjectivity demands philosophical or cognitive-scientific investigation. In general, philosophy of mind has a more robust tradition of theorizing subjectivity than cognitive and neurosciences, though scientists like the Nobel-winning neurobiologist Francis Crick maintain that subjectivity calls for scientific rather than philosophical inquiry (1995). Cognitive theories and experiments studying subjectivity define it variously. This is because, as neuroscientist Anil Seth points out,

> selfhood is a constellation concept that involves not only representation and control of physiological homeostasis, but also the experience of owning and identifying with a particular body, the emergence of a first-person perspective, intention and agency, and metacognitive aspects that relate to the subjective 'I' and the narrative linking of episodic memories over time. (2013, 565)

Given that selfhood is a complex assortment of phenomena, philosopher Dan Zahavi (2010) voices the need for complementary approaches to account for its many facets. Subjectivity, in short, demands explanatory pluralism, and in so doing, inspires speculative exercises in sciences and philosophy of mind and experiments in literary narration.

Narrative's modeling of subjectivity engages prevailing theories about the concept and simultaneously enfolds contemporary forms of self-experience. Keeping in view the affinities of narrative constructions of subjectivity with scientific and philosophical attempts at grasping and codifying the self during the twenty-first century, this chapter of *Out of Mind* examines multimodal narratives that are thematically concerned with "selfieing." Extrapolating from the familiar understanding of the selfie as a self-portrait taken to be shared on social media, I deploy selfieing to mean the salient processes, including those of self-representation, through which one functions as a self in society. I situate the depiction of selfieing in fictions amid interdisciplinary discourses, intending to fathom how we perceive ourselves and interact with other people, where interaction with others is a special case of agent–environment interaction.

The pair of narratives studied here, Steve Tomasula's *The Book of Portraiture* (2006) and Aleksandar Hemon's *The Lazarus Project* (2008), incorporate pictures (sketches, photographs, computer-generated images) to trace how experiences and conceptions of selfhood change based on broader cultural

---

specific metaphysical dimension of his argument: what Metzinger denies is the idea that the self is "real." He endorses here and now versions constituted through functional processes.

shifts, including changes in media technological cultures. W. J. T. Mitchell has distinguished pictures—that is, "constructed concrete object or ensemble (frame, support, materials, pigments, facture)"—from images, which he defines as "the virtual, phenomenal appearance" pictures provide their beholders (1994, 4). Hemon's and Tomasula's narratives include pictures that mediate and illustrate how the characters' surroundings appear to them. That is, the pictures are artifacts that aid in the narration of the characters' phenomenal and social experiences. In addition to including artifactual pictures, *Book of Portraiture* and *Lazarus Project* forthrightly articulate the priority given to pictorial concepts in thinking about subjectivity and call for us to grasp their implications. Extant criticism of Hemon's novel has focused on its treatment of grief and trauma related to migration (Mihăilescu 2014; Weiner 2014) and tension between fiction and documentary activated by the presence of photographs (Fjellestad 2015). The material design of Tomasula's novel and its representation of posthuman embodiment as well as the relationship of representational modes with power have been fruitfully studied (Venkatesh Ghosh 2013; Hayles 2015; Chevaillier 2015; 2019). Drawing upon these prior studies, my chapter attends more specifically to the two narratives' dramatization of the cognitive processes and actions involved in selfieing through the register of their multimodal forms.

There is a long-standing intellectual tradition of using pictures—the concrete object—as a *vehicle* in metaphors explaining aspects of subjective experience. Illustrations, photographs, and mirror-images belong with other optical instruments and analogs used to explain cognition and perception in sciences and philosophy of mind (see Draaisma 2000). In the late nineteenth and twentieth centuries, photography and cinema significantly influenced such undertakings: Jean-Paul Sartre, Henri Bergson,[4] W. E. B. Du Bois,[5] Maurice Merleau-Ponty, Jacques Lacan, and Roland Barthes, among others, borrowed the technical language of photography to reflect on selfhood, consciousness, and experientiality.[6] For instance, Lacan observes, "in the scopic field, the gaze

---

4. See Trifonova (2007) for the role of the "image" in twentieth-century French philosophy.

5. Smith (2000) argues that Du Bois centred a "visual model of subjectivity" in his conception of the Black experience (581).

6. Given the recurring representation of psychic faculties in terms of the camera and its contents (like memory and perception) as photographs in theories of consciousness, Eduardo Cadava writes, "the question is not whether or not the camera or the photograph are successful figures for the work of the psyche, not whether or not the psyche is indeed a kind of photograph, but rather what is a photograph, what is the psyche if it can be represented by a photograph. For if there can be no camera or photograph that does not have a psychic-origin and this seems to be what Benjamin and Freud think—then there can be no psyche without photography, without a process of writing and reproduction. To say that everything

is outside, I am looked at, that is to say I am a picture" (2018[1973], 106). He swapped mirror-image with "pictures" and "photographs" in his writings and, like Roland Barthes after him, opined that others' gaze reconstitute us as photographs (Lacan 2018[1973], 106; Barthes 1977).

Between the early twentieth century and the present, the dominance of analog photography and cinema has given way to digital images and graphics. These technical shifts influence both theoretical and experimental approaches to subjective experience. Cognitive psychologist Stephen Kosslyn, a proponent of computationalism, describes mental images into which sensory perceptions are supposedly converted as "displays on a cathode ray tube screen attached to a computer" (Tye 1991, 34; see Kosslyn 1994). Steven Pinker (1997) also likens pictures on a computer screen with the symbolic representations he claims the mind produces. The narrator of *Curious Incident* picks up and muses on this metaphor (discussed in chapter 1). Empirical studies on self-recognition frequently rely on photographic portraits, some of them morphed to blend multiple faces, as sensory stimuli (Sforza et al. 2010). In the 1970s, the psychologist G. G. Gallup designed a self-recognition test for primates using mirrors as "scientific tools for measuring self-awareness" (Keenan 2004, 8; Gallup 1970). Gallup claimed that recognizing oneself in the mirror proves the existence of an idea of self in the subject. Newer studies designed along the same lines use pictures in place of mirror images. Some of these studies appeal to the proliferation of profile pictures and selfies in the present visual culture for establishing the urgency of probing the role of visuals in self-experience (Chakraborty and Chakrabarti 2018). Pictures thus continue to inspire accounts of subjective experience in the twenty-first century both as tools and analogs.

My analysis of Tomasula's and Hemon's novels brings to the fore their interest in pictorial modeling of subjectivity across historical periods. *Book of Portraiture* touches on those technological epochs from the fourteenth-thirteenth century BCE to the present day that afford new ways of thinking about oneself. *Lazarus Project* follows the uses of photography, as it goes from being a new analog technology in the nineteenth and early twentieth centuries to a more ubiquitous technology in the twenty-first century. However, notwithstanding the diachronicity of the various ideas of selfhood thematically explored in segments of the novels, the novels' multimodal macrostructures, I show, jostle around cognitive-scientific and theoretical positions of the present. Both narratives show the characters' senses of self to be contextually

---

within the psyche begins with writing and reproduction is to say that the psyche begins with photography" (1997, 100).

variable, emerging through purposeful social interactions, rather than imply that the self is a stable and amodal mental construction.

Lazarus Project's and *Book of Portraiture*'s emphasis on the sociality of the self is strikingly resonant with evolving digital forms of self-representation, particularly the selfie. Jörg Metelmann and Thomas Telios explain that though artistic self-portraiture "has undergirded the Western cultures of individualism and individualization from the Renaissance to the present day," a salient feature of selfies is their pronounced sociality, given that a bulk of them are meant to be shared online (2018, 324). As opposed to an intuitive understanding of self-portraiture as expressing the priority of the individual, sociality and sharedness are technologically and conventionally inscribed in the selfie. What is more, one does not take and upload a single, distinctive selfie. Clicking and sharing selfies are repeated and repeatable actions. Selfies capture 'little selves' and subjectivation becomes "an endless process and a media spectacle" (Metelmann and Telios 2018, 327). As such, Metelmann and Telios contend that in the selfie culture "being oneself boils down to being a content-free, relational form. It is . . . not something, but anything; it is the constellation of a purely formal relation" (2018, 336). *Book of Portraiture* and *Lazarus Project* predate the popularity of selfies by a few years, but their representation of subjectivation through verbal-pictorial means adopts the same social and relational attitude to the self as these artifacts of the digital media ecology. My purpose in remarking upon the similarities among narrative presentations of subjectivity and the habitual staging and sharing of subjective experiences on social media platforms is not to propose that any one of these caused or determined the other. Rather I intend to emphasize the semiautonomous co-emergence of concepts and practices during a particular historical period. Co-emergence of aesthetic, technological, and epistemic frameworks is itself a complex phenomenon that can accommodate plural explanations and logics of causation.[7]

Multimodal Social Selves

The understanding of selfhood as a dynamic process that involves social interactions will not be met with opposition from most second-generation cognitive-scientific researchers and philosophers of mind. Once the stronger versions of computationalist explanations are dispensed with, amodal representations take a backseat in accounts of cognition, including those that

---

7. For possible links between explanatory and causal pluralism, see Lombrozo (2010).

deal with the contentious notion of selfhood. The theoretical waters, however, become muddied the moment we try to find explanations for how these processes and interactions work. Terms such as emergence, generation, negotiation, and regulation permeate contemporary cognitive-scientific and philosophical language, as their vocabularies do away with rigid dualistic (mind–body / self–other / internal–external) explanations for cognition and consciousness. Accounting for the various forms and functions of the brain-body-world entanglement, second-generation cognitive theories tell us: the mind emerges, the self emerges, and so on. Of course, *Out of Mind*, too, appropriates this language.

Mutually incompatible but workable descriptions come from different quarters about the terms and conditions of "emergence." Predictive processing is an explanation receiving widespread attention at present, one that is championed by Clark and Seth. In the predictive processing model, "perceptual content is seen as resulting from probabilistic, knowledge-driven inference on the external causes of sensory signals" (Seth 2013, 565). The model foregrounds relations of reciprocal causality between percepts and learned concepts, but in a "top-down" fashion, meaning learned conceptualities and causes form probabilistic models—called "generative models"—that serve predictive functions. Downflowing predictions meet upward flowing sensory signals, wherein the selection of signals both guides and constitutes action. The causal flows are continuous, and generative models also routinely update when perceptions do not match expectations or predictions (Seth 2013; Clark 2016). In fact, learning happens when the models reconfigure. Seth proposes a predictive model of selfhood, in which versions of the self emerge through the reciprocal integration of sensory information with interoceptive feelings, metacognitive and narrative awareness as well as forms of self-representation. Predictive processing's position on mental models and predictions overlaps with those adopted in theories of grounded cognition. Lawence Barsalou, Léo Dutriaux, and Christoph Scheepers, too, maintain that processes of conceptualization exist to facilitate an embodied agent's goal-directed action in their experiential and social worlds. However, unlike Seth and Clark, Barsalou, Dutriaux, and Scheepers suggest that subjects conceptualize during experience—"a concept is typically coupled with its referents in the body and the world"—rather than tackle experiences through context-independent preestablished concepts (2018, 1–9). In other words, while one side argues for a top-down relation between generative models and perception, the other argues for a bottom-up relation between perception and knowledge representation.

A contrasting description of emergence comes from the enactivists, though Clark has sought to assimilate this description within the predictive processing model so that it may constitute a "truly fundamental and deeply unified science of the embodied mind" (see Clark 2016, 297). According to enactivists like Varela, Rosch, and Thompson, embodied interactions, based on common biological linkages among brain-body-world, lead to emergent patterns (2016 [1991]). The units constituting emergent patterns are self-organizing and self-maintaining but cannot be understood independent of the "structural couplings" in which they necessarily partake. That is, the units have a phenomenal, irreducible core. The enactivist explanation resonates with phenomenological accounts such as those of Zahavi that argue for minimal, pre-reflective forms of selfhood[8] as bases for more complex self-awareness.

As must be clear from my, admittedly, simplified overview, the latter account is anti-reductionist unlike the former. Predictive processing combines machine learning, computational neuroscience, and accommodates tentative, though not amodal, internal representations within its schema. Selfhood is a thematic preoccupation of both *Book of Portraiture* and *Lazarus Project*, and I have already stated that they treat selves as emerging through purposeful social interactions. Then, which of the said frameworks do the narratives emulate for showing the emergence of selves? I am going to argue that they combine the two: they illustrate predictive relations among characters, and at the same time, insist on more primordial forms of sensorimotor linkages among them.

The exploration of subjectivity and self–other relations in *Lazarus Project* is prompted by a conundrum its character narrator Brik faces: how does one explain the constant generation and sustenance of harmful social stereotypes—the human proclivity for finding perceptual justification for biased expectations, while one also apprehends, at a fundamental—cellular, neurophysiological level—we are "just like everybody else" (5, 13, 284, 236). Brik is an immigrant in post-9/11 America, a society that discriminates against people based on their "foreign" appearance. He sets out to write a multimodal, fictional narrative that dwells on the use of pictures in psychopathological studies at the turn of the twentieth century and its connections with anti-Semitism. His fiction serves to remind us that experimental psychology, neuropsychiatry, and criminology relied on portraits as diagnostic tools to deduce certain racialized subjects' antisocial tendencies in the late nineteenth and early twentieth centuries. The mind sciences of the era operated on the assumption that "degeneracy," conflated with criminality, could be inferred from bodily appearance. Brik interweaves the historical fiction he composes with his own

---

8. Zahavi's minimal self is dependent on bodily primacy rather than sociality. Social interactions would be engendered by rather than be constitutive of the pre-reflective self in his formulation.

experiences of living in twenty-first-century Chicago, where he must contend with bigotry in his personal life and confront politically motivated mass media representations of migrants as violent and deranged.[9] Hemon includes archival photographs of Chicago taken between 1902 and 1933 to depict Brik's encounter with history. He also incorporates more recent photographs shot by Velibor Božović to portray Brik's attempts at grasping and reimagining his relations with his own surroundings.

Lazarus Project is, in part, Brik's self-constituting narrative or "self-narrative." Psychologists Kenneth J. Gergen and Mary M. Gergen define self-narratives as an individual's account of the "relationship among self-relevant events across time" (1988, 19). For Gergen and Gergen, Jerome Bruner (2003) and Kim Atkins (2010), among others, the self is a sophisticated narrative construction; that is, in their views, narratives allow for the synthesis of diverse lived experiences necessary for being and knowing oneself. My understanding is that the narrative account is one of several facets of subjectivity. This will become clear in my discussion of the concept here and in the next chapter. I take my cue from Seth's and Zahavi's understandings of selfhood as a constellation concept, and also from Hemon's and Tomasula's novels, which locate narrative self-making within a variety of other modes of selfieing. At the same time, however, I recognize that the narrative version of a (fictional) self emerges distinctly and explicitly through first-person narration such as Brik's.

Self-narratives have a prominent social dimension, since in the actual world, we tell them "to identify ourselves to others and to ourselves" (Gergen and Gergen 1988, 17). In literary texts, as Marco Caracciolo (2014a) observes, self-narratives need not always be presented as first-person accounts. They may emerge as the

> thread of a larger story that focuses specifically on the interplay between a character's behavior and his or her mental states, allowing (a version) of his or her identity or self to emerge ... It may be told by someone else (the narrator, another character)—what matters, however, is that the story makes claims about the character's experiences, values, and motives, linking them to the way he or she interacts with a physical and socio-cultural world over the course of a larger text. (Caracciolo 2014a, 139)

---

9. Shaista Patel (2014) considers the propagation of the figure of the mad Muslim terrorist in discourses and the racialization of madness after 9/11. In Hemon's novel, Brik faces bigotry in Chicago, not directly related to the stereotype of the mad Muslim terrorist. It is Rora, Brik's friend, who is stereotyped when he says he is Muslim while travelling through Europe.

Brik tells his own story in *Lazarus Project*, albeit his first-person account integrates perceptual experiences and beliefs of other characters. These "others" include characters from Brik's world—individuals in the textual actual world—and subjects who populate the fiction he composes by extrapolating from historical records.

Seth leaves open the question of if and how predictive models of selfhood can accommodate narrative self-making (2013, 571). My discussion of Hemon's and Tomasula's fictions in the following sections of the chapter show that the characters' experiences and expectations of others in a given context have a reciprocal causal relation with their more long-term self-narratives. Nevertheless, the novels also depict moments in which sharing experiences among subjects is not strictly causal or inferential—living beings' experiences resonate owing to the basic sensorimotor structures of their bodies. Brik observes that "nobody can control resemblances, any more than you can control echoes" as his self-narrative shows the impossibility of clearly distinguishing oneself from others, selfieing from othering (2008, 106). Božović's photographs, credited to Brik's friend Rora in the storyworld, accompany the narration. These pictures are supposed to elucidate and document Brik's experiences. But they also effectively demonstrate that Brik's experiences threaded into the self-narrative are not uniquely his own. He has appropriated experiences shared with others—particularly Rora—to tentatively constitute his subjectivity.

Tomasula's *Book of Portraiture* is more modular and prismatic in form than Hemon's novel. *Book of Portraiture* is made up of five chapters, and each features disparate groups of characters. The characters come from different walks of life—the ensemble includes a prophet, a painter, a psychiatrist, a model, photo and video editors, an investigator, bio technicians, and so on. While *Lazarus Project* moves between the turn of the twentieth and twenty-first centuries, Tomasula's novel jumps from the fourteenth century BCE to the seventeenth century to the twentieth and twenty-first centuries. The verbal style of narration changes over the course of the five chapters as do the layout and pictorial styles, establishing an analogous relationship between evolving visual and linguistic cultures. As opposed to Hemon's exclusive use of photography in *Lazarus Project*, *Book of Portraiture* includes sketched portraits, photographic portraits, and digitally manipulated pictures of the human body.

The thematic import of the macronarrative of *Book of Portraiture* depends on the agglomeration of meaning across the five chapters. As an experimental novel, the text requires readers to integrate the various fragments in order to arrive at the bigger thematic picture that links understandings of selfhood with self-representation technologies through history. A painter and a psychiatrist narrate their own stories in the second and third chapters of *Book *of Portraiture*, while in the other chapters, heterodiegetic narration reveals the intentions and beliefs of groups of characters. What connects the host of characters in *Book of Portraiture* with one another and also with Hemon's protagonist Brik is their attempts at making and remaking themselves—clicking selfies repeatedly, as it were—based on feedback from their social worlds. For example, through the diary of Diego Velazquez, a low-born figure, modelled after the early modern Spanish painter of the same name, Tomasula depicts the deliberate construction of a verbal-pictorial self-narrative. Velazquez's contemporaries attack his lowly origins and his artistic practices. These attacks cause him to record and theorize his daily experiences and interactions in court. His diary entries contest the expectations others seem to have of court painters; expectations he has extrapolated from their shared social world. He defends himself by reimagining what a court painter should be like, and he himself, of course, fits the role he imagines. But, even as the diary entries project him as a model artist, they also show that the conceptualities he has generated are founded on the aesthetic disposition and practices of other artists like Rembrandt, Michelangelo, and Titian. Rembrandt and Titian, as part of Velazquez's training environment, influence his conception of what an artist should be like and of himself. His inferences about their art and reflective appropriation of their practice allow a particular version of his self to emerge in the diary entries. Tomasula's novel thus illustrates the causal flows guiding the selection of words and pictures constituting Velazquez's self-narrative.

Rough sketches of the historical Velazquez's celebrated paintings such as *The Jester Calabacillas, Rokeby Venus, Las Meninas,* and *Las Hilanderas* accompany the fictional character's diary entries. Velazquez inserted Titian's *The Rape of Europa* within his painting *Las Hilanderas*. Tomasula's Velazquez even justifies his repurposing of Titian's painting by saying he has made "fair-use" of it (Tomasula 2005, 63). In a chapter following the one presenting Velazquez's diary, a Japanese artist pastes his own face into a "life-sized, digitally remastered duplicate" of Velazquez's *Las Meninas* (2005, 161; see Figure 2.1).[10] Just as *Las Hilanderas* reframes and offers a new context to *The Rape of Europa*, the Japanese artist's creation offers a new frame and context to *Las Meninas*. *Book of Portraiture* thereby stresses how the character's selves emerge through reciprocal relations. If I were to use Metelmann and Telios's phrasing to describe *Book of Portraiture*'s attitude to subjectivity, "being oneself boils down to being a content-free, relational form" (2018, 336). Whereas some of these relations are causal—that is, relations founded on social rank,

---

10. In the French edition of *Book of Portraiture,* Tomasula had the Japanese photographer stand in place of all of the court characters other than the Infanta Margaret Theresa.

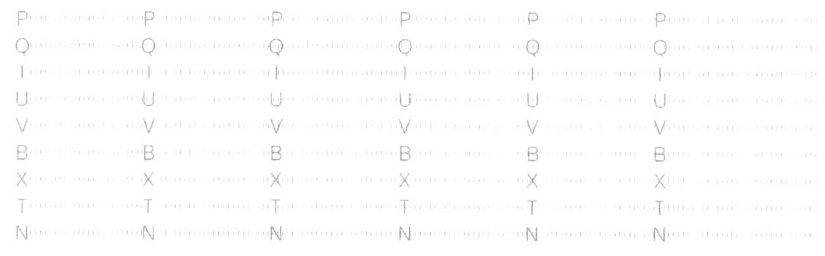

PQIUVBXTN PQIUVBXTN PQIUVBXTN PQIUVBXTN PQIUVBXTN PQIUVBXTN

The Next Day....

FIGURE 2.1. Digitally edited *Las Meninas* in *Book of Portraiture,* showing both Velazquez (extreme left) and the unnamed Japanese photographer (center) in place of the Infanta Margaret Theresa. Image courtesy Steve Tomasula.

envy, admiration, aspiration,—others are based on more fundamental, shared sensorimotor capacities. Tomasula's Velazquez reflects on how "the processes by which we see" serve as a kind of meeting ground for subjectivities when he describes *Las Meninas* as a "fusion of you King and Queen viewer-subject and me viewer-subject looking at you looking at me—they, we—everyone making each other in a world already made—for it is only the I that can give expression to this world that precedes us while the only expression possible is the I itself" (84). The embodied act of looking couples the various agents in the picture, the artist, and the viewers. "King," "Queen," "I," "you," and "we" thus jointly structure and "enact the world"[11] of *Las Meninas*.

The same enactive conception of looking—that is, of looking as embodied coupling—is implied in a photograph on the verso to the title page of *Lazarus Project*. The photograph shows a man facing a mirror, but he is not looking at his own image. His gaze is directed at the camera (and thus, also at the viewers). Fjellestad observes that "what makes the photograph [in *Lazarus Project*] perturbing is the fact that the man is not looking at his reflection in the mirror but at something else, something unavailable to our gaze: the photographer taking the picture. The photographer's position is aligned with the position of the readers/viewers: it is as if the man in the photograph were looking at us looking" (2015, 209–10). The interplay of perspectives and the triangulation of attention (since the gazes of the subject, photographer, and viewer converge) implied in the mirror-portrait is meant to make viewers metacognitively aware of their own embodied process of looking. The contemporary form of the mirror selfie shared online initiates a similar triangulation, whereby the photographer who is also the subject seems to be saying to the viewers, 'I am staging myself for you.'

Like *Lazarus Project*, *Book of Portraiture* is a metafiction that depicts characters' self-conscious modelling of themselves. The pictures included in both novels rarely graphically illustrate the key characters, though they serve the purpose of characterization.[12] In this respect, Hemon's and Tomasula's narratives resemble other twenty-first-century novels such as Teju Cole's *Every Day Is for the Thief* (2007), Lance Olsen's *Theories of Forgetting*

---

11. The phrase "enact the world" is borrowed from Varela, Rosch, and Thompson (2016 [1991]).

12. Torgovnick (1985) and Burrows (2008) discuss how modernists like Henry James, Zora Neale Hurston, and Virginia Woolf, among others, used visual arts to represent characters' perception and thoughts. Some modernist narratives also included artifactual pictures. In these novels though, pictures are not usually marked as artifacts belonging to the storyworld. By contrast, in the twenty-first-century novels pictures are either commented on by a character or are referenced in the discourse in another way. For more discussions on photography and literature, see Entin (2012), Armstrong (1999) and Novak (2010).

(2014), Zinzi Clemmons's *What We Lose* (2017), Amitava Kumar's *Immigrant, Montana* (2018), Lynne Tillman's *Men and Apparitions* (2018) and Valeria Luiselli's *Lost Children Archive* (2019). The narratives are all thematically concerned with the complex phenomena of selfhood, and pictures serve as keys to understanding the characters' manner of interacting with their worlds. Tillman's narrator, an ethnographer, even titles an early segment of his narrative, "Self-narration, Or Wildness of Origin Myths" (2018, 3). He announces his rhetorical goals as such: "How I came to be, not you, how I'm shaping me for you, the way my posse and other native informants do for me, how I'm shape-shifting" (2018, 3). The self-consciousness of Tillman's narrator is prototypical of the character narrators in these books. Compositional elements (tone, texture, framing) of the pictures included in the narratives often manifest these characters' cognitive and emotional states, and in this context, what is especially interesting is that the pictures in *Lazarus Project* and *Book of Portraiture* do not remain anchored to the perspective of a single character. That is, the pictures ultimately manifest the entangling of subjectivities rather than exemplify individual ways of seeing the world. Clark and Chalmers begin their essay on "Extended Mind" with the question, "Where does the mind stop and the rest of the world begin?" *Lazarus Project* and *Book of Portraiture* raise and address the question, Where does the self stop and others begin? Moreover, how are borders between selves and others negotiated?

Clark and Chalmers have argued that an individual's mental life can be "partly constituted by the states of other thinkers" (1998, 17–18). Combining the extended mind hypothesis with the predictive processing model, Clark further states that "socially interacting agents benefit from nested and self-reinforcing cycles of ongoing mutual prediction" (2016, 288). An enactivist description about the sharedness of minds and subjectivities comes from Jordan Zlatev, Timothy P. Racine, Chris Sinha, and Esa Itkonen when they announce that "the human mind is quintessentially a shared mind" (2008, 2). They note:

- Human beings are primordially connected in their subjectivity, rather than functioning as monads who need to 'infer' that others are also endowed with experiences and mentalities that are similar to their own.
- The sharing of experiences is not only, not even primarily, on a cognitive level, but also (and more basically) on the level of affect, perceptual processes and conative (action-oriented) engagements.
- Such sharing and understanding is based on embodied interactions (e.g, empathic perception, imitation, gesture, and practical collaboration).

- Crucial cognitive capacities are initially social and interactional and are only later [understood] in private or representational terms. (2008, 3; sic)

They lay down these propositions against another, older model of social cognition—the Theory of Mind—that takes distinctions between self and other to be pre-given. In the Theory of Mind, since the self and other are taken to be distinct in advance, attribution and assigning of motives and beliefs from one to the other bridge the gap in social communication. Daniel D. Hutto (2008) explains that the Theory of Mind, also sometimes called folk psychology, assumes that "contexts in which we make sense of others are, at root, spectatorial," but, taking an enactive approach, he argues that interpersonal responding is more immediate and visceral than inferential. To be clear, neither Zlatev et al. nor Hutto are referring to an undivided, collective unconscious—as Carl Jung would have it—as the basis for shared mind but appealing to neurophysiology. Hutto's contention is that interpersonal responding is characterized by emotional contagion and motor mimicry, and natural history accounts for the "basic organismic capacities for recognition and response to agency, emotions, and goals" (Hutto 2008, 114, 116).

Cognitive literary criticism on narrative representations of selfhood and social cognition pursues two interwoven themes: one examines how storytelling strategies possibly cue readers to attribute mental states to characters; another considers the representation of how characters know each other and interact with each other within the storyworld. My chapter is more concerned with the latter theme. By far the most popular cognitive-scientific framework appropriated for the purposes of these studies is the Theory of Mind. Lisa Zunshine and Alan Palmer draw on the Theory of Mind to account for how readers infer the selfhood of characters and characters grasp each other's intentions. Zunshine does refer to mirror neurons and mirroring as the basis for sociality, but her theory privileges a spectatorial stance. The self is a reader—specifically a mind reader—and another's body is the text (see Zunshine 2008, 69). Palmer (2010) identifies the subjectivity of the self as "internal" opposed to the subjectivity of others inferred by the self through reasoning as "external," as he sets out to study how narratives depict the bridging of these poles through the construction of what he calls "social minds." The Theory of Mind—the foundation for "social mind"—supposes that an individuals' mental states can be extricated to some degree from the external environment in which they are embedded and that this individual mind, constituted in advance, imputes others' mental states during social communication (see Baron-Cohen 1995; Keenan 2004 for claims to this effect). Like much of narrative criticism referring to the Theory of Mind, Palmer too relies on the human capacity for assigning thought based on other people's appearances and behavior to connect internal and external states, the self and the other. He observes, "Social minds are possible because much of our thought is *visible*" (2010, 4). It is worth adding here that the Theory of Mind framework associated with researchers like Baron-Cohen—the framework I am summing up here—has been challenged by both cognitive scientists and philosophers of mind.[13] There are also internal partitions and debates among the Theory of Mind's proponents, with philosophers like Alvin Goldman (2006) arguing that mental states are "simulated" rather than inferred during social interactions: the self understands others by generating or replicating others' mental states. Goldman refers to empirical findings on mirror neurons to explain the simulation of mental states and emotions. Despite offering a different and more embodied account for how selves bridge the gulf with others, Goldman's simulation-oriented theory does not explicitly question the premise that there indeed is a clear gulf between selves and others waiting to be bridged. Thus, his simulation-oriented approach absorbs some of the founding assumptions of the initial Theory of Mind framework.

My present chapter will not try to account for the social dimensions of subjectivity either in the actual world or in narratives using any one explanatory framework—instead, I will show that certain positions on selves and self–other relations are implied in particular narrative contexts. Hemon's and Tomasula's novels arrive at a picture of the mind that is primarily social and interactional. While doing so, they critique spectatorial and estranging stances toward the "other" endorsed in the Theory of Mind, but this critique is made through the association of thought attribution and "mindreading" with nineteenth-century brain sciences and psychiatry. In the two novels, the borders between what an individual experiences as self and who they distinguish the self from are shown to be malleable, and these borders are negotiated through predictive reasoning as well as perceptual and sensorimotor resonances (see Figure 2.2. for some assumptions in the Theory of Mind, predictive processing models, and enactive thinking).[14] In the remaining three sections of this chapter, I elaborate on the narratives' critique of thought attribution à la the Theory of Mind framework and their depiction of alternate relational forms.

---

13. See *Against Theory of Mind* (2009), edited by A. Costall and I. Leudar, for assumptions different versions of the Theory of Mind share and objections raised against them.

14. This diagram is a simplification—it distils complex scientific and philosophical positions in the way these enter narrative criticism. As I stress throughout this book, the scientists and philosophers who use similar approaches are not always in complete agreement about every tenet of those approaches. Different proponents of the Theory of Mind, predictive processing, and enactivism have somewhat distinct accounts of social interactions with certain shared assumptions.

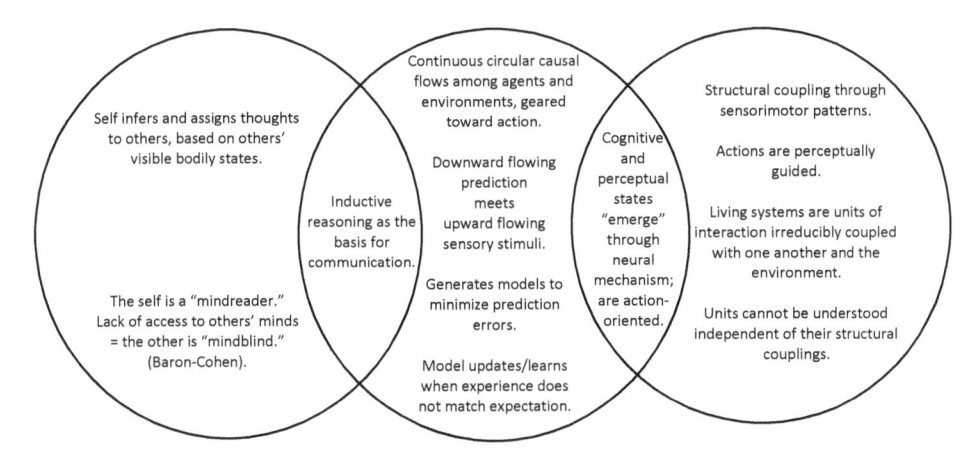

FIGURE 2.2. Initial ToM framework (left), predictive processing (middle), enactive approaches (right)

Among narrative theorists, Caracciolo takes an enactive view of self–other relations and discusses how readers possibly latch on to the experiential substratum of characters' behavior (2014a, 112). His explanation relies on the shared condition of embodiment rather than inferential relations among individuals.[15] Karin Kukkonen (2020) refers to predictive processing to explain the dynamic unfolding of narrative plot and its reciprocal relations with readers' expectations. And while I have mentioned Palmer's professed commitment to the Theory of Mind, I should also note that he refers to Clark and Chalmer's extended mind thesis for clarifying how individual minds "pool" resources to become social minds (2010, 43, 88). Palmer thus performs explanatory pluralism in his own right, combining attribution theory with the extended mind hypothesis.[16]

In the novels I am examining, the very constitution of the self is irrevocably social, and various configurations of self–other relations unfold over the course of the narratives. *Lazarus Project* and *Book of Portraiture* attempt to present selfieing in all its messiness and interrogate assumptions about pre-given or unchanging self–other distinctions.

---

15. Melba Cuddy-Keane (2020) adopts a complementary approach to study sociality in modernist narratives. She refers to distributed cognition and rejects both mind–body dualism and the supposed separation of the individual mind from those of others.

16. Palmer briefly mentions Zlatev et al. as well and casts the debates between the Theory of Mind and their "shared mind" hypothesis as a terminological one (2010, 22). However, the rift between Zlatev et al.'s position and an inference-oriented Theory of Mind is deeper than that between Chalmers-Clark's hypothesis and the Theory of Mind.

Mindreading, or, How Not to Read Pictures

The chapters of *Lazarus Project* move between two timelines—the embedding narrative that channels the textual actual world is introduced with two sentences in the first chapter but begins in earnest in the second chapter. It chronicles Brik's experiences in post-9/11 Chicago and eastern Europe. Embedded within Brik's account of his own experiences is a fictional narrative he is writing about a historical figure. This narrative follows Lazarus Averbuch, a Jewish young man and pogrom survivor from Kishinev who came to Chicago in 1907 as a refugee. Lazarus was shot by George Shippy, the chief of Chicago police in 1908. Subsequently, his corpse was photographed, and these photos were published alongside newspaper reports accusing him of being an anarchist and having an unstable state of mind.[17] Brik (like Hemon himself) found the photos he uses to imagine Lazarus's life and death in archives. He subsequently gathers funding and travels to eastern Europe with his friend Rora to find more information for writing the Lazarus story.

At the center of *Lazarus Project* are two posthumous portraits of Lazarus Averbuch from 1908 (52, 240). In both photographs, Lazarus's corpse has been made to sit upright on a chair with his head supported by a police officer. One of the photos shows Lazarus's side profile. In the other, he faces the camera (see Figure 2.3). The officer's hands frame his face as though it were a picture within the picture. The attention drawn to the face in the photo is further accentuated by the verbal reports that accompany it.

In the storyworld, William P. Miller, a correspondent of the *Chicago Tribune*, notes that Lazarus's face has a "foreign cast of features" (7).[18] He diagnoses Lazarus as a diseased individual, "a dreamlike Jewish boy whose mind was distorted with inflammatory ideas," "an anarchist degenerate," and opines that the boy embodies symptoms of collective maladies like "congenital laziness" (58, 119, 137). Miller goes on to cover the Lazarus incident and speculate about what happened just before Lazarus was shot, and these reports appear as italicized excerpts throughout Brik's narration. During his research, Brik stumbles upon a report in which Miller profiles Lazarus as an "anarchist type." Brik narrates:

---

17. *Chicago Daily News* published the photographs. *Tribune* covered the incident with headlines like "Would-Be Slayer a Russian 'Red,'" and quotes from his sister were grouped under subheadings like "Too Much Reading and Brooding" and a postcard photo of Lazarus was labelled "Slain Anarchist . . ." (March 3, 1908; March 4, 1908).

18. Miller is a historical figure for Brik, but a fictional character constructed by Hemon. Hemon bases Miller on "Judith Miller, the former *New York Times* reporter criticized for her coverage of the lead-up to the US invasion of Iraq" (Hemon quoted in Johnson 2009, n. pag.).

FIGURE 2.3. Archival photo of Lazarus reproduced in
The Lazarus Project. Original negative in Chicago History Museum.

THE ANARCHIST TYPE the heading says; numbers are strewn around his [Lazarus's] face. Below it, the numbers are explained:

1. *low forehead;*
2. *large mouth;*
3. *receding chin;*
4. *prominent cheekbones;*
5. *large simian ears.* (143)

Miller's index replicates the detective's gesture of framing Lazarus's face. Scholars of literature and art have observed that representational "frames" can mediate the "emergence [of scenes or objects] out of the big confusing mess of pre-reflexive sensation" (Beaujour 1981, 33; also see Torgovnick 1985, 30–35; Wolf 2006). When imported from art into cognitive science, framing denotes habits of conceptualizing and organizing perceptual information. Marvin Minsky offers a computationalist definition of cognitive frames as a "data structure for representing a stereotyped situation" (1977 [1975], 355).[19] Minsky notes that a "frame's terminals are filled with 'default' assignments" that may or may not be warranted by the situation at hand and discriminates between top- and lower-level frames (1977 [1975], 356). At higher levels encoded and represented information are supposed to be fixed, while the lower levels are populated during an individual's present experiences. Note that much of this sounds like predictive processing with frames standing for what Seth and Clark call generative models or models of expectations. The difference lies in Seth and Clark's insistence on the instability of generative models and the inevitability of their reconfiguration. By contrast, even though Minsky admits the possibility of changes to cognitive frames, he stresses the stability of encoded and represented information that supposedly enables individuals to parse reality. In a branch of cognitivist theories, frames continue to be discussed as though they are ready made slots to fill with experiences and memories (see Andersen, Barker, and Chen 2006, 46, for instance). Through the character of Miller and his practice of ascribing of stereotypical mental states to Lazarus, Hemon's narrative demonstrates this sort of framing behavior. The default assignments filling Miller's cognitive frame are probably a mix of personal biases and broader cultural viewpoints. Miller reads beliefs,

---

19. Jahn (1997) builds on Minsky's cognitive frames to model how readers process third-person narrative situations. In Minsky's theory, Jahn finds a more flexible account of framing than the earlier structuralist description of narrative frames and situations. My engagement with Minsky here differs in kind. Instead of extrapolating from the theory of cognitive frames to understand the dynamics of reading narratives, I am considering the assumptions of the theory and their consequences as materialized in a narrative situation.

values, and norms about the mind dominant in his time into Lazarus's photograph. Hemon characterizes Miller as a subject who adopts an estranging and spectatorial stance toward another individual. Miller is confident about both the veracity and fixedness of the codes that enable him to see criminal tendencies manifested in Lazarus's face, justify his removal from the society, and enlist public support for police brutality.

The index Miller attaches to the photo is similar to classifications created by Cesare Lombroso. Lombroso cataloged physiological features that, he claimed, predisposed individuals to criminality. He popularized the idea that people could be "born criminals" (see Lombroso 2006 [1876]). Apart from burgeoning discourses in criminology, anti-immigrant discourses circulating in American mass-media also aid in the creation of Miller's index. Newspaper reports perpetuated a general suspicion of anarchist agitators and immigrants from eastern Europe, following the Haymarket affair of 1886 in Chicago. Miller is borrowing and combining these frameworks to mindread Lazarus.

Miller's specific action of mindreading a photograph is also revealing. It was a conventional belief in the early brain sciences that madness showed itself as deviance from accepted standards of beauty. Aesthetic objects, including illustrations of the "manic," the "hysteric," and the "degenerate," were involved in the conceptualization of insanity. In the nineteenth century, medical and neuropsychiatric photographs replaced sketches and engravings as tools for detecting and classifying symptoms of psychological disorders present on the surface of the body. In the tradition of neuropsychiatric photography, practiced by James Crichton-Browne and Hugh Welch Diamond, among others, patients were shown to have severely distorted facial expressions. And although these photographs were meant to be mechanical records of "reality," often patients would be subjected to electric shock to achieve the facial distortion recorded in their images. Simply put, the photographs were usually 'staged.' Georges Didi-Huberman (2004) has explored the role of photography in the very invention of the category of hysteria.

Contemporary cognitive-scientific theories and literary criticism that accept the idea that bodily behavior and appearance make mental states visible replicate the assumptions of early brain sciences, and also neuropsychiatric photography. Alan Richardson (2010) has traced the Theory of Mind back to Charles Bell and Charles Darwin's studies of facial expressions. Darwin's understanding of human subjectivity was partly indebted to neuropsychiatric photographers.[20] In other words, the Theory of Mind's direct roots may be in

---

20. Crichton-Browne supplied forty close-ups and medium close-ups of his patients to Darwin when the latter was writing *Expression of Emotions*. The representational conventions of Victorian theatre also inform Darwin's *Expression* (see Smith 2006, 215).

computationalism, but the beliefs it gives credence to have a longer history, and thus, a longer ideological history, too, going through eugenics.

Lazarus Project takes photography's pervasive influence on the conceptualization of subjectivities as its point of departure—photos brace Brik's amateur theorizations on perception and memory. At the same time, the novel is critical of reading artifactual photographs as transparent indexes of thought. A host of the photographs included in *Lazarus Project* are worn out, blurry, and poorly lit, making it difficult to see *through* the medium. Hemon's questioning of the diagnostic powers that early psychological sciences and criminology invested in pictures is reminiscent of similar efforts made by W. G. Sebald. Sebald was interested in psychiatry, mental pathologies like psychosis and schizophrenia, and read widely on these topics (see Etzler 2014; 2019). The relationship of pictures with words is complicated throughout Sebald's multimodal novel *Austerlitz*,[21] but especially so when photographs are included in connection with the question of mental pathologies. For example, Jacques tells the narrator that the assistants at a nursery where he worked "all bore the scars of their mental suffering" (2018 [2000], 326). The metaphor of scarring implies that there are markers of madness expressed on the bodily surface. The portrait depicting one of these volunteers, though, shows the subject to be cheerily smiling at the camera. The ordinariness of the portrait undercuts the verbal description of its subject as aberrant. Thus, the photograph refuses to "other" the character by visually presenting him as partaking in a shared visual convention—that of smiling at the camera.

In *Lazarus Project,* Brik's narrative includes the photograph of an unnamed man staring fiercely toward the camera (and the viewers). The muscles of his face are tight, his lips are sealed, and his chin is tilted downward. Hemon does not caption photos in the novel but its placement at the beginning of a chapter in which Brik's friend Rora mentions clicking photos of a man named Cormac prompts us—readers—to associate it with this man. Rora says that when he shot the photo, Cormac was "grinning like a lunatic" (33). None of the particulars in the description match the photograph in the book. Yet, there seems to be a "family" resemblance between description and picture, mediated by Rora's simile that likens Cormac to a "lunatic." This resemblance (and viewers'/readers' perception of it) depends entirely on the subject's divergence from the conventions of portraiture. If we identify Rora's subject with the included photograph, we are replicating the fallacy of construing cognitive difference as deviance from shared aesthetic norms.

---

21. See Linkis (2019) for a discussion of *Austerlitz*'s multimodal features.

Brik self-consciously mimics Miller's gesture of mindreading dead and absent subjects. He appropriates Miller's reading of Lazarus's portrait to model other minor characters in his fiction. He imagines that when Lazarus goes to the police chief's house (where he would be shot), the police chief's maid,

> recorded as Theresa, opens the door (the door certainly creaks ominously), scans the young man from his soiled shoes up to his swarthy face, and smirks to signal that he had better have a good reason for being here. The young man requests to see Chief Shippy in person. In a stern German accent, Theresa advises him that it is much too early and that Chief Shippy never wishes to see anybody before nine. He thanks her, smiling, and promises to return at nine. She cannot place his accent; she is going to warn Shippy that the foreigner who came to see him looked very suspicious. (1)

Theresa takes a moment to observe the stranger's—Lazarus's—body, and immediately, the cognitive frames in her mind activate. The sensory evidence she selects focuses on Lazarus's foreign appearance. He looks suspicious to Theresa not because of anything he is doing in the present moment, but because of the default assignments filling her cognitive frame. That is, her perceptual experience becomes a source of epistemic justification for preestablished beliefs, a condition technically known as "cognitive penetrability." Cognitive penetrability, Susanna Siegel explains, "is a kind of causal influence on visual experience. Not every kind of influence by a cognitive state on visual experience is a case of cognitive penetrability" (2012, 203). We can diagnose Theresa as having an especially distorted visual experience at this moment. However, the problem is, every detail we learn about Theresa except her name has been made up by Brik. In Miller's report he reads, "There was a look about that slim, swarthy young man—clearly a Sicilian or a Jew—that could send a shiver of distrust into any honest man's heart" (7). Brik assigns some of these words and ideas to Theresa, and some similar ideas to the owner of a grocery store around the Shippy residence who scrutinizes Lazarus's "foreign" appearance and movements (5). Brik's retelling also puts an emphasis on Theresa's accent, which makes her remarks on Lazarus's foreignness all the more noteworthy. As a writer, Brik is assigning mental states to subjects who can "never again be unreadable" because they are dead and by doing so, is showing how investing others with mental states constitutes a deliberate process of framing, a representation, and often enough, a misrepresentation (107).

Miller rather than Lazarus embodies otherness from Brik's perspective, and this is typographically illustrated in the representation Brik is developing—the narrative that is *Lazarus Project*. Excerpts from Miller's reports are italicized in the book and distinguished from Brik's writing. The typography signals the strength of his disidentification with Miller, especially because Brik usually does not use quotation marks or any typographical marks to distinguish dialogue or the voices of characters other than Miller throughout his narration.

Another instance of performative mindreading that exposes its contrivances ensues when Rora shows Brik the photos of an insurgent called Rambo. Brik learns how Rambo liked to be photographed and observes that "he imagined himself a hero, someone who would always be remembered . . . : here was Rambo bare-chested, pointing his silver gun at the camera; here he was clutching in jest the hair of a young woman smiling, painfully, next to him; here he was sitting on top of a corpse of one of our soldiers" (183). Rambo's photographs resemble either posters or stills from the *Rambo* movies starring Sylvester Stallone—"bare-chested Rambo pointing his silver gun at the camera" for example closely corresponds to the poster for *Rambo: First Blood Part II* (1985). The correspondences between the photos of the insurgent and the stills from *Rambo* cause Brik to read the desire for heroism into the insurgent's portrait, although the pictured actions (pointing a gun, clutching a woman's hair) are not heroic. Brik's thought attribution to the insurgent's photographs self-consciously mimics the ways in which reporters read Lazarus's images to frame him as an anarchist.

Lazarus Project underscores how social interactions mediated via photographs, especially when photographs are not contextualized enough or mischaracterized, can turn into one-way spectatorial processes. Brik's interest in exploring the limitations of assuming an estranging spectatorial stance has to do with his own experiences. It is the profiling of immigrants and refugees in twenty-first-century America that leads him to the Lazarus incident in the early twentieth century. Once marginalized people are assigned mental states—and mental pathologies—anything a particular subject does can serve as epistemic justification for the preestablished frame. Brik's sense of urgency about pursuing the 'Lazarus Project' is fueled by learning from Rora that the San Francisco police shot a Bosnian man smoking on the patio of a nonsmoking Starbucks: "They couldn't understand him, and they wouldn't wait for someone to interpret" (43).

Miller's character finds a counterpart in a Boston-based psychiatrist whose typed journals make up the third chapter of Tomasula's *Book of Portraiture*. The journal entries, dated 1917, document the psychiatrist's treatment of "Miss P." and are reminiscent of Freud's case study of Dora. The psychiatrist strives to remove all traces of himself from his "medical diagram" in order to achieve a scientific gaze—he equates this gaze with a view from the camera. Furthermore, he borrows expressions from evolutionary theories, psychoanalysis, and criminology, and glosses ideas taken from Darwin's *Expression of Emotions* and ethnographer William B. Seabrook's *The Magic Island* (1917). In *Expressions of Emotions*, Darwin projects a normative self and attends to how aberrations in others ("idiots" and animals) shed light on normative self-expression. And, as I have already mentioned, Darwin used neuropsychiatric photographs to codify these expressions. In the psychiatrist's journal, the page glossing Darwin's views is headlined "The Camera Does Not Lie." Two copies of the same portrait, flipped horizontally, are presented side by side on the page. In one instance, the portrait is captioned as demonstrating rage and in another as demonstrating surprise (89). Tomasula's multimodal design emphasizes that the relationship between pictures and the language that frames them (whether in the form of a caption or narrative) is neither stable nor does it default to "truth." The psychiatrist's journal also includes a sketch titled "Curing a Hysteric" dated 1889 that recalls the history of medical photos and illustrations of hysteria (125). A common diagnosis in the nineteenth and early twentieth centuries, hysteria essentially identified women as deviant subjects and pathologized their expressions. For example, a front-page article in the *Tribune* (in our actual world) published on March 3, 1908 identifies Lazarus's sister as hysteric for crying out "Mama! Mama!" on seeing her brother's corpse.

Given that the psychiatrist in Tomasula's novel imagines himself as a camera, he interacts with Miss P. as though she is the subject in a picture he is simultaneously capturing and reading. He edits details of their sessions "to make those of scientific import stand out," which means he is selecting and manipulating information (91). He is taken aback by her behavior when she first walks into his cabin and lays down on a couch where he has earlier treated veterans through electroshock. He observes, "Perhaps P. read something of these dolorous experiments in my face and felt a twinge of empathy for me. Or perhaps . . . she had a distaste for ceremony . . . Not knowing what else to do in the face of such boldness, I took my station" (93). At this point, he is having difficulty investing P. with mental states, but then he begins to read her fluently—every perceptual information he encounters serves as epistemic justification for a diagnosis he seems to have arrived at even before meeting her. "The rhetoric of her corset" along with "her talk of liberation" come across as "an attempt through fashion to code her body as available" to him (95); her "gloves falling away" is "obviously a token of her shedding her dress" (99). His cognitive frame is that of "the psycho-analyst who knows what to look for and concentrates until he sees it" (99). In other words, his prior expectations can neither be corrected nor adjusted, since he is simply looking for justification.

Like Miller of *Lazarus Project*, the psychiatrist views madness as deviance from accepted codes of behavior and appearance. Both take their estranged stance toward others to be "objective." They are also convinced of their own distinction from the subjects—the anarchist degenerate, the woman—they study. Their assumptions encourage them to continue attributing—indeed misattributing—intentions and motivations to others. The psychiatrist diagnoses his patient as suffering from "frustration of sexual nature," and he speculates that her disease will manifest itself in "lesbian hysteria" or "nymphomania" (109). The details he offers as "proof" of the woman's disorders, like the physiological features of Lazarus Averbuch listed by Miller, do not prove or disprove anything. As Chevaillier observes, "The young woman's therapy ends up revealing more about the psychologist's own sexual needs than about those of his supposedly neurotic patient" (2015, 118–19). The psychiatrist's medical diagram of his patient is *his* selfie.

Tomasula's novel thus folds critiques of psychiatry and the pathologies it discovered like hysteria and sexual repression into his novel. The psychiatrist is shown to rely heavily on thought attribution. *Book of Portraiture*'s critical representation of the psychiatrist reveals how we, in the twenty-first century, think about the methods of the mind sciences of the late nineteenth and early twentieth centuries.

After the psychiatrist anticipates that Miss P. may break into "lesbian hysteria," he spots her laughing with another female friend, and his encoded cognitive frame activates. He wonders whether what he is seeing is "the perfect portrait of an older and more experienced woman who had already begun to instruct her young initiate in the ways of the world. Or was it a portrait of nascent Sapphism?" (127). He is so sure of his own diagnostic powers that he fails to see how his patient frames or deceives him after the initial sessions. She tells him that she is seeking but not finding a husband, an inference that he had earlier made about her and related to her. She gives him the pleasure of thinking he is curing her. The "other" he thinks he has cured is of his own making. Even when he finds out that "she had fabricated the entire story [his] analysis was based upon," he does not question his methods (112). Instead, he finds justification for them and observes, "as Lombroso and Ferro have shown, the female of our species, being nearer to the savage, has an actual physiological incapacity for telling the truth" (112). Evidently, the psychiatrist manifests problems with thought attribution by taking attribution to extreme lengths. Through him, Tomasula explores fixedness of preestablished beliefs that will not be reconfigured, no matter what perceptual signals one encounters. The cognitive reward for mindreading in the instances I discussed is the confirmation of a preexisting cognitive frame.

If attribution occurring in this spectatorial way was the primary means of communication, then social cognition would be quite impossible. Predictive processing approaches thus stress probabilistic embodied exchanges among brain-body-world rather than endorse the idea that one subject attributes mental states to another. In predictive processing, a mismatch between sensory data and predicted data is understood as a condition that leads to learning and minimizing future prediction errors.

Predictive Processing or Adjusting Expectations

Frames in narrative and art direct perceptions and judgements, but as Brian Richardson observes, they

> invite their own deconstruction because they appear so definitive yet are obviously partially arbitrary and capable of being reconstructed or placed themselves within a larger, different frame; this can be easily demonstrated by any painter who depicts a fly on the wood surrounding the painting proper, or any author who ends a story by saying, "At least that was one version. Of course, there are other, different ones." (2002, 330)

Lazarus Project and *Book of Portraiture* construct and violate representational frames (pictorial and narrative borders) in ways that figuratively establish how conceptual frames—including those that distinguish selves from others—are malleable. In *Book of Portraiture,* as I have already mentioned, a rough outline of *Las Hilanderas* (by Maria Tomasula) is included and framed by the narrative of chapter two attributed to Velasquez. *Las Hilanderas* itself copied and incorporated Titian's painting *The Rape of Europa* as though it were a tapestry woven in the competition between Athena and Arachne (62). A picture framed within another bigger picture underscores endless possibilities of framing and violating frames. Because representational frames are open to endless reconfigurations, Brik can reframe Lazarus's picture.

Though early cognitive sciences appropriate framing as an analogy from art and architecture, the cognitivist understanding underplays the extent to which frames invite and anticipate reconfiguration. Stressing the probability and inevitability of reconfiguring downward flowing predictions is an important way predictive processing frameworks are distinguished from first-generation cognitivist positions. Prediction errors are common, and so, predictive processing entails feedback and embodied exchange among agents and environments. For example, when Brik spots a can in the kitchen and reads its label as saying SADNESS, his mood (not yet articulated in the narrative) is likely penetrating his visual experience. However, soon enough, he realizes that "it was not SADNESS but SARDINES" (73). The upward flowing sensory stimuli reconfigures his perception and inference drawn from it. The correspondences in the spellings of sadness and sardines also emphasize that it was the label that was the basis for his misperception. If he had discerned a few letters in "sardines," it was probable, based on his knowledge of the language, that the arrangement of letters could lead to "sadness." It was a probabilistic inference supported by both the sensory signal at hand and his emotional state, albeit a wrong inference that is later corrected. What he momentarily perceives due to his expectation and mood becoming manifest as a can's label then begins to impact his narration. After the mood becomes expressed as a word, the word begins to permeate his sentences. He remarks, "Sadness was now the dark matter in the universe of still objects around me . . . My country's main exports are stolen cars and sadness" (73). Brik's experience as presented by Hemon demonstrates the circular causal flows between conceptual thinking and sensory experience, continuous exchange of information between subjects and their surroundings.

Causal flows and feedback also characterize the social interactions through which Brik's sense of self emerges. Brik's experiential background of being an immigrant in America guides his interest in the figure of Lazarus. The experience generates expectations concerning the trajectory on which he can take his fictional retelling of history. It is his experience that prompts him to not provide an "intellectual niche"[22] to the stereotype of the harmful immigrant through narration. Also, what he infers from extant historical records and how he imagines Lazarus is ultimately geared toward action—the action of constituting a self-narrative in response to his present social experience. He mentions that his wife and father-in-law seem to speak of his past in Bosnia as though it were an exhibit in a museum or a piece of fiction. So, he sets out to, quite paradoxically, compose a well-researched fiction to authenticate his autobiographical experiences. The rift between his wife, Mary, and him shows when Mary indicates that his desire to pursue the Lazarus story is pretentious because his "own American life was nothing to complain about" (42). Given their experiential backgrounds, the cultural niches they have inhabited, Mary and Brik actively sample their environments and experiences differently.

As I have mentioned, Brik draws conceptual borders between himself and Miller, while refusing to assume a spectatorial position with respect to Lazarus. The first chapter of Hemon's book primarily consists of the Lazarus story, which leaves room for a reader to have an initial impression that the 1908 sections of the novel are an "objective," heterodiegetic retelling of what happened

---

22. This is Clark's (2016) term for agents who make up an extended network.

to Lazarus. Only after readers settle into the pattern of the book—its alternating chapters—and recognize the unremarked upon, inobtrusive "I" that surfaces from time to time in the Lazarus narrative as Brik, do they realize that it is Brik fictionalizing and authoring Lazarus's story. Brik reconstructs his own childhood memories (e.g., of playing hide-and-seek) to imagine Lazarus's subjectivity. He offers his own epiphanies to Lazarus's sister (30, 7). Like Brik, Lazarus becomes an aspiring writer in the fictional retelling. While assigning his ideas and inferences to Lazarus, Brik also attempts to use what he learns of Lazarus as a medium to transmute his sense of self. The structure of Brik's narrative, the priority given to the Lazarus story in its arrangement, drives home the centrality of the historical episode in the causal networks that constitute Brik as a subject. That is, the narrative establishes the extent to which Brik's project of selfieing depends on his perception of another person.

The boundaries of Brik's self are neither fixed nor stable because they can only be realized in interactions with the wider social world. Beside Lazarus, the character of Rora becomes an intrinsic part of the dynamical unfolding of Brik's selfhood. Rora and Brik grew up and knew each other in prewar Bosnia. In the later years, Rora witnessed the war (1992–1995) but Brik did not, since he had moved to America by then. They find each other at a gathering of Chicago Bosnians in 2004. Like the other Chicago Bosnians, they share the feeling that they do not quite belong in America. More significantly, they share certain ways of parsing their present environments.

When Brik first tells Rora about the Lazarus incident, Rora immediately connects it with the lynching of Mexican farmhands in Indiana and police brutality in San Francisco (unlike Mary, who treats Lazarus's death as an event removed from the sphere of their everyday experiences). It is Rora who first suggests that Brik should go to "where [Lazarus] came from" because "there is always a before and an after" (46). Once they reach eastern Europe, they begin to negotiate their idea of home and also their relationship with each other. Brik constantly asks Rora about the war years in Bosnia, partly out of curiosity, and partly because Rora is an expert storyteller (Brik mentions how he admires "Rora's narrative embroidery" [103–4]). It is implied in the narrative that Brik will subsequently appropriate these stories. He has done it before—he has presented to Mary stories he picked up from other people as autobiographical incidents. He can only be himself by being others, and that is why the belief "the only one who was not me was myself" runs like a refrain through his narration (235). What is more, Brik's epiphanies, observations, and ideas are frequently echoed by Rora, and vice versa; so, it becomes impossible to track their source. For instance, even Brik's silent identification with others around him, whereby Brik looks at an individual and thinks "that's me" (235) is articulated by Rora as a joke (237–38) and surfaces in Lazarus's sister's (fictionalized by Brik) thoughts (172). The order in which readers encounter the repetition confounds attempts at source tracking—the origins of the beliefs, motivations, and thoughts that make up the characters in Hemon's novel are blurred. The circulation of phrases and events between the embedded and embedding narratives undercuts the singularity of subjective experiences. *Lazarus Project* thereby presents subjectivities as inextricably entangled, part of nested loops.

That Brik's interactions with Rora reconfigure his prior beliefs and expectations becomes especially apparent in his changing attitude to photography. Brik initially wants Rora to photograph their surroundings during the research trip because he wants to consult them for writing the Lazarus story. He is interested in photographs for their epistemic value—what they can tell him about the past and what they can record of the present. Brik often describes conditions of low visibility in both the narrative documenting his journey and his fiction (for instance, "We left the city on a poorly lit road" [100]). He expects Rora to overcome these conditions with the help of a flash. Rora, on the other hand, has little interest in pursuing such epistemological projects. He is of the opinion that "what does not need to be seen will not be seen" (71), and his embodied activities have a reciprocal relation with his theories. He does not bring a flash to their trip to eastern Europe. The photos he ends up taking are blurred and foggy, capturing what exists on the fringes of intelligibility, transforming rather than mirroring and magnifying Brik's perception of his surroundings (I discuss the blurred photos further in the following section). Rora understands that other people value photographs as records, but he does not care for their documentary functions. He tells Brik that he takes photos simply because he likes to look at them. Eventually Brik too begins to value photographs almost exclusively for aesthetic reasons and for their affective import rather than as memory aids. He observes, "The pictures would offer no revelations; I would have seen all that mattered, because I was present at the moment of their creation" (228). Brik can approach photographs as something other than a recording device once he has "achieved the freedom of being comfortable with the constant vanishing of the world" (229). This is an attitude Rora models for him. Progressively Rora's attitudes regulate Brik's expectations. Brik's emergent self depends on a multitude of such reciprocal exchanges with agents and objects around him throughout the novel.

Book of Portraiture's chapters similarly chart circular causal flows among characters and their worlds: characters in the narrative become self-aware through interactions with their surroundings. Chapter One follows an initially unnamed character who invents symbols for transcribing sound. The character's invention is grounded in his immediate experiential life world, dependent on his knowledge-driven parsing of sensory stimuli: he hears an ox low while dozing off and recalls seeing a symbol resembling an ox head. It also occurs to him that the West Semitic word for ox is *aleph* and he draws a simple ox head in sand (4). What he draws is a remediation of Middle Bronze Age glyphs he has earlier seen carved in stone. While drawing, he pronounces "not the animal's whole name, aleph, but only its first sound: Aa" (7). Thus, the process of inventing a semiotic system is represented as distributed among a host of entities in the storyworld.

Realizing *Book of Portraiture*'s sustained thematic interest in selfieing, the unnamed narrator decides to "transform" and "transmute" himself with the technology he has invented. He begins to portray himself in words, beginning with "I, Moses, born of the Nile . . ." (15). The emergence of "I," the first-person pronoun, and an accompanying mode of self-consciousness are prompted by the nexus among brain-body-world. The self-constituting narrative Moses composes draws upon Assyrian legends: he models his origin story after that of King Sargon, just as Velazquez in Chapter Two models himself after artists like Titian and Rembrandt. The opening chapter of *Book of Portraiture* thus sets up a multidirectional causal network constituting selfhood: Moses's subjectivity is shown to emerge from his interactions with novel media as well as other actual and imagined entities in his world. The self so formed defies an internalist or mentalist description given how it is bound up with the surroundings. This dynamic repeats with variation throughout the novel. As the chapters (and centuries) progress, the number of agents and media that constitute the characters' sense of self multiply. Even the psychiatrist who believes he has an "objective" gaze is, first of all, negotiating his idea of perception and of himself with the affordances and constraints of a camera. He is also proactively selecting perceptual stimuli to match his downflowing predictions and drawing (incorrect) inferences about the situation. That is, though the psychiatrist does not recognize it, due to his dogmatic beliefs and expectations, he too is situated within a series of relations that include his patient.

Chapters Four and Five of Tomasula's novel trace the rise of digital photography, video surveillance, and transgenic art in the late twentieth and early twenty-first centuries. The fourth chapter depicts the continuous flow of thought and perceptions through eight strangers identified with a letter each. The letter reflects an aspect of their profession (e.g., P__ for a programmer/hacker; U__ a model; I__ a private investigator). The chapter layout wherein paragraphs and sentences cascade across pages without being clearly tagged as originating in the consciousness of a single character visually represents the extended dynamic network this chapter imagines. There are micro feedback loops nested within the larger network: so, particular characters cross paths while accomplishing specific tasks. The chapter opens with an investigator, I__, observing that he is being watched. I__ tries "to make out the face looking at him through the glare of an apartment window across the courtyard . . . as steadily as a camera" and fails (150). Based on his past experiences as an investigator, he equates the gaze of the observer with a surveillance camera and assumes that he is under surveillance (221). The knowledge that he is being watched guides his embodied activity in his social world. Given that the letter identifying the character is also the first-person pronoun, the opening move of this chapter is to establish that self-consciousness emerges through one's correlation of current sensory signals with prior self-related events.

In an essay that speculates about the history of subjectivity and self-representation along the lines of *Book of Portraiture*, Tomasula identifies the Gutenberg printing press as the tool that "helped create Renaissance individuals with unique, individual features" as opposed to "the generic character types in Medieval mystery plays written by anonymous authors" (2018, 40). The digital media ecology seems to revert subjectivities to almost medieval genericness in *Book of Portraiture* as the narrative becomes invested in showing the continuous flow of expectations, information, and perception across diverse characters. The twenty-first-century characters in the novel are generic, but generic in the sense of being "content-free, relational forms" rather than fixed stereotypes (Metelmann and Telios 2018, 336). Characters tentatively emerge out of patterns of online and offline behaviors.

Tomasula's narrative is critical of the extent to which such relations and networks can be tracked and commodified in a digital ecology. The professions of several characters in this chapter require them to monitor patterns and make predictions to maximize the consumption of various products. They are involved in data analysis, but the irony of course is that they are the data they analyze. Chapter Four also features website links and advertisements underlining how behavior is monitored in the storyworld: for example, a swimsuit advertisement says, "YOU ARE ON SURVEILLANCE AN AVERAGE OF 10 TIMES A DAY . . . ARE YOU DRESSED FOR IT?" (238). Such an advertisement further establishes that I___'s form of self-consciousness that integrates the view of a surveillance camera is not uniquely his; rather, the awareness of being tracked is a shared condition in the storyworld.

A video graphic designer in the same chapter, identified as V___, dwells on the idea that the sociality of the self may possibly precede self and other, internal and external, conceptual and perceptual distinctions. During busy shifts at work, she experiences images "flow[ing] like ghosts through her head, through her hand and mouse (for during these times they seemed as one), onto her screen, then out over the airways, through satellites and other nodes and systems and onto everyone's screen as if there were no boundary between images in her head and images in their heads, which is probably where the images in her head came from to begin with" (164). The condition V__ reflects on—in which images are shared across networks of subjects and technologies—is also multimodally illustrated in the novel.

Pixelated photographs appearing throughout the chapter show a human body without the face (179, 236, 248; see Figure 2.4). The picture is generic rather than recognizable as a particular person. The verbal discourse identifies the model for the generic body circulating in the storyworld as U__. The second person pronoun, like mirror selfies and *Las Meninas,* calls attention to the readers'/viewers' position and can make them self-conscious, though U__ is also a specific character, a high-end fashion model in the storyworld. The pixelation obscures information that could individuate U__ and mediates how other characters experience her photographs.

While characters in Chapter Four of Tomasula's narrative lead distinct lives, ubiquitous images of U__ on billboards, magazine covers, and products serve as touch points among them. B__, the character who edits the model's photographs, intends to capitalize on the possibility of having a picture stimulate collective fantasies. He observes, "The lesson is to imagine a body that can be all things to all people, at least to most shoppers, i.e., the great bulge in the demographic bell curve" (218–19). He predicts the hypothetical roles into which viewers fit the picture of a female body. The social-cultural world he inhabits and its conventions of representation influence his predictions. He understands that individuals see photographs in slightly different ways and contexts—their familial and familiar surroundings regulate their perception. So, his imperative is to produce a picture that minimizes the gap between the sensory information the artifactual picture of the model offers and the models generated by those individuals who interact with the picture. In this sense, he is designing a "generative model" for an extended cognitive system, given that, as Clark says, the task of the generative model is "to capture the simplest approximations that will support actions required to do the job" (2016, 291). In this case, doing the job entails selling the product with which U__'s image affectively connects individuals. The editor succeeds in his probabilistic guessing game (supported by data analysis), and a character perceives the picture to be that of her mother, and another character makes it into an object of his sexual desires (173). The pictures of U__ that the characters encounter are

P............P............P............P............P............P............
Q............Q............Q............Q............Q............Q............
I............I............I............I............I............I............
U............U............U............U............U............U............
V............V............V............V............V............V............
B............B............B............B............B............B............
X............X............X............X............X............X............
T............T............T............T............T............T............
N............N............N............N............N............N............

Back in the FBI, the only Rabbit they ever lost was that Spy for Airbus. Not shackled to the politics of purchasing committees, the Rabbit's corporate-backed counter surveillance team had used the latest in de-encrypting scanners to trump their counter-counter-surveillance, outfitted with an old administration's government issue, and the first thing that occurred to I__ now was that he had stumbled onto a bigger, more sophisticated operation than one nineteen-year-old Cashier.

Aberration Reports
Region 0008District 0389
Scoring Type: All Cashiers

Number	Score	Title
Report 1	3	Cash Return/Sales
Report 2	3	Avg. Check Returns
Report 3	4	Returns to Same Acct
Report 4	3	Exchanges
Report 5	3	Post Voids/% Sales
Report 6	3	Cash Post Voids/Sale
Report 7	4	Post Voids/No Sales
Report 8	3	Post Voids/5 Trans.A
Report 9	4	Voids Employee Purch
Report 10	4	Transact. Voids
Report 11	3	Line Item Voids
Report 12	4	Price Modifications
Report 13	4	Sales Not Scanned
Report 14	3	% Sales Keyed
Report 15	4	% Credit Card Scan
Report 16	3	Gift Certificates
Report 17	4	Payouts
Report 18	2	No Sale Transactions
Report 19	2	Sign Off Transaction
Report 20	-	Cashier Profile

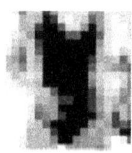

Breasts & Bones
Models who have protruding hipbones, ribs or other features that could deflect attention from a swimsuit or article of lingerie will not be selected....

On-Going Management (Cont.)
...if response is poor, consider adding lithium or switching the patient to another drug. Other antidepressants include: Tricyclics: amitriptyline (Elavil®); imipramine (Tofranil®); doxepin (Sinequan®) clomipramine (Anafranil®); haloperidol decanoate (Haldol LA®); benztropine mesylate (Cogentin®); trihexyphenidyl (Artane®); procyclidine (Kemadrin®); amantadine (Symmetrel®); benzodiazepines: flurazepam (Dalmane®); nitrazepam (Mogadan®); lorazepam (Ativan®); chlordiazepoxide (Librium®)....

FIGURE 2.4. Layout of a page from chapter 4 of *Book of Portraiture* showing a pixelated photo of U__ alongside generic instructions for selecting a model. Image courtesy Steve Tomasula.

not pixelated or of poor-quality in the storyworld. They are most likely sharp, commercial photos. The pixelated photos included in the book thus figuratively represent what the editor does to the model's appearance and what other characters approximate from that appearance.

That these segments of Tomasula's narrative match so well and so overtly with the expectations set out in a predictive processing model is not incidental: Tomasula pursues a self-reflective and self-conscious style of writing. He is depicting how subjectivities begin to be configured as variations in statistical patterns within a digital media ecology. It is the same ecology, the same media substrate that generates predictive processing as a framework to think about thought.

A seemingly direct match of sensory information with prior expectations or knowledge-driven hypothesis, however, does not guarantee that the subject will be able to draw the appropriate inference and act in an appropriate manner. In the chapter of *Book of Portraiture* I am discussing, Queenie, a character who had for a time operated statistical modeling programs and then served in the army, recalls an incident wherein a little girl ran in front of her jeep. Queenie recalls how "framed by the windshield, the girl smiled, enigmatic as Mona Lisa, and as though that smile was their cue, others opened fire on the convoy" (183). Queenie compares the girl who may have been instrumental in the ambushing of a convoy with Mona Lisa and in another instance with the Infanta with "an enigmatic smile" in *Las Meninas*. The visual echoes made possible by the frame of the windshield had misled Queenie and the jeep's driver to assume that they understood the girl's intentions. It is only in retrospect that Queenie realizes that what the girl, Mona Lisa, and the Infanta share is a common unknowability.

Sensorimotor Entanglements

I have already discussed how *Lazarus Project* and *Book of Portraiture* illustrate two methods of establishing self–other relations (mindreading, predictive processing) and their cultural implications. Here I will trace a third approach to social cognition implied in the narratives. Earlier in this chapter, I had mentioned that enactivist thinkers like Hutto put forward hypotheses about visceral, organismic sharing of experiences as opposed to the early Theory of Mind's and predictive processing's inductive reason-oriented understandings of interactions. Sharing experiences need not require the self to infer others' thoughts. Zahavi and Philippe Rochat (2015) observe that while the separation of self from others is empathy's precondition,[23] sharing is "a dynamically emergent and negotiated we-experience" (Zahavi and Rochat 2015, 545). Sharing rather than empathy suggests the possibility of living with another without assuming self–other distinctions.

In *Lazarus Project,* Brik and Rora visit a cemetery in eastern Europe with a woman called Iuliana as their guide. As soon as they enter the cemetery, Brik recalls, "the birds were suddenly quiet; there were no sounds whatsoever coming from the outside; indeed there was no outside. The leaves did not move as we brushed past them; there was no sun, though there was light, heavy and vicious. This was all, the world of the dead: Rozenberg, Mandelbaum, Berger, Mandelstam, Rosenfield, Spivak, Urrman, Weinstein. I could not remember how long I had been away, how I had gotten to this point. Hoydee-do, haydee-hi, all I ever do is die" (234). Brik's description evokes a self-organizing, self-sustaining ambience—he says, the place seemed to have "no outside" (234). Within this ambience, every agent co-enacts and lives through the same experience. The birds, the leaves, Brik, Iuliana, and Rora cannot be understood independent of their commingling and coupling in this scene. This experience is analogically described by Brik as though it were a photograph: there is no sound, no movement; only light. Brik is stretching the linguistic mode to develop a photograph, reaching for Rora's expressive mode in the process. Every element that has been photographed (in language) is still. This stillness prefigures death, the condition that all the agents in the ambience will experience. As Rora says, "Everybody who has ever been photographed is either dead or will die" (189).[24] Brik's experience of embodied connectivity within the ambience leads him to identify other agents involved in it as himself. He observes:

Iuliana was flustered, blushing, a globule of sweat sliding down past her ear, then curving at the jawline. She smiled at me—I could have kissed her right there, those living lips, those gloaming eyes, that pale face. That's me, I thought. That woman is me. Somewhere beyond the roof of tree crowns the sky grumbled, gearing up for a storm. Rora took a picture of her, then of me, then of us.

It took a while to find a way out. Rora's hair was sweat-pasted to his skull and neck, a gray oval perspiration growing on his back—the closer we got to exit, the bigger it was. And again, I thought: that's me. The thought bounced

---

23. Empathy "is the experience of the embodied mind of the other, an experience which, rather than eliminating the difference between self-experience and other-experience, takes the asymmetry to be a necessary and persisting existential fact" (Zahavi 2014, 151).

24. Barthes has called photographers "agents of Death" (1981, 92).

in my head deliriously, I couldn't get to the end of it, could not fold it up into meaning. Iuliana walked behind; I heard her gentle panting. She was me, Rora was me, and then we came upon the man on the bench, drooling asleep, his mouth open enough for us to see a graveyard of teeth, his hand wedged inside his pants' waist—and he was me, too. The only one who was not me was myself. (235)

It is a moment of heightened emotional arousal in which Brik almost exclusively perceives the shapes and rhythms of bodies around him: Iuliana's blushing, pale face, her jawline, ears, the rhythms of her breath; Rora's perspiring skull, neck; the agape mouth of the sleeping man. His body identifies with the cadences and experiences of other bodies. His identification with Rora and Iuliana may still be understood in terms of imputing and inference—he has interacted with them earlier and so, perhaps likens himself with them based on what he knows about them, but such an interpretation cannot quite explain how he identifies with the sleeping man. Brik's identification with the sleeping man is primarily somatic. The manifold connections and resemblances that Brik sees generate a particular version of his subjectivity. By negotiating distinctions with the various individuals around him he is arriving at a "we-experience." Even while narrating the experience, Brik admits that he "could not fold it into meaning" because this self-generating experience cannot be specified in any terms other than those making up the experience. There is an irreducible core to the experience, Brik's narration insists.

Brik and Rora's travel photographs visually manifest these sorts of embodied experiences, wherein I and you blur, and with it blur conditions for inferential sense-making. The historical photographs included in *Lazarus Project* are sharper and convey more visual information than most of the recent photos taken by Rora (taken by Božović for Hemon's novel). The blurred and foggy newer photographs that are part of Brik's self-narrative illustrate his doomed attempts at making sense of not only the fragments of history available in archives but also his lived experiences. The quality of the photographs challenges assumptions about the camera affording greater perceptual clarity. When Rora gets film rolls developed, Brik reports, "I could discern next to nothing" (228). Sonia Weiner observes, "Smudged, distorted, and blurry land- or-cityscapes parallel Brik's sense of disorientation in eastern Europe, and his utter lack of direction, experienced by him as an 'ontological warp' (LP 68). In this dream-like reality, Brik becomes a 'confused character' within a 'narrative that has gone completely haywire,' and feels caught within a plot from which he is 'unable to escape' (126–27)" (2014, 229). The photographs foreshadow the frustrating ends of Brik's epistemological quest to resurrect Lazarus and the journey through eastern Europe. He aspired to play the writer-investigator using archival photographs as evidence. However, the archival photographs sustain contesting possible explanations for Lazarus's intentions, and so he knows they can always be framed again. Moreover, his Lazarus project itself leads to Rora's accidental death. After Brik and Rora reach Sarajevo, the city that used to be their home, Rora gets shot in a café. Brik was not there with Rora at the time and later tries to make sense of it through the many stories Rora told him about the war years. He tries to make it fit longer cause–effect chains, but eventually learns that a petty thief was trying to steal Rora's camera and the man's "gun went off" (291). As if seized by the very action he initiated, the man kept on firing at Rora.

The blurred photos suggest that Rora used long exposure to make up for the poor lighting conditions in which he shot them, and either his hands or the objects within the frame moved. The photographs make visible the movements of his eyes and hands. They also show that Rora, at times, tried to capture motion through still photography and failed. It is analogous to Brik's attempt at developing photographs in language. Rora's failed photos visually capture the state of "emergence"—they depict a condition in which things are in the process of coming into view but never quite arrive (see Figure 2.5). Brik will never understand what happened to Lazarus. He will also fail to make sense of Rora's death.

Hemon's collaborator Božović points out that blurred photographs render a shared experience of transition. He had travelled to eastern Europe with Hemon to develop photos for the novel. When asked about the blurred photos, Božović says,

> long exposures are result of, and speak to, different things. We travelled a lot in a relatively short period of time (one month). Scenes were coming up quickly and unexpectedly. Sometimes a long exposure was just necessary to take the photograph. Not all long exposures were there because I wanted to say something with them. Many were a result of the camera setting that I didn't have time to alter, or even forgot to alter. So, in retrospect, they are the reflection of the road trip, they expose duration and maybe "the collision of past and present," they also refer to transition in which that part of the world was going through (and still does) from Communism to Capitalism. The transition was brutal to the vast majority of people. And that transition is blurry, just like some of those images, in which only a few have the means to clearly see what is and was going on. (Zelnick n.d)

FIGURE 2.5. Blurred photo illustrating Brik-Rora's experience
of journeying through Eastern Europe

Within the narrative, the photographs disclose Brik's and Rora's shared experience of being in transit as migrants and travelers. They also encapsulate the bodily feeling of being in flux, not only during travel but also more generally, during any experience.

Brik remarks that "a human face consists of other faces—the faces you inherited or picked up along the way, or the ones you simply made up—laid on top of each other in a messy superimposition" (105). In Hemon's fiction, the self is a product of such "a messy superimposition"—Brik picks up Rora's beliefs and intentions, makes up Lazarus's, and so on. Both the verbal discourse and the included pictures insist on the presence of the other in the self and the self in the other.

Like Brik, characters in the fifth and last chapter of *Book of Portraiture* experience togetherness in ways that are primarily somatic. Chapter Five of Tomasula's novel is both formally and thematically interested in forms of embodied connectivity that are primordial rather than inferential. Two apparently distinct narratives, one set in America and another in the Middle East, progress simultaneously in the chapter, bordering each other. The bodily makeup of organisms—human and nonhuman—determine all relations and expressions in both narratives. Mary, one of the two main characters of the US-based narrative, is a biotechnician and creates transgenic art. Her partner, Paul, had been a premed major and assists her in her projects. The narrative follows his perspective. The Middle East-based narrative follows Saroush, who is a bench technician and has just lost his daughter, Fatima. Tomasula's choice of characters and situations in this chapter ensures that the bodily dimensions of experiences and the infinite affective potential of bodies (that is, their ability to affect and be affected) remain at the forefront. The narration identifies bodies as a locus of sociality; bodies afford and constrain patterns of interactions, initiate and enact structural couplings.

For helping Mary to create an embryo, Paul has to kill lab mice and, despite training and experience, responds to the animals' predicament at a visceral level. We are told, "the killing always got a reaction from him. Holding the soft underbelly of the dead mouse between thumb and forefinger, he snipped it open with surgical scissors. Not a big reaction; but a little one, like anyone might get when it was their turn to gas the used rats, or do anything unpleasant" (286). Other bodies—that of the mice—prompt a particular form of awareness in Paul. Tomasula's sentences convey the affective involvement Paul feels with the animal he is holding and with which he is negotiating a "we-experience." The bodily details of the animal are presented only in relation to Paul's body—in fact, there are more references to his body parts and actions (thumb, forefinger; holding, snipped) than those of the mice (underbelly). The somatic interaction between Paul and the animal induces feelings of similarity and difference. Not the mice's carcass, but Paul's embodied coupling with it prompts his "reaction" or emotional arousal. The following sentence further suggests that Paul is not alone in experiencing this form of biological connectivity, but that bodies are attuned to respond to one another the same way. The narrative thus leaves open the possibility that readers, too, will realize this bodily connectivity and become affectively invested in Paul's as well as the mice's biological states.

To show how basic, biological attunement cuts across social and cultural borders, Tomasula's narrative parallels Paul's experiences and awareness with Saroush's. As Saroush witnesses his daughter's death, his responses are first and foremost somatic. He notes the frailty of his daughter's body, and realizes that "her body, like all bodies, determined to have the last word" (288). It is in moments of profound unsettlement or disorientation that characters become mindful of connections that were always there. Another instance of the same phenomena, that is, structural couplings founded on bodily resonances, materializes when an Imam tells Saroush that they will identify Fatima as a "martyr," and as Saroush hesitates to overtly politicize his daughter's death, the Imam says, he can fire a gun near Saroush's ear: "Fear will make you know with your entrails" (298). Subsequently, Saroush realizes that what the Imam is trying to induce is not fear but terror, because "fear was always fear of something. Terror was what the body did while in that unknown something's fury" (304). Fear and terror, the narration indicates, are familiar to all bodies. The Imam's threat is effective because it recognizes and capitalizes on this shared bodily makeup.

Both Paul's and Saroush's narratives and contemplations flourish into descriptions of corporeal connections that fuse subjectivities. Paul reflects on his grandmother's migration from war-torn Lithuania to America. She landed in the Midwest in the wake of rumors that people from her country had moved there, but, as it turned out, only the windows of a church in the city had come from Lithuania. However, her movement determined Paul's life and identity. As he begins to consider the chances and circumstances "so old and interwoven" (315) that account for who he is, he perceives the essential similarity among organisms, because "if a person counted back 120,000 generations to Adam, the first ameba, even words like fish and mammal began to blur—forget about monkey/man" (316). His grandmother was penniless and did not know English when she got on a boat to come to the US, but he feels, she came with "an understanding deeper than marrow that she was part of something larger than herself" (316). An analogous picture of relatedness surfaces in the Middle East-based narrative. Saroush's grief for his daughter comes to be embodied by the hordes of mourners who trail Fatima's corpse, beating their chests, wailing, and lashing their own bodies (321). The rhythm of this bodily performance of mourning is familiar to Saroush from Ashura processions, but the ritualistic mourning in this instance also reveals how an experience he assumed to be personal is interpersonal (and political).

Hayles observes that while an individual chapter of Tomasula's novel works "with a set of characters we can understand in the ways typical of realistic novels, the entire scope of the text is much, much larger" (2015, 134). The macronarrative structure manifests connections that defy straightforward causal explanations. These connections are simultaneously primordial and technological, given that technologies engender particular modes of selfieing throughout the novel. Across the five chapters, Tomasula presents experiences to be transnationally and transhistorically resonant. It is a playful affirmation of the extensive possibilities for social cohesion should such resonances become the basis for societies, but in the novel itself, social cohesion is always coming into view but never quite arriving. The shared enactment of grief for Fatima, for instance, is ultimately going to serve the Imam's divisive politics.

Book of Portraiture is a novel about selfieing in which the self is not an individual but a recurring, emergent pattern. The last chapter of *Book of Portraiture* thus gives way to grids of empty frames. Since the events described in the chapter include Fatima's death and also a plane crash, Pawel Frelik interprets the frames as coffins (2014, n. pag.). Chevaillier (2015) observes that the empty frames are suggestive of thumbnails, a commonplace template into which profile pictures and selfies are made to fit. Both interpretations bring forward the commonality and sharedness suggested in the scaling down of representations to specific frames. One of the pages displaying the frames is captioned, "All people are shaped in Your Image" (316, 322–23). The caption and the frames together recall Metelmann and Tolioc's claim about the self becoming a "content-free, relational form" in the process of habitually clicking and sharing selfies. In the end *Book of Portraiture* makes clear that everyone can be shaped in the image of the self because there are no predetermined or stable divisions between selves and others.

State of Mind

Tomasula's and Hemon's novels consistently explore the sociality of selves and dramatize the constitution of subjectivity through interpersonal interactions. In this chapter, I traced how the narratives depict particular self–other relations during specific historical periods and cultural experiences. The narratives, as I show, remain interested in exploring the cognitive tendencies that play a role in the disenfranchisement of certain groups of individuals (immigrants, the "degenerate," and so on) in our societies. By presenting how characters' experiential backgrounds and proactive inferences result in their identificatory and discriminatory stances, the narratives contend the idea that one's assimilation of cultural stereotypes is inevitable.

Lazarus Project and *Book of Portraiture* opt for epistemological heterogeneity to account for the variable relations among selves and others, presenting both predictive and enactive forms of couplings in the process. My reading of the two novels with reference to cognitive-scientific and philosophical approaches to subjectivity and social interactions reflects on the complex, dialogic relations between aesthetic representations of minds and psychological and philosophical models of thinking. In closing, I return to my argument from the introductory chapter. Cognition, or contemporary knowledge of it at any rate, relies on historically and culturally contingent representational strategies. Formal properties of pictorial representations, from neuropsychiatric photographs to selfies, modulate conceptualizations about the self and play significant roles in cognitive theories of normative and divergent thinking.

In the following chapter, I continue analysing contemporary narratives' representation of subjectivity and subjective thinking as dynamic processes. Whereas the narratives I discussed in this chapter concern the sociality of the self, those I study in chapter 3 are concerned with its spatial groundings.

CHAPTER 3

Cartographic Minds

Spatial Thinking, Spatial Reading

"A home is also wherever there's good Wi-Fi. That connects me to the world in a way that is irreducible and essential to my experience of the world," Teju Cole says in an interview[1] following the publication of *Blind Spot* (2017), a book-length multimodal lyric essay (Paulson 2017, n. pag.). *Blind Spot* pairs travel photographs that are mystifying rather than traditional landscape shots with fragmentary notes. The notes loosely correspond to the pictures. Siri Hustvedt observes that Cole's project is a "phenomenological one. It is a study of a person's embodied consciousness in relation to the visible world" (2017, xvi). Given that the photos and notes track Cole's travel and flânerie, spatial navigation is fundamental to the experientiality of the self in *Blind Spot*. In a note titled Lugano Cole writes that he had a dream in which his iPhone's camera stopped working just as he was about to click a selfie with Princess Diana. The appearance of the long-deceased Diana does not worry Cole—"There was no shadow of death at the meeting," he reports—but for years after his anxiety dreams feature malfunctioning cameras and other mechanical faults (2017, 302). In both the interview and the book, Cole expresses how ubiquitous technologies—the Wi-Fi, the camera—ground one in the world. Subjectivation is imagined as a dynamic process involving repeated interactions with media technologies for spatial navigation in *Blind Spot*.

---

1. Paulson asks Cole "Do you consider Brooklyn home?" Cole elaborates on the idea of "home" to refer not only to a place but also to an experience (Paulson 2017, n. pag.).

While discussing Tomasula's and Hemon's fictions in chapter 2, I focused on their use of pictures and concepts related to pictorial compositions to present the sociality of the self and the malleability of self–other relations. In this chapter, I concentrate on narratives that reflect on the influence of spatial environments on an individual's sense of self—how our experience of who we are integrates our experience of where we are. Cognitive psychologists and philosophers Michael J. Proulx, Orlin S. Todorov, Amanda Taylor Aiken, and Alexandra A. de Sousa note, "There are a myriad of ways in which our spatial coordinates and our 'selves' are intertwined. Investigating the self in humans and non-human animals from social and spatial perspectives may help explain how spatial factors interact with personality, self, and perception" (2016, n. pag.). To carry out the simplest daily tasks, individuals must navigate their environments. Navigation requires a variety of cognitive skills, including "object recognition (what), localization (where), and obstacle avoidance (how; Maguire et al., 1999)" (Proulx et al. 2016, n. pag.). Learning topographies is an essential dimension of everyday experience.

H. Porter Abbott observes that narrative "is the principal way in which our species organizes its understanding of time" (Abbott 2008, 3). However, spatial factors are so central to our lived experiences that any narrative will also mediate our understanding of space. Traditionally, literary narratives use spatial language to indicate distances among objects and agents in the represented world, present characters' strategies for navigating their environments, and anchor the readers' perceptions of these agents and environments. As the historical conditions of mobility change in the actual world, so do spatial experiences, and narratives of particular eras find ways to represent these shifts. This chapter studies how twenty-first-century narratives render the generative relationship of individuals' experience of spaces with their senses of self. The term "space" in the context of my study includes the built topography of the storyworld as well as the semantic spaces developed by readers as they experience that topography. Specifically, I focus on the representation of mapping as a navigational strategy adopted by characters to find their bearings within their worlds, and the critical claim embedded within such representation about how readers, too, map textual topologies in order to orient themselves in relation to represented objects and entities. Whereas mapping as a cognitive skill for characters is more directly concerned with places and sites, mapping textual topologies implies semantic networking.

By identifying reading with cartography, associating mapping with how readers track their knowledge of storyworlds, the narratives under consideration in this chapter, I argue, self-reflexively prop up the spatial dimensions of the reading experience. In addition, they call attention to the transformation of this experience in a digital media ecology wherein technologies multiply the possible trajectories of movement and channels for distributing attention. The interest in the overlaps of reading with spatial thinking in twenty-first-century print narratives mirrors that of digital literature and arts. As David Ciccoricco observes, "Spatiality constitutes a metadiscourse of digital art and literature," reflected in the coining of terms like Netspace, hyperspace, cyberspace, World Wide Web, and so on (2007, 44). Organizing metaphors employed in early hypertext literature, like the garden (Moulthrop 1993) and the quilt (Jackson 1995), foregrounded spatial logics (Ciccoricco 2007, 44–45). More contemporary mobile narratives and games that utilize location-based information for their progression further highlight the convergence of spatial cognition with narrative comprehension (see de Souza e Silva 2013). The inclusion of maps and their metaphorical implications in codex-based contemporary narratives bespeak the influences of such digital literary practices.

The postscript to Cole's *Blind Spot* traces the book's genesis to Cole's recognition that the map of his movements had become a "map of the world" (2017, 324). However, *Blind Spot* does not include maps as artifacts in the body text (a map appears in the appendix). The notes and photographs connect places Cole visited for research and literary events with texts, dreams, and memories that become associated with his perception of these places. Place names title his notes and photographs. The resulting book, *Blind Spot,* is like a "map overlay," where Cole's experiential relation with places, his perception of distance and proximity, interpose the names of the cities, towns, and villages he visited. The phrase "map overlay" is extensively used in Geographic Information Systems to denote the processes whereby different thematic maps of the same place are layered to visualize relations among them. When I say Cole's book of photographs and notes resembles a "map overlay," I mean the book's structure has much in common with cartographic representations in which different kinds of geographic data are layered and integrated to generate a novel model of spatial relations. *Blind Spot*'s similarity with overlaid mapping is informed by Cole's approach to subjectivity as constituted through encounters with spatial environments of several different kinds, across several different modalities at once.[2]

Like *Blind Spot,* twenty-first-century fictions such as Kamila Shamsie's *Kartography* (2002) and J. J. Abrams and Doug Dorst's *S.* (2013) overlay dif-

---

2. Gehlawat (2020) argues that *Blind Spot* contests the distracted perusal of digital media content and instead offers "a vision of what it might look like to look within, thereby advancing the practice of self-reflection as a form of intersubjective support" (211–24). I agree with Gehlawat that Cole's photos do not emulate dominant social media aesthetics (such as those of selfies), but I do not think *Blind Spot* construes self-reflection as an inward turn, given its interest in the configuration of experiences at the nexus of brain-body-world.

ferent kinds of spatial information to depict the characters' emergent self-awareness. The narratives plot the characters' sites of attention across the same (*Kartography*) or distinct diegetic levels (*S.*), their situated views of objects and people around them, and delineate how spatial knowledge informs their thinking, including their conceptions of who they are. Layering and integrating of spatial information are made possible by semiotic multiplicity in *Kartography* and *S.*: that is, map-like and tour-like linguistic descriptions, innovative use of deictic signposts and the materiality of books, alongside hand-drawn maps attributed to characters in the storyworld, culminate in the intricate design. The aesthetic construction of consciousness in terms of spatial relations reflects an engagement with notions like "cognitive map" and "mental mapping," that grew in popularity through the twentieth century. Moreover, *S.* and *Kartography* include artifactual maps that either illustrate or challenge the "cognitive maps" the characters develop through embodied movements in their worlds. The plurality of maps incorporated in these novels after the style of map overlays compounds and complicates the spatial experiences they afford their readers.

Map overlay in GIS refers to a composite multimodal representation. For example, if one thematic map plots population density, another plots precipitation, and yet another plots water consumption in the same region, a sequence of overlay operations can layer these plots and show new patterns of interdependencies and correlations. Prior to the advent of digital cartographic platforms, an overlay would refer to a clear or semitransparent sheet with information plotted on the same visual scale as a map on which it would be placed to supplement information. This method eventually proved inadequate for representing complex geospatial patterns and in the 1970s, the overlay method migrated to digital platforms. At present, GIS's digital map overlays are not only able to store and layer multiple kinds of plotted data but also synthesize the existing layers in a given order to generate a new layer. While it can be argued that even a single thematic map constitutes different orders of information and multiple semiotic modes, my assertion is that the popularity of GIS and computer-aided cartographic strategies have made the layered, multimodal nature of mapping more legible. Contemporary fictions adopt strategies of layered mapping to present characters who typify the increased mobility of people amid the proliferation of communication technologies in the twenty-first century. A subject can be located at an airport while also staying connected to home through the airport's Wi-Fi, and contemporary narrative constructions of consciousness reflect this dynamic.

The experience of being here and elsewhere at once is not completely "new" in either storyworlds or the actual world. Modernist authors, such as

Marcel Proust, Virginia Woolf, and James Joyce, interweave lived and imagined experiences through what Joseph Frank calls a "spatial form" of narrative; that is, a narrative governed by "space-logic," where thematic resonances among episodes and intertextual references are foregrounded over temporal progression (1991, 115). Cole has expressed his indebtedness to Woolf and Joyce (see Paulson 2017). Christina Ljungberg (2010) has compared the descriptions of diagrammatic representations in Woolf's fiction with maps and other icons included in an overtly multimodal novel by Reif Larsen. However, as Fredric Jameson (1988) observes, in the late nineteenth and early twentieth century, "the phenomenological experience of the individual subject" concerned "a tiny corner of the social world," and novelists adopted narrative techniques that resembled "a fixed-camera view of a certain section of London," although the "truth of that limited daily experience of London . . . is bound up with the whole colonial system of the British Empire . . . Yet those structural coordinates are no longer accessible to immediate lived experience and are often not even conceptualizable for most people" (1991, 349). For Clarissa Dalloway, the realities of the Empire, the life that her friend Peter Walsh led in India for instance, are inconceivable. By contrast, as present-day technologies facilitate actual and virtual movement across places, individuals confront the "elsewhere" (what lies beyond their familiar environments) more frequently and to a greater degree.

The narratives I discuss in this chapter evoke spatial experiences familiar to twenty-first-century readers—the increased frequency of being "here" and "elsewhere" concurrently—through the multiplicity of modes and maps. My analysis of *S.* and *Kartography* traces how their map overlay forms direct attention to the role of cognitive and artifactual maps in grounding subjects (characters and readers) in imagined and actual worlds. In my analysis, I take into account changes in cartographic technologies and accompanying shifts in understanding cognitive activities—like movement, reading, and writing—that are figuratively aligned with mapping. Advancing *Out of Mind*'s diachronic approach to aesthetic forms and cognitive models, this chapter charts the co-emergence of novel strategies of spatial representation and theories of spatial cognition.

Cartographic Minds in Twenty-First-Century Fictions

A number of twenty-first-century narratives, such as Kamila Shamsie's *Kartography* (2002), Mark Haddon's *The Curious Incident of the Dog in the Night-Time* (2002), Steven Hall's *The Raw Shark Texts* (2007), Reif Larsen's *The*

Selected Works of T. S. Spivet (2009), J. J. Abrams and Doug Dorst's *S.* (2013), and Zachary Thomas Dodson's *Bats of the Republic* (2015), include artifactual maps as parts of the narrative discourse. They also thematically address a range of philosophical and experiential issues related to mapping. Though Hemon's *Lazarus Project* does not include artifactual maps, as a narrative concerned with travel and migration, the novel necessarily represents the protagonists' spatial thinking. Brik compares Sarajevo with Chicago, Eastern Europe with America. Transposing knowledge of one territory onto another is critical to his migrant consciousness. His subjective experience of places also blends with those of others. While listening to Rora's stories of wandering through Europe, he notes that he would "follow his roaming all over Europe on the imprecise, incomplete map in my mind, planting little Sarajevo-youth flags in the European capitals" (21). *Lazarus Project* thus engages with the issues I consider in this chapter, but its more pronounced feature is the coupling of subjectivities, manifested and mediated through photographs (discussed in chapter 2).

In *Kartography* and *Curious Incident,* mapping is an adaptive tool for the characters Karim (*Kartography*) and Christopher (*Curious Incident*), though the two novels diverge in their attitudes to this kind of adaptation. Karim and Christopher draw maps to navigate a world in which they feel out of place. Since multimodal sensory stimuli result in Christopher's cognitive overload (as discussed in chapter 1), he maps unfamiliar and busy areas through which he must move, such as the London train station. He flattens the three-dimensional experiential world into a two-dimensional representation on paper in order to simplify and better tackle it. Maps serve the same purpose as the formulaic pictorial icons he draws to encode and decode the multimodal stimuli he encounters in social situations. The cartographer in Larsen's *T. S. Spivet* is also a precocious child similar to *Curious Incident*'s Christopher. *T. S. Spivet*'s narrator creates "diagrammatic maps" of "people doing things," "zoological, geological, topographical" information, and "insect anatomy" (3). By contrast, Karim of *Kartography* maps the city of Karachi, where he spent his childhood, to come to terms with the fissures in South Asian society, specifically the sectarianism that forces his family to leave the city and migrate to London. Nadia Butt notes that scraps, letters, diaries, and digital maps function as objects mediating "transcultural" and intergenerational memory in *Kartography* (2015, 169). After moving to London, Karim's parents split. The breaking up of his parents, as Karim learns much later, can be traced to events that transpired right after the war between East Pakistan (present-day Bangladesh) and West Pakistan (modern-day Pakistan) in 1971. Mapping the world and, particularly, mapping Karachi become Karim's means of coping with Pakistan's divisive history as well as his own broken family. For a period, Karim maps to impose order on his otherwise chaotic experience of places,[3] akin to Christopher. He intends to arrive at a more complete and authoritative view of Karachi from a distance (London) than those who continue to live in the city. He emulates practices of colonial and political mapping to recover the lost world of his childhood in one piece. Shamsie's novel though, as Butt observes, "seeks to show the reader how political maps ignore one's personal associations with home/land, and how individuals themselves have to struggle to overcome cartographic violations of one's own country and territory" (2015, 175). So, Karim must learn to acknowledge and deal with the tension between personal and political cartography. By the end of the narrative, he understands mapping as a practice meant to engender novel connections, foster a sense of community, and decides to create an interactive digital map that would archive geotagged stories.

Kartography thus goes on to depict the limitations of hierarchizing authoritative spatial representations of a kind (the maps Karim creates to stake a claim to Karachi) over experiential relations with spaces (realized through his "mental maps" of Karachi). Whereas, in *Curious Incident,* maps remain formulaic diagrams that Christopher creates for his mind-as-computer to process his surroundings, maps in *Kartography* are more multifaceted and realize the characters' embodied and affective relations with spaces. Through Karim's changing approach to mapping, Shamsie's novel advances a dynamic understanding of what maps can do to connect people—how they can carve bustling virtual communities out of divided populations. Published in the early 2000s, the novel is steeped in optimism about the inclusive possibilities of digital media that Shamsie's later novels call into question.[4]

In J. J. Abrams and Doug Dorst's metafictional novel *S.,* mapping features once again as a communicative and connective practice. *S.* shows characters creating topographic and topologic representations to track polyvalent relations among entities in their world and also the fictional world of a novel they are supposedly reading. The protagonists of *S.* are fictionalized readers. They map terrains described in or associated with a possible world that is at an ontological remove from them (i.e., removed from the textual actual world).[5]

---

3. Jani (2010) argues that *Kartography* "pay[s] attention to the problems of historiography and memory without reducing the nation to . . . an inexplicable site of chaos" (243). I agree with this reading of the narrative, though at a more local level and especially from Karim's point of view the city seems to be forever splintering.

4. In her 2017 Man Booker long-listed novel *Home Fire,* Shamsie explores how Twitter and other social media platforms generate choric chatter that fuel exclusionary politics.

5. See chapter 1 of this book for definitions and discussion of actual and possible worlds.

What is more, they write notes to one another to locate things from their surroundings in the world of the fiction and vice versa. As a story about stories and how we read and write, *S.* exemplifies the many ways in which mapping operates as a semiotic mode and metaphor in contemporary narrative fictions. Mapping is imagined as an essential aspect of reading, instrumental in furthering readers' embodied engagement with narratives and overall narrative comprehension of *S.*

Among contemporary narratives that present characters' lived, remembered, and imagined spatial experiences in cartographic terms, I take *S.* and *Kartography* to be representative case studies. The maps in *Kartography* and *S.* demonstrate the characters' ways of perceiving their world and chart their relations within it. Additionally, through the organization of information on the surface of the page and within the material space of the book, *S.* seeks to illustrate how readers develop and map semantic spaces when engaging with narratives.

While it is not uncommon for maps to be included in narratives to offer an overview of the setting, the presence of artifactual maps in the twenty-first-century narratives I am examining generally implies that mapping will also operate at a conceptual level, as a figure for certain modes of thinking within the storyworld. This makes maps in multimodal fictions stand apart from the instances in which authors draw maps while writing, wherein "a map is the first step in a deliberate act of world creation" (Ryan, Foote, and Azaryahu 2016, 59). As opposed to genres like Fantasy, Historical, Science or Speculative fictions where maps, typically placed at either the opening or closing of the text, establish the fictional space—the terrain where the narrative action takes place—and aid in readers' interpretive efforts,[6] maps in multimodal narratives are not particularly concerned with revealing the geography of the storyworld. It is not as if this function is necessarily abandoned. Some included maps lay out fictional sites (e.g., *S.*) and others have actual world referents (e.g., Karachi in *Kartography*) that are recontextualized in fiction. However, how and why certain characters are mapping their worlds is of more immediate consequence than the mapped narrative space in fictions like *S., Kartography, Curious Incident,* and *T. S. Spivet.* For instance, a map included halfway into *Kartography* shows a part of Karachi but is not particularly important as a representation of narrative space (126–27). Rather, the placement of the map in the narrative accompanied by Karim's annotations distinguishes his attitude to places from that of the narrator Raheen's. In other words, mapping in

---

6. For examples of such usage see Jonathan Swift's *Gulliver's Travels* (1726), Robert Louis Stevenson's *Treasure Island* (1882), and Omar El Akkad's *American War* (2017).

twenty-first-century multimodal narratives establishes the ways in which certain characters think, and in turn, prompts actual readers' identification with or alienation from such structures of thought.

Although digital cartographic practices and spatial experiences influence twenty-first-century narratives, the included maps often reproduce hand-drawn diagrams or older prints annotated by hand. The combination of pictorial design features and inscriptions resembling handwriting that stand apart from the standard printed fonts stress the multimodality of mapping as an activity. Maps make use of geometry, color, handwriting or calligraphy, and a multitude of other design features to represent relations. As Denis Cosgrove observes, "Acts of mapping are creative, sometimes anxious, moments in coming to knowledge of the world, and the map is both the spatial embodiment of knowledge and a stimulus to further cognitive engagements" (1999, 2). Mapping as a figure for cognitive habits underscores the multimodality of thinking itself, affirms thought's multisensory and relational nature. The frequent association of handwriting with mapping and the exaltation of old media in contemporary narratives makes palpable the same aesthetic of nostalgia I mentioned when discussing Hall's *Raw Shark Texts*. But beyond the nostalgic celebration of old media, these narratives represent thinking as happening at the seams of embodiment and materiality by associating handwriting with maps. They direct readers' attention to their own bodily grounding in space, localized among objects—particularly the book object they are reading. In so doing, the narratives attest to a renewed interest in the sensory bases of writing and reading in the twenty-first century.

Spatial Cognition and Cognitive Maps

Phrases such as "mental map," "mind map," and "cognitive map" permeate the specialized vocabularies of disciplines as diverse as behavioral geography, cognitive science, cognitive linguistics, political theories, and narrative studies. With slight variations in meaning, the phrases refer to the ways in which embodied subjects organize and network perceptual knowledge to navigate situations. When used in the narrowest sense, cognitive maps are supposed to emerge through a subject's interactions with and learning of the environments around them. This understanding of cognitive maps can be traced back to psychologist Edward Tolman. However, through repeated elaborations across disciplines "cognitive maps" have acquired a broader meaning. When used in the broader sense, the term becomes a figure for semantic networking.

S. and *Kartography* thematize the role of spatial experiences in constituting subjectivities. So, artifactual and cognitive maps in both narratives have a specific interest in representing spaces and spatial relations. At the same time, both narratives to some degree, and S. in particular, play with the various associations of maps with embodied, enactive thinking, and thus, engage with the broader meaning of cognitive maps. A close look at the connections drawn between mapping and thinking across disciplines in the mid-twentieth and early twenty-first centuries sheds light on how artifactual maps and the idea of cartography inform the surface and deep structures of these narratives.

Despite the pervasive presence of map-related analogies for cognitive habits in common parlance and cognitive-scientific studies today, as geographer Sébastien Caquard (2015) observes, the association of maps with cognition was not formalized until the late 1940s. Caquard identifies Arthur Robinson's *The Look of Maps* (1952) as a key text that formalized this relation. Robinson examined how readers make meaning from visual design features (like lettering and color) in order to refine cartographic techniques. Approaching maps as a means of communication, Robinson tried to improve them through what he called cognitive map-design or cognitive cartography. Mapping and thinking, however, were also aligned from another direction in the mid-twentieth century: Tolman (1948) formulated the notion of "cognitive maps" while analyzing the place-learning abilities of rats in mazes.

Whereas Tolman was interested in the mental representation of places (though Tolman was not a cognitivist but a behaviorist), Kevin Lynch (1960) was concerned with the perceptual experiences afforded by particular spatial designs. In this light, he studied the ways in which acquiring spatial data through everyday activities contributes to the formation of what he interchangeably calls "mental maps," "cognitive maps," and "city images." According to Lynch, "The [cognitive] map, whether exact or not, must be good enough to get one home" (9). While Robinson was studying artifactual maps, both Tolman and Lynch concentrated on hypothetical, mental maps.

John O'Keefe, Jonathan Dostrovsky, and Lynn Nadel offered a neurophysiological description of cognitive maps in the 1970s. O'Keefe and Dostrovsky (1971) discovered place cells in the hippocampus of rats, and O'Keefe and Nadel (1978) identified cognitive maps with these newly discovered hippocampal place cells. By doing so, they traced the psychological experience of space to the structure of the neural system. Pursuing this line of research, Edvard I Moser, Emilio Kropff, and May-Britt Moser (2008) found that place cells are part of larger circuits that help conceptualize self-location and identified entorhinal grid cells as components of the same circuits.

Caquard notes that although Robinson's and Lynch's research drew attention to the phenomenological and communicative implications of mapping, the broader sociocultural context within which cognitive maps are produced was not recognized until much later (Caquard 2015, 226–27). The sociocultural foundations of both artifactual and cognitive maps began to be seriously considered in the 1990s. For instance, Ervin Laszlo, Ignazio Masulli, Robert Artigiani, and Vilmos Csányi, editors of *The Evolution of Cognitive Maps* (1993), observe that "the relationship between individual thinking and societal context can be fruitfully elucidated in terms of the dynamics that manifest the creation, preservation, change, and transcendence of publicly shared cognitive maps" (xii). Laszlo, Masulli, Artigiani, and Csányi's notion of shared cognitive maps complements hypotheses about social distribution and the extension of individual cognition.

In linguistics and literary studies, the French linguist Gilles Fauconnier's (1985) explanation of discourse construction and comprehension in terms of mapping remains influential. Unlike the previous scholars I mentioned (Robinson, Tolman, O'Keefe), Fauconnier's approach to "cognitive maps" no longer restricts it to thinking about observable spatial relations. Mapping denotes the "semantic networking" fundamental to linguistic comprehension in his usage. Thereby, Fauconnier links cartography with the cognitive processes instrumental for language-based communication. He also suggests that the habit of semantic networking he terms "mapping" has been found to be scalable—"the same mapping operations and principles are at work in elementary semantics, pragmatics, and so-called higher-level reasoning" (1997, 5). Fauconnier thus sought to establish "mapping" as an explanation for a range of cognitive functions around the 1980s, the heydays of "computationalism." His argument was that "neural architectures might provide a good computational implementation of the theoretical constructs but still be equally well suited for alternative theories, thus, providing at best a weak compatibility" with computation (1985, xxxii). For Fauconnier, mapping was a more compatible and useful analogy for understanding thought processes than the equation of cognition with computation. In a similar vein, Laszlo, Masulli, Artigiani, and Csányi observe, "nature has not programmed the human being for interaction with artificial information processing systems: there are no 'operating instructions' in our genes for life in an information society" and as such, "the required cognitive functions can be viewed as a kind of 'map' of the world, a map capable of orienting people bent on the achievement of their objective along the complex pathways of the emerging socio-technical system" (1993, xiv). In short, these researchers found maps as analogs to support more interactive, dynamic, and contextually attuned understandings of thought than strong computational explanations. Accordingly, in "Contemporary Theory of Metaphor" (1993), George Lakoff describes "conceptual metaphors" and the metaphorical structure of thought as mapping: metaphors map information from the source domain onto the target domain (206–16). Lakoff and Mark Johnson (1999), following Fauconnier, reinforce this interpretation of mapping as a method of analogical thinking.

Initial cognitive-scientific understandings of mental maps held them to be abstract representations. Second-generation cognitive-scientific approaches, of course, contest the existence, degree, and pragmatics of mental representations. Theories of radical embodiment do not admit the possibility of abstract, amodal, and arbitrary representations at all. However, theories of extended and grounded cognition acknowledge the possibility of producing adaptive, hypothetical representations (Clark 1998, 2016; Barsalou 1999, 2008, 2009; Barsalou et al. 2003). From a second-generation viewpoint, then, cognitive maps would not be abstractions transduced from sensory cues and stored in the brain. They have to be constituted by the reactivation of neurons associated with the learning of places and remain modality-specific. Semantic networks, too, would be grounded in sensorimotor and bodily variables.[7]

"Cognitive mapping" as a term used in literary studies generally builds on Fauconnier's, Lakoff and Johnson's, Mark Turner's, and Raymond W. Gibbs Jr's discussions of mental spaces, metaphors, and linguistic form. Theories of cognitive mapping in narrative studies oscillate between an engagement with narrative's spatial poetics and readers' semantic networking of objects and entities represented in the narrative. The latter usage is more commonplace in contemporary cognitive narratology, which focuses on the reader's perception of the storyworld more often than on the narrative's rendering of the characters' spatial behavior. David Herman's (2002) concept of "storyworld," for instance, refers to the reader's mental modelling of relations in the narrative. Herman takes the reader's mental modelling of spaces as a "core property of story." Though he does not thoroughly equate this sort of modelling with mapping, what he calls "storyworld reconstruction" is similar to what other narratologists understand as the "mental mapping" of narratives. As Joanna Gavins observes,

> A considerable range of approaches to narrative are based on the notion that human beings process and understand discourse by constructing mental representations of it in their minds. The detailed mental maps that readers form of narratives, variously also called 'frames' (Emmott 1997), 'worlds' (Gerrig 1993; Werth 1999) and 'mental spaces' (Fauconnier 1994; Semino

---

7. See Barsalou (1999) and Barsalou et al. (2003) for discussions of how conceptual processing involves the reactivation and enactment of perception.

2003), enable them, for example, to track the movements of characters and objects through time and space [. . .] and to understand focalized narration. (2005, 300)

Marie-Laure Ryan's scholarship productively combines the specific spatial sense of mapping with a broader interest in reading comprehension and semantic networking. Adopting a visual-spatial approach to narratives, Ryan argues that the comprehension and recall of narratives depend on the cognitive mapping of narrative spaces. To test the hypothesis, she asks a group of high-school students to map spaces constituting a fictional narrative (see Ryan 2003). Their drawings are disparate, which leads Ryan to conclude that although readers mentally model spaces, the models remain malleable. Since reading is a dynamic experience, mental maps of narrated spaces are continually readjusted based on new information.

Marco Caracciolo draws upon second-generation approaches to cognition and states that the mental modelling of spatial environments represented in narratives happens in embodied ways: readers simulate movements and imagine moving through described spaces to comprehend spatial references (see Caracciolo 2011; 2013). This sort of embodied, readerly enactments is represented in *S.*, as my discussion will show. Moreover, the actions of the fictionalized readers Eric, Jen, and Caldeira in *S.* suggest that readers can choose to create artifactual maps out of their "mental maps" of fictional spaces.

In addition to representing their characters' cognitive mapping of what is fictional or represented spaces for them, *S.*, and also *Kartography,* have their characters map their own surroundings (Karim maps Karachi). Some of the artifactual maps are thus semiotic articulations of cognitive maps that have emerged from the characters' learned navigation of their environments. The characters' experiential knowledge of places and their maps—artifactual and cognitive—co-evolve. Shamsie's and Abrams and Dorsts's representation of spatial thinking is multilayered, realized through their narratives' map overlay design. *S.* and *Kartography* show that one learns one's surroundings through not only the traversal of sites but also interactions with representations of locales in stories and maps.

The Structure of *S.* and *Kartography*

Abrams and Dorst and Shamsie utilize multimodal devices to build a multi-layered topography for their characters to navigate in *S.* and *Kartography.* The narratives' multimodality also offers intricate spatial experiences to readers.

Abrams and Dorsts's *S.* quite overtly depends on readers' media literacy of using ubiquitous communication technologies that position them "here" and "elsewhere" at once to engage with the storyworld. *S.* comes in a black slipcase that holds the book *Ship of Theseus,* which is said to have been the fictional author V. M. Straka's last novel. *Ship of Theseus* chronicles the adventures of a character—"a man in a dark gray overcoat" (3)—who has emerged from the sea into a "city in which even life-long residents find themselves lost" (4). The character—the protagonist of *Ship of Theseus*—who eventually names himself "S" interacts with other characters in the unnamed city to learn who he is and thereby constitute his subjectivity, though his self-knowledge is never stable or conclusive. Straka's narrator also mirrors the character's state of oblivion, observing that "it [is] difficult to know at any given moment whether he is heading toward the water or away from it" (3). The narrator asks questions about the storyworld that presumably mimic both the amnesiac character's and the actual readers' questions. Contesting the notion of omniscience, the narrator only offers tentative answers: "Why is the man in the overcoat so wet? Perhaps he has been walking in the rain for hours. Or perhaps he has been wading through the maze of half-submerged tunnels that underlie the twisted city" (6). In other words, the narrator of Straka's *Ship of Theseus* seems to be touring the city *with* the amnesiac man in the overcoat in search of answers and guiding readers to do the same. Multiple maps for this "tour" are offered by three fictionalized readers of Straka's *Ship of Theseus.*

The print narrative about S. in *Ship of Theseus* is framed by the (similarly printed) footnotes of a fictional editor-translator, F. X. Caldeira, and the handwritten commentaries of two other characters, Eric and Jen. Straka, Caldeira, Eric, and Jen are characters in Abrams and Dorst's *S.*, the novel within which *Ship of Theseus* is a novel, and thus, at an ontological remove from *Ship of Theseus*'s character S. Accordingly, Caldeira, Eric, and Jen comment on how the world of *Ship of Theseus* reflects their "real" world (the textual actual world of *S.*). In her notes prefacing *Ship of Theseus* Caldeira notes that Straka's novel dramatizes aspects of his authorial persona—"Who was V. M. Straka? . . . The world knows his name, knows his reputation . . . knows him as the most nimble of writers . . . But the world never knew Straka's face, never knew with certainty a single fact of the man's life" (v–vi). Eric's and Jen's marginalia similarly concern hidden connections between their conditions and the cognitive states of the character S. in Straka's novel. For instance, Jen underlines, "He does not know why he is here now" in *Ship of Theseus* and scribbles "and I don't know why I'm scribbling in a book with a stranger" next to it (4). Thus, these characters are engaged in synthesizing their world with the imaginary world Straka's S. navigates.

S., Caldeira, Eric, and Jen are characterized according to how they subjectively experience and interact with spaces, including represented sites like the city S. enters, the library where Eric and Jen find their copy of Straka's novel, and also the space of the artifactual book that mediates Straka's novel. Eric's and Jen's hands-on manner of reading, whereby they annotate and map the contents of Straka's novel, foregrounds the visual-haptic aspects of narrative comprehension. The artifacts Eric and Jen tuck into Straka's novel, on the one hand, reflect their desire to have Straka's fiction leak into their actual world. On the other hand, the artifacts and notes they enclose demonstrate how the material space of the book can become a placeholder for thoughts and ideas. Books, like other media technologies, function as nodes in extended minds, to use Clark and David Chalmer's extended mind hypothesis (1998). Reading is also represented as a social activity in *S.*, given that Eric and Jen exchange notes and build a relationship through their shared experience of *Ship of Theseus*. *S.* is thus a formally complex narrative that operates on an understanding of cognitive tasks like reading as embodied and contingent on an individual's embeddedness in social circles and spatial environments.

For the actual readers of Abrams and Dorst's novel, Eric, Jen, Caldeira, Straka, and S. are all equally fictional characters. Nonetheless, the visible markups on the book's pages, the enclosed objects, and the pages' texture invite readers to take an imaginative leap and accept the copy of the book in their hands as a well-worn library copy of Straka's novel. The accumulation of notes and documents within the book demand a degree of bodily interactivity and decision-making from the readers—do they read the various documents in the order they are tucked in the book or shuffle and read them in another order? Do they first read the print narrative and then read all the notes or read the print narrative and the notes around the page spread at once? Reading *S.* is a bodily performance, as is all reading, but *S.* self-reflexively draws attention to the bodily and sensorimotor variables determining our experientiality of texts.

Even as the novel *S.* requires its actual readers (distinguished from the fictional readers Eric and Jen) to continuously negotiate between the *mise-en-page* (the design of the page) and the imagined storyworld, the rules of this negotiation are not explicitly laid out. What is clear though is that the narrative, across the several ontological levels, intends to show that finding one's way, whether that is through a city (as in the case of the character S.) or a book (as in the case of Caldeira, Eric, and Jen), involves finding out something about oneself. Put another way, who one is will depend on where one is. The constitution of subjectivity entails spatial interactions that can take the form of touring a place, mapping it, or reading about it. Such a view of subjectivity is aligned with embodied and enactive cognitive-scientific approaches and philosophy of mind.

Shamsie's novel is a bildungsroman, with the story beginning in a garden in Karachi at a time when the two main characters—Raheen and Karim—can learn and follow each other's cognitive habits. They habitually spot anagrams while reading or listening to other peoples' conversations. They share perceptual and affective states and have, to use Zahavi and Rochat's terms, "a dynamically emergent and negotiated we-experience" (2015, 545). To Raheen, Karim is her "shadow-self," and her self-narrative[8] integrates his thoughts, beliefs, and goals (Shamsie 2002, 146). Over time, however, the characters in *Kartography* part ways. Karim's family leaves Pakistan and his parents' marriage begins to fall apart. Raheen's and Karim's subjective experiences begin to diverge. Shamsie distinguishes between the mindstyles of the two characters by bringing to the fore their irreconcilable approaches to spaces. Karim grows up to be a cartographer, and the older Raheen is the novel's narrator; thus, one makes maps of Karachi, and another tells stories set in Karachi to make sense of their relationship with the city as well as with each other.

Raheen's father had once been engaged to Karim's mother, a woman of Bengali origin, but humiliated her in a social display of loyalty to Pakistan during the war between East Pakistan (Bangladesh) and West Pakistan. Subsequently, Karim's mother and Raheen's father broke their engagement and married others, who also happened to be their mutual friends. The broken engagement is at the heart of the intergenerational conflicts driving the narrative. In this light, Butt notes, "By recreating the map of his city as it is increasingly drawn into violence, Karim not only tries to come to terms with the failed marriage of his parents, but at the same time seeks comfort in the thought of restoring the city in his memory by remaining loyal to official names of streets and grieving the loss of people at certain places" (2015, 177). However, for Raheen, memories "create their own maps of belonging" which "ought to be seen above official names and places on a map" (Butt 2015, 177). Shamsie's novel suggests neither Raheen's nor Karim's cognitive habits are without their flaws.

Mapping alienates Karim, and from Raheen's point of view, maps become a "symbol of everything that had gone so wrong, so inexplicably," in her relationship with him (163). To Raheen, Karim's maps reveal his ever-increasing ignorance about the "realities of this place [Karachi] and the people in it" (163). And yet, it is not as if Raheen really knows Karachi much better than

---

8. See chapter 2 of this book for definitions of self-narrative and further discussion of the concept.

Karim does. For instance, at one point she wonders, "How could the violence reach somewhere so familiar?" (282). Their surroundings often catch both Raheen and Karim unawares. Eventually, Raheen too accepts the limits of what she can know of her city through stories spun around her lived experiences. In a letter to Karim, she writes, "we belong to a city invested in storytelling. It is in our blood. But you can only be familiar with those you know well, you can only know the stories of those whom you've bothered to listen. What happens to all those streets that hold no stories for us?" (297). Once both characters recognize and accept the failings of their cognitive habits, they reconcile and this reconciliation is represented through Karim's conception of an interactive digital map of Karachi that will overlay locational signposts with stories. Thus, in *Kartography*, as in *S.*, the characters' experience of and conceptual approaches to spaces are vital to who they are at a particular juncture in the narrative and who they can become as the narrative progresses. Both novels functionalize multiple semiotic modes (language, maps) to represent characters whose self-narrative is grounded in their understanding of space: instead of before and after, Eric and Jen of *S.* and Raheen and Karim of *Kartography* think of their lives in terms of "here" and "there." This is not to say that temporal order is of no consequence for them, but spatial experiences determine the arc of their self-narratives in more conspicuous ways.

Caroline Herbert (2014) calls *Kartography* a "postcolonial city text." With an "emphasis on dialogue and active engagement," postcolonial city texts present "the complex experience of postcolonial urban modernity—the experience of being in the city. But they also invite us to reflect on the experience of reading the city and on the ethical implications of imagining its past, present, and possible futures in collaboration and in conversation with other writers, readers, and reader-walkers" (Herbert 2014, 213). By inviting us—readers—to reflect on the experience of "reading the city," *Kartography*, akin to *S.*, stimulates readers' spatial thinking. In both cases, the invitation and stimulation come in the form of:

> a. Linguistic descriptions: The description of the characters' movements and their interactions with the setting enable readers to experience the represented spaces that constitute the storyworld. The strength of the reader's perception of the represented space further affects the reader's sense of "spatial immersion" in the storyworld, which, as Ryan argues, is a challenging literary effect to achieve in language-based narratives. When spatially immersed, readers experience the spaces described in the narrative in embodied ways (2001, 120; see Caracciolo 2011; 2013).

b. Layout: The linguistic descriptions, deictic language, and visual design features draw attention to the material space of the codex. How the language is spatialized on the page and the presence of character-drawn maps and other pictorial-tactile elements form the threshold for the readers' bodily engagement with the narrative. Philosopher Hans Ulrich Gumbrecht has observed that a work of art (such as a literary text) can produce "presence." The production of presence is a dynamic process through which a textual form becomes tangible in and as space (2004, 17). *Kartography*'s and *S.*'s material layout contributes to making the storyworld feel "present" to the readers.

It is worth noting that many reviews of *S.* either celebrate the book's layout for its own sake or lament that the narrative's payoff does not justify the amount of labor readers are expected to invest in figuring out how to read it (see Lawson 2013; Roberts 2013). These responses point out that the concurrent semiotic modes and inscription systems that overlay spatial experiences of the different characters (especially the fictionalized readers) in *S.* may evoke fairly different responses in actual readers. The material design may even get in the way of readers' immersion in the narrative. *Kartography* is relatively less intricate than *S.* in its material layout. The narrative is language-based for the most part, though it uses an abundance of ellipsis, offsets the letters which characters write to one another, and includes maps. Karim's maps help him negotiate his plural identities (national, ethnic, diasporic) and experiences while he also navigates multiple geographies. In the following sections, I develop a comparative analysis of *S.*'s and *Kartography*'s presentation and evocation of spatial thinking through language and layout.

Spatial Immersion in the Storyworlds

Linguistic descriptions mediate characters' perception of spaces around them and cue readers into imagining the storyworld. The storyworld, comprising the sites and the environment which characters inhabit, is gradually built, as per the requirements of the narrative. As Ryan observes, language-based narrative "discloses its geography detail by detail . . . It does not normally represent by creating an illusion of presence to the senses, as do visual media" (2001, 122). The linguistic revelation of geography can take various forms. Linguists Charlotte Linde and William Labov (1975) name the two most popular varieties of spatial descriptions through language, the "map" and the "tour."

Map-like[9] descriptions offer a "bird's-eye view" or panoramic view of the space, while tour-like descriptions evoke spatial configurations from the point of view of a tourist or wanderer. Ryan, Kenneth Foote, and Maoz Azaryahu also suggest that the nature of descriptions dominant in a particular narrative can inform its overall structure at a macrolevel (2016, 32). *S.* and *Kartography* intersperse map-like and tour-like descriptions, integrate the organizational affordances of both maps and tours.

In *Ship of Theseus,* Straka's novel enclosed within *S.,* the city which the amnesiac character S. traverses is built by blending omniscient overviews that are map-like in their scope with more localized details from the character's point of view. We learn that S. has emerged from water, while the city itself is sinking because of its "strange," "flawed geometries" (2). A refrain in *Ship of Theseus* says that "what begins at the water shall end there, and what ends there shall once more begin" (12), and the chapter titles—"The Drifting Twins," "The Emersion of S."—evoke immersion-related imagery. In the handwritten notes, Eric commends Jen for "immersing" herself in Straka's world. Through such cues, *S.* proposes immersion or absorption within the storyworld as a way of reading. Ryan has observed that the "reader's sense of being there is independent of the verisimilitude of the textual world" (2001, 130). Despite its seemingly impossible geometric design, Straka's storyworld immerses the fictionalized readers Eric and Jen. Being spatially immersed, Caldeira—the editor of Straka's manuscript—maps parts of it (see Figure 3.1).

Straka's *Ship of Theseus* mentions that the character Sola showed a map to S., and a rectangular map is placed on the following page of the book. However, Eric's and Jen's commentaries explain that probably Caldeira, and not Straka, drew the map. The aerial view that the map affords differs from how actual readers may experience the spaces of a storyworld. Mark Turner has argued that most of our actions (which would include reading) involve the construction and execution of "small spatial stories," but these small spatial stories are usually grounded in our bodily affordances and constraints (1996, 19, 117–19). Small spatial stories tend to have singular and local viewpoints, but "we integrate over singularities" (1996, 117). In other words, readers semantically network actions and objects from a particular, bodily grounded point of view and from a particular location. Readers can draw artifactual maps of the storyworld in addition to cognitively mapping information revealed through language—as Caldeira does when reading *Ship of Theseus*—but in general, narratives rarely require readers to imagine, mentally or materially

---

9. Though Linde, Labov, and Ryan simply use "map" and "tour" for the description categories, I use "map-like description" to avoid potential confusion with the artifactual maps in the narratives discussed in this book.

[Margin notes, left top:]
I ASKED HER.
SHE SMILED. SHE SAID
SHE DIDN'T KNOW FOR SURE
THAT THE MAP WAS CORRECT
BUT YOU COULD TELL SHE WAS
REALLY PROUD SHE'D DONE IT.

Checked satellite maps.
Doesn't look like there's
anything there now.

BUT PLACES CAN BE
OBSCURED FROM SATELLITE
MAPS. SOUNDS LIKE
GARDEN-VARIETY
CONSPIRACY-THEORY
JIVE, BUT STILL...

We should go.
Look for ourselves.
It's not that far away.
Maybe a day by train?
Less?

[Margin notes, top right:]
Or Filomela put it in. That
would be so bad-ass: putting
a map to Bouchard's estate
in the goddamn book.
She's my idol.

NOT IN THE ORIGINAL MS.
MAYBE HE DIDN'T BOTHER TO
DRAW IT? THOUGHT SOMEONE ELSE
WOULD?

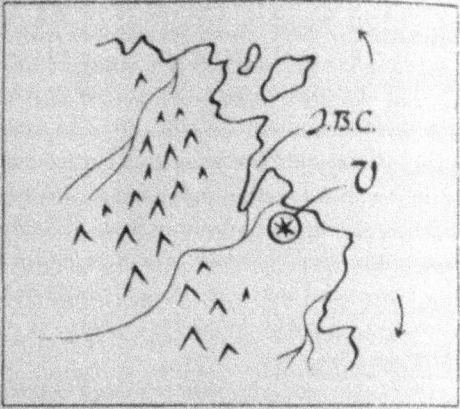

SHIP OF THESEUS

[Map image with labels "J.B.C." and "V" and a star symbol]

[Left margin, lower:]
CITY COPS CAME TO MY
APT. THIS MORNING.
I'M GUESSING THEY FOUND
ME B/C OF THE CAR
REGISTRATION. KNEW IT
WOULD HAPPEN EVENTUALLY
ANYWAY. TOLD THEM
THEY COULDN'T COME IN
W/O A WARRANT, WHICH
THEY WON'T BE ABLE TO GET
B/C THE ONLY THING THEY
HAVE IS MOODY ACCUSING
ME. NO PROOF I WAS
EVEN ON CAMPUS THAT
DAY — OR FOR MONTHS
BEFORE.

[Printed text:]
France. The foothills of the Pyrenees. S. had heard a rumor, years ago, that Vévoda's estate was in this region, but he never found evidence that it was anything more than another wild guess.

"How did you get this?" He barely recognizes the sound of his voice.

"If you mistreat many, many people for many, many years, eventually one of them will grow desperate enough to risk her life to stop you," she says. "One person's audacity: the only prerequisite for resistance."

"And the woman who drew this?"

[Bottom handwritten:]
— If they found you, then the suit guys can find you.

JEN: IF THEY HAVEN'T DONE ANYTHING BY NOW,
THEY'RE NOT GOING TO.

Maybe they're waiting for us to
find something. I don't know. All I know is I keep
seeing them.
— THEY MIGHT NOT EVEN BE
WHO YOU THINK THEY ARE.

{ 402 }

FIGURE 3.1. Caldeira's map within the print narrative of Straka's *Ship of Theseus*

model, a whole gamut of represented relations at once. If we bring a second-generation cognitive-scientific understanding to reading, we must agree that readers are pragmatic and adaptive. They would not conceptualize relations that have little bearing on their moment-to-moment experience of narratives. Thus, conventionally, reading a narrative feels less like looking at a map and more like taking a tour.

The copious marginalia, letters, and maps Abrams and Dorst use to showcase the fictionalized readers' (Eric, Jen, Caldeira's) immersive navigation of *Ship of Theseus* impact the actual readers' ability to do so. The "tour" on which *Ship of Theseus* could take actual readers is punctuated by speed bumps in the form of the myriad objects included in the book. For the actual readers, Eric's and Jen's handwritten notes are a source of visual feedback when they are trying to fixate on the printed narrative and vice versa. The extent of the page that the 60-degree radius of the peripheral vision covers depends on the distance and the angular direction at which the book is held. The closer a reader holds the book, the easier it is to limit the visual feedback. However, *S.* is designed to stipulate numerous saccades[10] and continually redirect the readers' attention. The visual feedback and the readers' rapid, non-linear eye movements are necessary elements constituting the experience of *S*. If "tours" are immersive narrative structures, then *S.*, given its pictorial-tactile form, resembles a composite "map" overlaying multiple kinds of spatial experiences.

The challenge of tackling several layers of spatial information (of the storyworld, the artifactual book with the inserts) is not wholly unfamiliar to contemporary readers who juggle several electronic devices, find themselves situated within a multitude of networks at any given moment. We are used to holding electronic screens closer to our eyes or hunching over them to limit the demands on our attention. Similarly, *S.* requires the book be held up close to limit the visual feedback.

The compounding of spatial experiences is also central to the poetics of Shamsie's *Kartography*. As the title indicates, Shamsie uses mapping as a metaphor, expansive in its scope, standing for modes of perception and the nature of experiences, encompassing the cognitive processes of thinking, knowing, and remembering. In the novel's prefatory chapter, the narrator Raheen adopts a "bird's-eye view" of the spatial relations that define her self-narrative while looking at a spinning globe: "The globe spins. Mountain ranges skim my fingers; there is static above the Arabian Sea" (1). As Raheen considers the globe, she notes the discrepancies between the world represented on a map and her

---

10. Saccades are the movement of both eyes between two phases of fixation. Saccadic eye movements and saccadic performance are studied in neuropsychological experiments as indicators of cognitive functions (see Matsuo et al. 2003).

lived experience of the mapped spaces. She observes that the scale of distance between the plotted sites does not measure up to the experience of surmounting that distance: "From there [Karachi] to here is no distance at all if you look at the map of the world. But distance is not about miles and kilometers, it is about fear" (1). The description of her immediate surroundings while she is reflecting on the globe is fuzzy. She is at an airport, but, apart from the fact that it is raining where she is currently located, the spatial configuration of the self-narrative she is about to spin around that globe takes precedence over her present location. Following the map-based spatial meditation of the prefatory chapter, Raheen's narrative takes a tour-like form.

Raheen takes readers to a garden within the city of Karachi in 1986. She reconstructs her world of childhood with vivid sensory details for readers to experience it with her: "We [she and Karim] were sitting cross-legged, side by side, on the grass that bordered the triangle of soil on which the rockery had been set out. Mud on his knees and chlorophyll on mine, though as we sat close, swaying back with laughter and forward with curiosity, the colours were mingling, dun shot through with emerald" (3). The name Raheen, as Karim later notes in the novel, means "guide," and accordingly, Raheen as *Kartography*'s narrator guides readers through the Karachi she remembers. She is primarily interested in "literary mapping" rather than "scientific mapping" (164). Raheen notes that Eratosthenes, the third-century BC Greek polymath, was the first to suggest that mapping concern itself with science and facts. Prior to that stories told by poets or travelers and sailors were considered valuable sources of geographic information. Strabo, the Greek geographer born around 64 or 63 BC, critiqued Eratosthenes' move of excluding poets like Homer from the "corpus of cartography" because geographic truths could be rendered in the language of poetry (164). Taking a cue from Strabo, Raheen wants to focus on telling stories that "define Karachi" rather than learn and relay names of streets where bombs blasted or people died (164). Since guiding and storytelling are equated in the novel, spatially immersed readers would be tourists generating experiential, cognitive maps based on Raheen's descriptions. Her position as both narrator and guide would cause readers to align their perspectives with hers while imagining represented sites until the narrative is broken by Karim's maps.

Karim's maps interrupt the tour and prompt readers to adjust their approach to Karachi. The switch in mode (from linguistic tour to artifactual map) offers readers an alternate way of configuring semantic spaces. The maps adopt a bird's-eye view of the city's topography, a perspective that Raheen refuses to adopt. However, coming on the heels of her linguistic descriptions, the artifactual maps that diagrammatically represent Karim's way of thinking, his modelling of spaces, can nonetheless begin to inflect the readers' understanding of the spatial relations making up the storyworld.

"I Know the Way": Grounding and Moving through Deixis and Marginalia

Raheen's final sentence in *Kartography* addressed to Karim is "Follow me . . . I know the way" (305). What Raheen, the guide, tells Karim echoes the ambition of several characters in both *S.* and *Kartography* as they attempt to find their way in the storyworld and while doing so offer readers competing directions for experiencing the narrative spaces.

While the protagonist S. wanders through the storyworld of *Ship of Theseus*, Eric and Jen, the fictional readers of *Ship of Theseus*, immerse themselves in the described spaces through the material affordances of the book. A painstakingly designed artifact, *S.* highlights how books are spaces capable of containing not only inscribed information but also objects such as maps, postcards, photographs, and so on. The inserted objects and Eric's and Jen's notes function as signposts, marking up passages of *Ship of Theseus*, pinpointing certain locations in the narrative, revealing new meanings. The inserts and notes thus add layer after layer of information to the fictional author Straka's writing. From the vantage point of the actual readers of *S.*, it is as though previous readers have left marks to facilitate their wayfinding through the narrative space as well as the space of the artifactual book. Put another way, the notes of the fictional readers (Eric and Jen) are like the "footprints" of earlier "tourists" that actual readers of *Ship of Theseus* can follow. In fact, Jen sketches a footprint next to Straka's prose (192). *Kartography*'s garden scene, where the tour-like narrative structure begins, also features a quest for footprints: in this case, the younger Raheen and Karim search the "footprints" of Alexander the Great, who as per apocryphal stories once came to Karachi.

In *S.* the placing of the footprint along the margin aligns it with the numerous handwritten notes in the book. The visual analogy invites reflection on what it means to leave one's trace in the spaces through which one has moved. It is a concern with which the character S. grapples—he frequently encounters the letter "S," which he used to name himself, in unlikely places and wonders about its relationship with him. Eric and Jen similarly leave their traces within Straka's book and return to it at a later time to remind themselves of who they were at an earlier time as well as to look for one another. The actual readers of *S.* encounter these signposts—the marginalia—attributed to Eric and Jen as they also encounter Straka's omniscient narrator charting the movements of S. within the storyworld of *Ship of Theseus*. It is up to the readers, then, to choose their own adventure.

Through Eric's and Jen's annotations Abrams and Dorst's novel visually illustrates the dense semantic networks that are formed during reading. Though not explicitly resembling an artifactual map as the one Caldeira draws, Eric's and Jen's annotations offer glimpses into the cognitive maps they develop of Straka's storyworld. The visualization of their emergent understanding of Straka's narrative in the form of colorful handwritten notes scattered across the surfaces of the pages stresses the sensory modality-specific nature of semantic networking—that is, they suggest that semantic networks are not amodal representations encoded and stored in the brain but are tentatively configured through somatosensory interactions with contextual information.

The abundant marginalia attributed to the two fictional characters serve as a reading map of *Ship of Theseus* for the actual readers of *S*. The relation among the structure of the text, the characters in the storyworld, Eric and Jen, and the readers is established by the deictic signposts that "encode a language user's position in the world" (Gibbons 2012a, 30).[11] Each use of the word "here," the spatial deictic center for the characters in the handwritten commentaries of *S.*, suggests multiple spatial relations. For instance, the pages between which actual objects (such as postcards, letters) are inserted often have Eric's or Jen's note saying that the object can be found "here." In such cases, "here" signals a specific position within the book (Abrams and Dorst 2013, 99). Then there are instances when characters write that what they need to tell cannot be told "here," in which case "here" refers to the spatial limitations of the page (100).

Ryan (2001) has argued that the deictic elements of language such as "you" in second-person narration as well as the spatial adverbs "here" and "there" relocate the reader to the inner circle of the narrative and "show" them the storyworld from the perspective of a participant in the narrated scene. Caracciolo (2011) underscores the embodiedness of such perspectival alignment by suggesting that readers simulate movements or take on a character's body to tour the narrative space. These arguments about perspectival alignment hold for the occasions in which the word "here" is used within the printed narrative of *Ship of Theseus*: Caldeira, the fictional reader-translator-editor, sums up her experience of reading *Ship of Theseus* in one of the printed footnotes by saying that she "saw the world through the eyes of his [Straka's] characters" (x). Caldeira's remark indicates that she enters the storyworld of *Ship of Theseus* by

---

11. In literature, words such as "I," "here," "there," "now" can momentarily shift the reader's perspectival, spatial, or temporal deictic center and align it with the entities or elements within the storyworld (see Herman 2002).

aligning her point of view with those of the characters, who are participants in the narrated scene. The actual readers, when going through the printed narrative of *Ship of Theseus* might, like Caldeira, align their points of view with the omniscient narrator following Straka's character S. However, when readers encounter the second-person pronouns and the spatial adverbs within the handwritten notes in the margins, the ensuing experience differs: the epistolary exchange within which the deictic shifts in pronoun occur resists sustained alignment of the actual readers with any of the characters, Eric or Jen, though the spatial deictic signposts align the book within the actual readers' grasp with the fictional book in which Eric and Jen wrote. To use Gumbrecht's (2004) terminology, the deictic signposts within the epistolary framework make Eric's and Jen's library book feel present to the readers.

The identification of an actually reproduced copy of *Ship of Theseus* with the fictional copy of *Ship of Theseus* is an aesthetic illusion[12] in which S. invites readers to participate. The aesthetic illusion is strengthened by the discursive import of the handwritten markups that show how Eric and Jen proceeded through the book. The discursive import of a given system of inscription results from our associating it with the contexts in which we frequently encounter it (see Nørgaard 2003, 118). While distinguishing handwriting from typography, Gerrit Noordzij, a Dutch typographer and professor of typeface design, observes that typography entails "writing with prefabricated letters" (quoted in Bil'ak 2007, n. pag.), whereas in hand-lettering the configuration of letters designed for a surface is unique and not reproducible. With the spread of digital illustration techniques, it is no longer technologically impossible to extract hand-lettered characters and paste them elsewhere, outside the configuration in which they occurred. Nevertheless, handwriting on the margins of a printed fictional text can bring its customary site-specific associations to bear on the actual reader's experience of the inscription and work in tandem with the spatial deictic signs to establish the actual reader's relation with the storyworld.

The layout of the handwritten notes undermines the chronology of Eric's and Jen's communication. The material layout of *S.* suggests that the fictional copy of *Ship of Theseus* was read and reread. Ideas and relationships were revised over the course of these readings and the surface of the page has synchronized the diachrony. The textual logic is such that, when Jen picks up the book, she writes notes about Straka's prose, responding to Eric's previous set

---

12. Wolf (2013) understands aesthetic illusion as a variety of immersion and points out that audiences are "experientially" immersed in aesthetic illusions. As an instance of what Wolf terms "illusionist representation" (11), *S.* offers readers the quasi-experience of being present in the storyworld through deictic language and the book's material form.

of notes, and then Eric follows the same process. For instance, on page 5, Jen asks Eric to see her response on page 10. On page 10, there is a doodle of an empty square. Next to it Eric has written, "That's your response?? Um, there's nothing there" (10). Jen's response follows Eric's. Yet, on page 5, we also learn that Jen stopped writing for a while after drawing the square. The exchange in blue and black ink that flows almost like an instantaneous chat transcript must have been written over weeks. The organization of the handwritten notes[13] ensures that the readers continually receive visual feedback from temporally disjointed clusters.

Using the visual import of the sprawling hand-drawn lines, *S.* further layers the different ontological planes of the narrative. Andrew Piper has observed that electronic literature and its technologies such as the hyperlink depend on topological connections and these often move readers toward the likely, the proximate, and the scalar (2013, 377). In *S.*, handwriting hyperlinks, by bending, stretching, and shaping communication on the topos that is the page. Eric's and Jen's handwriting in the margins brings out the verbal-pictorial correspondences among the many narrative layers: a phrase or a word from Straka's prose or Caldeira's notes serves as a hook for Eric and Jen to draw swirling lines. Visually, these designs recall and illustrate descriptions of spaces from *Ship of Theseus* such as a "twisted city" (6), a "maze of tunnels" (10), cave walls with a "kaleidoscopic swirl of images" (178), a river that "snakes darkly" (351) and, most significantly, as on page 272, the shape of the hand-drawn lines resemble the letter "S." (see Figure 3.2). The hand-drawn strokes flag sections of the printed text for the characters' future selves and for the readers. Their markups are accompanied by explanatory notes, moving in different angles and directions. For instance, on encountering the word "burden-shirt" in Caldeira's annotation, Jen draws a line across the body of Straka's prose, pointing to another section of the page where she can carry on her commentary, taking the conversation with Eric in another direction, both literally and metaphorically (52). Overall, the placement of the handwritten notes and the hand-drawn strokes entices readers of *S.* to forgo temporal order and instead follow information that is spatially proximate. The seemingly random placement of the handwritten notes undermines the actual readers' behavioral bias

---

13. Eric's and Jen's digressive notes are reminiscent of Charles Kinbote's commentary in Vladimir Nabokov's *Pale Fire* and Johnny Truant's in Mark Z. Danielewski's *House of Leaves*. However, Nabokov's as well as Danielewski's novels enforce a spatial hierarchy: in *Pale Fire*, the notes are placed at the end of John Shade's poem, while in *House of Leaves*, Truant's footnotes might be lengthy—sometimes taking up almost an entire page—but the design still establishes a top-bottom hierarchy between Zampanò's narrative and the notes.

Ship of Theseus

heads poke down from the tops to watch the big man, as if to verify that they have heard the song correctly. The sails luff and whack. S. feels a dark mood sweep over the ship, dark as the storm-clouds that descended upon them off the coast of B——; what he cannot tell is whether that mood is one of fury or fear.

The monkey, sitting atop a barrel mid-deck, amuses itself by tearing pieces from a ship-biscuit and tossing them to the wind. S. is heartened to see a few surly looks thrown its way, including one by its companion from the ghost ship. For once, S. feels as if he is not the least-liked creature on the ship.[11]

Maelstrom blows the same sequence again, and the crew responds with more stillness and silence. Only after he blows it a third time are there nods and whistled rejoinders. A whistle comes from the woman at the wheel, and the ship changes course sharply, heading off until it is racing on a dead run. Jibs are hoisted; a spinnaker flies; the ship seethes with velocity. There's been a change of plans, a significant one, and time—however elastic it may seem on these waters—is of the essence.

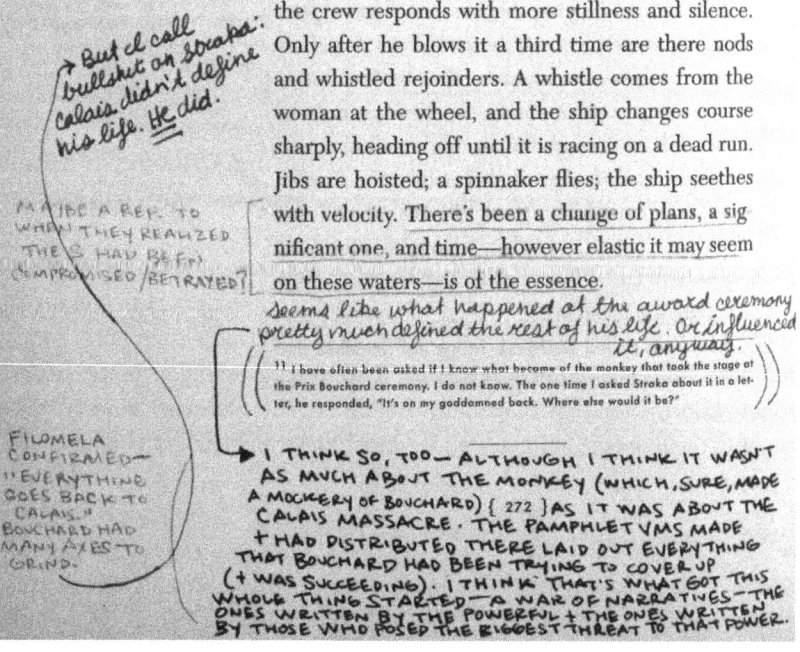

[11] I have often been asked if I know what became of the monkey that took the stage at the Prix Bouchard ceremony. I do not know. The one time I asked Straka about it in a letter, he responded, "It's on my goddamned back. Where else would it be?"

Margin notes:

→ But I call bullshit on Straka. Calais didn't define his life. He did.

MAYBE A REF. TO WHEN THEY REALIZED THE S HAD BEEN (C)OMPROMISED/BETRAYED?

Seems like what happened at the award ceremony pretty much defined the rest of his life. Or influenced it, anyway.

FILOMELA CONFIRMED— "EVERYTHING GOES BACK TO CALAIS." BOUCHARD HAD MANY AXES TO GRIND.

→ I THINK SO, TOO — ALTHOUGH I THINK IT WASN'T AS MUCH ABOUT THE MONKEY (WHICH, SURE, MADE A MOCKERY OF BOUCHARD) {272} AS IT WAS ABOUT THE CALAIS MASSACRE. THE PAMPHLET VMS MADE + HAD DISTRIBUTED THERE LAID OUT EVERYTHING THAT BOUCHARD HAD BEEN TRYING TO COVER UP (+ WAS SUCCEEDING). I THINK THAT'S WHAT GOT THIS WHOLE THING STARTED—A WAR OF NARRATIVES—THE ONES WRITTEN BY THE POWERFUL + THE ONES WRITTEN BY THOSE WHO POSED THE BIGGEST THREAT TO THAT POWER.

FIGURE 3.2. Eric's and Jen's commentaries in the margins of *Ship of Theseus*

toward reading print texts from top to bottom and left to right (for readers primarily familiar with left-to-right writing systems).

According to cognitive-scientific studies, readers respond to handwriting as they would to embodied movements. Summing up the findings of experiments conducted by Sonia Kandel, Jean-Pierre Orliaguet, and Paolo Viviani (2000), Raymond Gibbs asserts that "people perceived handwriting displays based on the gestures that produced them," which means that "production-related knowledge is implicitly involved in perceptual processing, as well as in perceiving causality" (2005, 56). Marieke Longcamp, Yevhen Hlushchuk, and Riitta Hari (2011) conducted functional magnetic resonance imaging (fMRI) to determine the different brain activities involved in the perception of handwritten alphabets as opposed to printed letters. Statistical analysis of the data collected showed that the left primary motor cortex and the supplementary motor area in the frontal brain regions that are involved in hand-movement triggering are activated more strongly while processing handwriting. Both Gibbs's and Longcamp's inferences suggest that the visual perception of handwriting involves the perception of movements that readers understand to have produced the written content. In addition, Longcamp et al.'s study also confirms that readers map the writing movements onto their own bodies as there is a remarkable similarity between the brain activities during reading handwriting and hand movements. Even as handwriting is often regarded as the expression of the writer's "selfhood," it presents a kinesthetic stimulus to the reader, whereby the reader locates her body as the originator of the writing movement. *S.* utilizes these embodied, locative dimensions of handwriting. The neurophysiological activities elicited by the perception of handwriting bolster the novel's attempt to "move" its actual readers and demonstrate how reading is a spatially and bodily grounded process.

Within the storyworld, the handwritten clusters move Eric and Jen closer to each other. This closeness is for a long time realized solely on the shared surface of the page: Eric, in fact, refuses to meet Jen initially, preferring the topological proximity inside the book to intimacy outside it. The actual readers, oriented by the deictic references to be found throughout the handwritten notes, also share Eric and Jen's space of proximity—the marked-up book. At a later time, when Eric and Jen start to live together, they still use the book to communicate and negotiate their proximity. Encircling a phrase where a character in *Ship of Theseus* is said to be freezing, Jen writes "Ok, seriously. It's freezing in here," and Eric responds, "You just walked past the thermostat," to which Jen says "so did you" mimicking Eric's handwriting (447). They use the book as a fixed point as they engage in allocentric spatial measurements. Allocentric spatial processing refers to the modelling of object-to-object distance.

The book's and the thermostat's co-presence within Eric's and Jen's perceptual fields brings out their spatial proximity. Jen reinforces their sense of closeness by imitating Eric's handwriting. Eric and Jen thus continue to use the pages of *Ship of Theseus* to both shape and articulate their relationship.

In Shamsie's *Kartography*, the temporal order of reading is not compromised except in the rare instances when the traditional print narrative gives way to a more visually elaborate design. For example, scraps from letters Raheen wrote to Karim over several years are juxtaposed to show what Karim makes of their correspondence in a fit of anger (122–23). As I have already mentioned, Raheen's divergence from Karim has to do with his fondness for maps or representations of a place over what Raheen considers the "reality." She thinks of herself as firmly situated in this "reality." So, when Karim is leaving Karachi as a child, she recalls he was "whispering street names . . . drawing a map of the route" (101–2). Although Raheen was in front of him, she assumes that she was already absent to him. She remembers thinking, "*Look up,* I had wanted to say then. *I'm here*" (163). "Here" in Raheen's narration encodes her position in the world, impresses upon readers her presence, even when Karim remains oblivious to her being there with him, because, as Raheen observes, Karim's "here"—his spatial center—has shifted. The page facing Raheen's narration of this departure scene shows the map Karim was drawing *en route* to the airport. At the bottom of the page, Karim has scribbled "start here," where "here" indicates the home in Karachi he is abandoning (see Figure 3.3). On his way to London, Karim is mapping to record the past to which he cannot return.

The map locates the point from where his embodied traversal of places began. His bodily experiences are thus immediately identified as a variable for the distances calculated and represented on the map. As such, this map is not so much an aperspectival view of the city as it is a representation of how Karim navigated the city when it was his home. In other words, what is materialized as an artifactual drawing in this instance is a map of his memories. It is the visual illustration of his cognitive map, emerging from his habitual movements through sites, and not an official or authoritative representation of a city from the outside. The parenthetical comments he adds beside place names stress his emotional attachment to them. For instance, he signposts a "squash court" on the map because of its significance in the history of his friendship with Raheen. He leaves out sites and landmarks that do not carry personal significance for them. Thus, at this moment, Karim is engaged in a more complex, memorial process than Raheen seems to realize.

Handwriting and hand-drawings, their scope and scale, depend significantly on the shape and contours of the page. What one sees of one's own

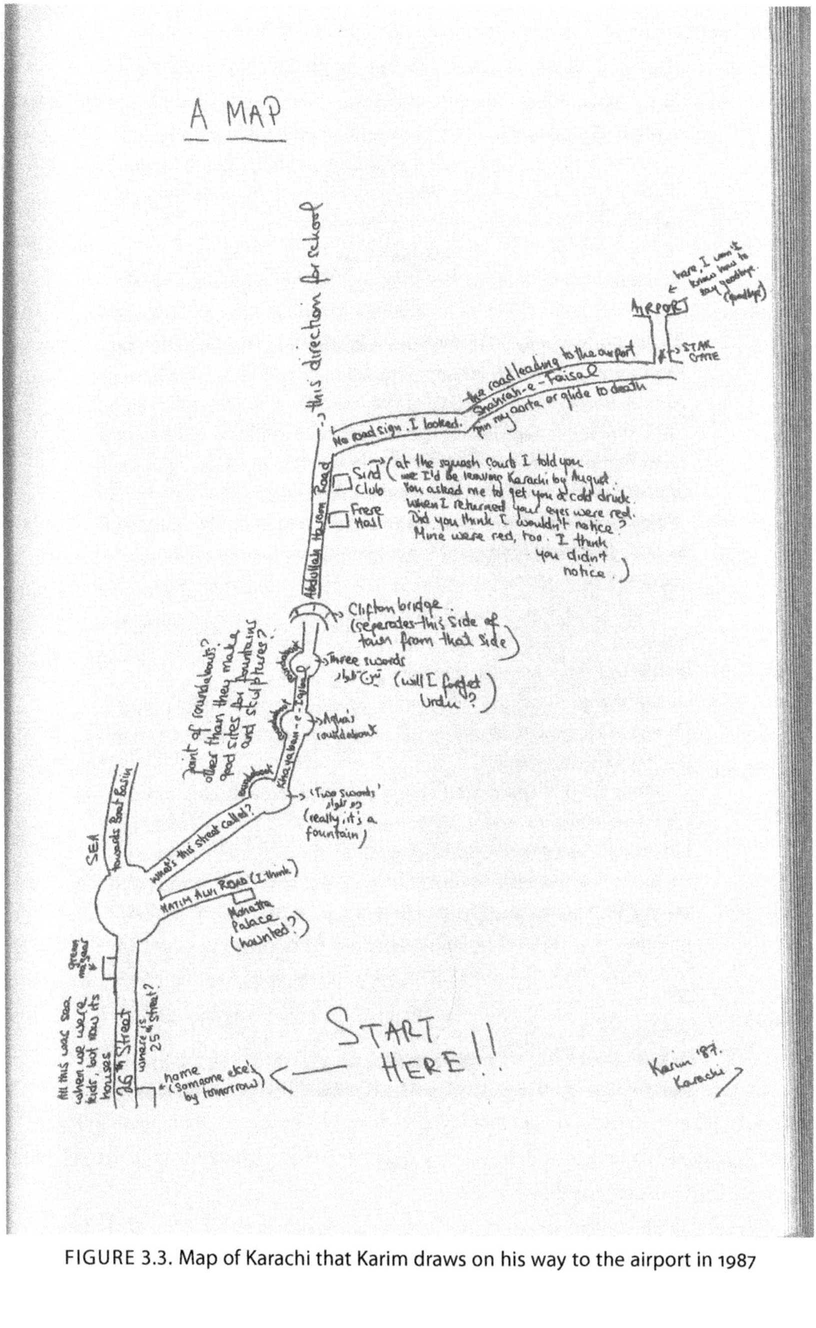

FIGURE 3.3. Map of Karachi that Karim draws on his way to the airport in 1987

writing, based on the layout of the page, affects the direction as well as the content of handwriting. Prior writing traces on the same page can provide guidance and feedback for the execution of the subsequent movement sequences required for the graphomotor transcription of a text (see Olive and Passerault 2012). Karim's handwriting on the map is oriented around the shapes he has drawn. They do not proceed horizontally. His parenthetical comments remain clustered around certain spots rather than use the abundant white space. The clustering visually realizes his attempt at overcoming the linearity of language—the need for it to be laid out in lines—while rendering experiences associated with one particular spot in the city that is now a point on the page. Like Eric's and Jen's notes, Karim's hand-drawn map too requires readers to forego their behavioral bias of reading from top to bottom and left to right. He instructs us to start at the bottom of the page, thereby locating the book's margin closest to the reader's body, should the book be held horizontally, as the starting point. It is a kinesthetic stimulus for the reader. Offering a navigator's view of the city, Karim's map invites us to experience the city, read the city with him. In most multimodal narratives that use handwriting or hand-drawings, the erratic organization of these features critically reflects on the regularity of organization enforced by the horizontal line of printed texts and the standard spacing between typed letters. It is most likely the non-trivial relationship of handwriting and hand-drawing with the page that accounts for the exclusion of maps from the electronic editions of Shamsie's *Kartography*.

Years later when Karim returns to Karachi, he persuades his friends to ask him directions, "from here to somewhere I used to know" (150). When asked he accurately names the streets leading to the destination—"Straight down Shahrah-e-Faisal and right on to Abdullah Haroon Road . . . ," but Raheen objects, saying, "in Karachispeak, go straight straight straight straight straight and then turn right" (150). The point of this exchange is for Karim to show he still belongs "here," that is, in Karachi; and for Raheen to contest that claim by using language ("straight straight straight . . .") that can only direct someone intimately acquainted with the city. Karim's formal answer is more political map-like and aperspectival in this instance. It differs in kind from the subjective map he drew on his way out of the city as a child. He has prioritized the artifactual representation of the city, presumably by more official-authoritative cartographers, over his memories and experiential history, and this is what Raheen finds unacceptable.

Given the thematic preoccupations of *Kartography*, "here" and "there"—spatial deictic markers—also call attention to historical contingencies that determine proximity. The spinning globe with which Raheen's narration opens shows an undivided (pre-1971 Pakistan) and, thus, an out-of-date Pakistan. Political maps change when national borders do, and what is "here" can become "there" over the course of history. Cognitive maps, however, need not necessarily follow the same logic or pattern. In privileging her cognitive maps, Raheen is, at least from Karim's point of view, ignoring historical contingencies. He accuses her of remaining confined to the "comfort of [her] own streets" and explains that he sent her the political, aperspectival maps to show that "the city is falling apart" (164, 219).

When they reconnect over a shared joke, Raheen remarks on his prolonged departure not simply from the city of Karachi (she too had left to study in the US) but from the affective states they were able to share in their childhood. She asks him, "Where have you been all these years, Karim?" (155). Through all those years, Raheen and Karim wrote to each other, but Raheen unlike Eric, Jen, and Karim distrusts manifestations of topological connections on paper and finds artifactual maps inadequate.

The Effects of Cognitive and Artifactual Map Overlays

Ryan points out that

> maps, because they represent a vertical, disembodied perspective—what philosopher Thomas Nagel has called 'a view from nowhere'—are not well-suited to express a subject's lived experience in an environment, while language-based narrative, because it relies on a temporal medium, is not well-suited to convey a mental image of what we have called 'strategic space' ... namely a network of relations between objects. But when language and map complement each other, space can be represented in both its emotional/phenomenological and strategic dimensions. (Ryan, Foote, and Azaryahu 2016, 45)

Linguistic descriptions, layout, and maps are put to complementary uses in *S.* and *Kartography*. Maps exchanged by the characters in the narrative contexts communicate the characters' affective relations with spaces as well as with each other.

In *S.*, Caldeira's map reinforces her closeness to, or specialized understanding of, the narrative spaces represented in Straka's *Ship of Theseus*. The map simultaneously accentuates the actual readers' relative distance from *Ship of Theseus* since they can only ever experience *S.*, the book into which Straka's novel has been transformed thanks to the copious marginalia. The various fictionalized readers' semantic networking of elements from *Ship of Theseus*, visually represented through the annotations, hand-written notes, and hand-drawn strokes, make *Ship of Theseus* inaccessible to its actual readers. Karim's maps in *Kartography* are meant to serve a similar function—of asserting his superior access to Karachi—vis-à-vis Raheen and the actual readers, whose perspectives up until that point are aligned with hers.

A map Karim annotates and sends to Raheen does not represent the whole city of Karachi, only the city's southern part, where Karim and Raheen spent their childhood (see Figure 3.4). However, Karim does not send the map to reminisce about their shared experience of southern Karachi; rather it is one of his many attempts directed at making Raheen see how little she knows of the city, even though she has lived there longer than him. His attitude replicates the colonial vanity of knowledge production—the pretense of assuming an objective, third-person perspective—inscribed in political cartographic processes.

Mapping becomes Karim's tool for staking a claim to the land where, he worries, he no longer belongs. For Raheen, the process of looking at the world of their childhood flattened on a piece of paper with landmarks that are peripheral in her memory signposted for their significance in official accounts of the city is a defamiliarizing experience. Presumably, her cognitive maps of south Karachi are at odds with the artifactual map Karim sent her. At the end of the narrative, however, Raheen gets to pull Karim into the music of Karachi's streets (305). Of the two characters' competing modes of understanding space, Raheen's mode—that of the storyteller and guide—ostensibly triumphs when she shows Karim the way toward the end of the novel. Notwithstanding who triumphs though, the fact that both became involved in such a competition shows that they recognize their relation with Karachi to be pivotal to their senses of self, an integral component of their identities.

Like Raheen and Karim, whose artifactual and cognitive maps stake a claim to the city, Eric and Jen are also initially inclined to compete with Caldeira, who has mapped a part of Straka's narrative space, to claim greater proximity with Straka's storyworld. Eric's and Jen's desire to "be there" in the storyworld of *Ship of Theseus* prompts them to look for objects and people mentioned in *Ship of Theseus* in their own world—the textual actual world. What is more, objects from the world of *Ship of Theseus* seem to be available around them. For instance, they track the small-bore wooden whistles mentioned in *Ship of Theseus* at an auction (see 40). Due to their interest in conflating the imagined spaces, objects, and entities of Straka's novel with their own, Eric and Jen read the novel as a love story between the characters S. and Sola, mirrored in the relationship they conjecture to have existed between Straka and the editor, Caldeira. Finally, Eric and Jen's own relationship reflects those other relationships played out across the ontological levels of the narrative.

The structure of *S.* recalls Frank's notion of spatial narrative form. According to Frank (1991), spatial narratives approach "simultaneity of perception." While analyzing Flaubert's *Emma Bovary* as a modernist novel with spatial form, Frank observes that in particular scenes, "attention is fixed on the interplay of relationships within the immobilized time-area. These relationships are juxtaposed independently of the progress of the narrative, and the full significance of the scene is given only by the reflexive relations among the units of meaning" (17). Flaubert's narration accounts for several different actions occurring in different parts of the same frame at once (as in a painting, for instance). However, in *S.*, the "reflexive relations" constitute discrete ontological planes and the narrative form overlays distinct experiences of spaces with little regard for temporal coordinates.

Apart from the love stories, the entanglement of reading and writing processes is another element reflected across the various ontological planes in *S.* Just as Eric and Jen fill up the space around the printed paragraphs of *Ship of Theseus,* S.—the character in *Ship of Theseus*—fills the space between the printed lines in newspapers with his handwriting and typewriting (378). S.'s reading and writing habits are reported by the omniscient narrator of *Ship of Theseus,* while Eric's and Jen's reading and writing habits are presented via the multimodal arrangement of typeface and handwriting in *S.* Thus, *S.* overlays elements of the different narrative levels, visually and conceptually.

As the multiple storyworlds of *S.* reflect one another, the actual readers are presented with a mise-en-abyme on page, which they may choose to enter. Writing notes in the margins is one of the older habits that accompany reading (see Jackson 2001). Readers as tourists want to record their experiences— as Eric's and Jen's notes indicate. Marginalia are the equivalent of "tourists' pictures," but *S.*, while dramatizing this situation, also makes it difficult for the actual readers to annotate; the margins are already full and where there is space, readers may decide to leave their tracks—add their commentary—or resist adding notes in order to avoid confusion and losing the way.

S. stipulates readers' embodied decision-making and in doing so, affirms the sensorimotor and spatial groundings of reading. The layers of handwriting and mapping in *S.* engender what Gumbrecht calls presence-effect by consolidating an aesthetic illusion that turns tangible features of the book into elements of the storyworld. The result is that the spaces of the storyworld—such as the book in which Eric and Jen write—seem to be available at hand for the actual reader.

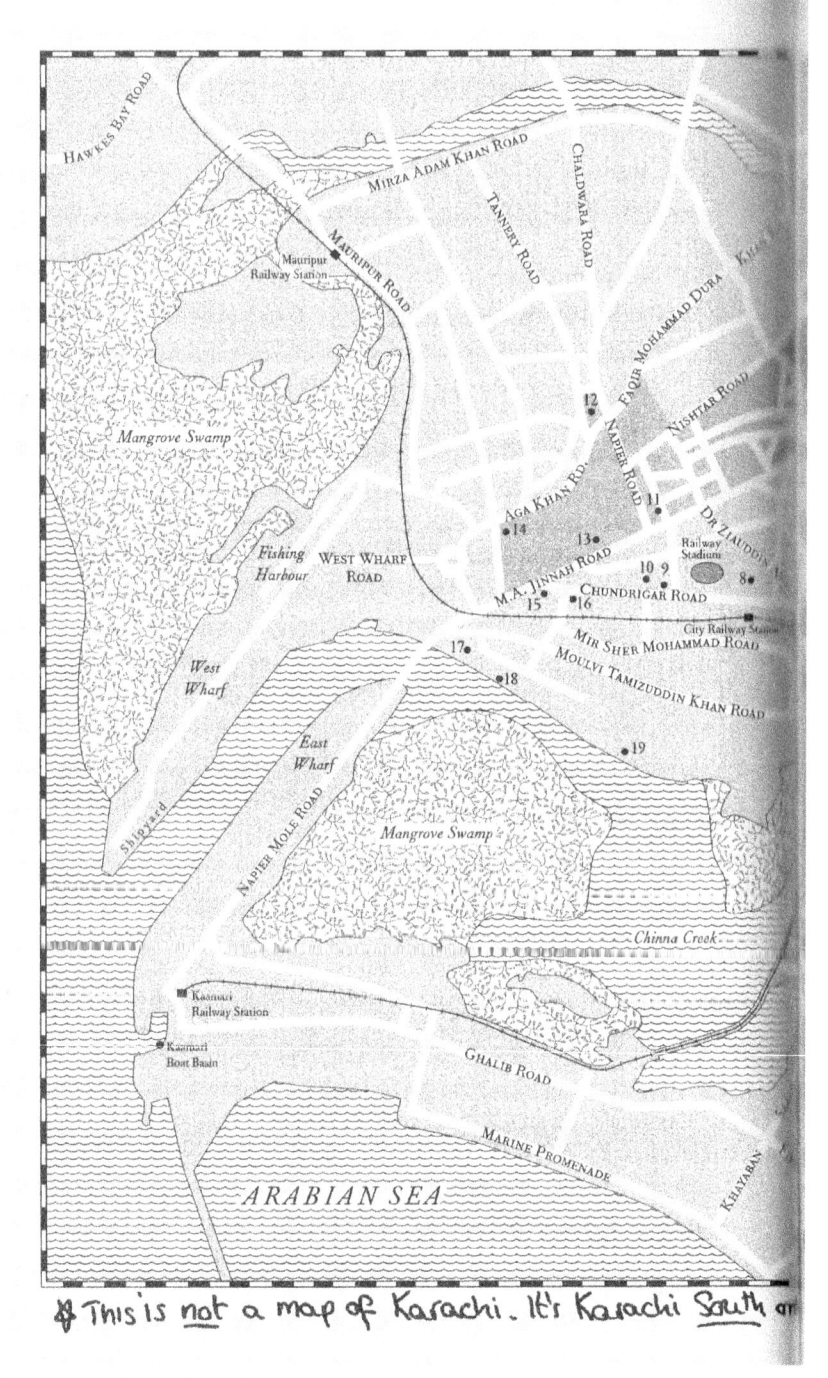

FIGURE 3.4. The annotated map of Karachi that Karim sends Raheen from London in 1990

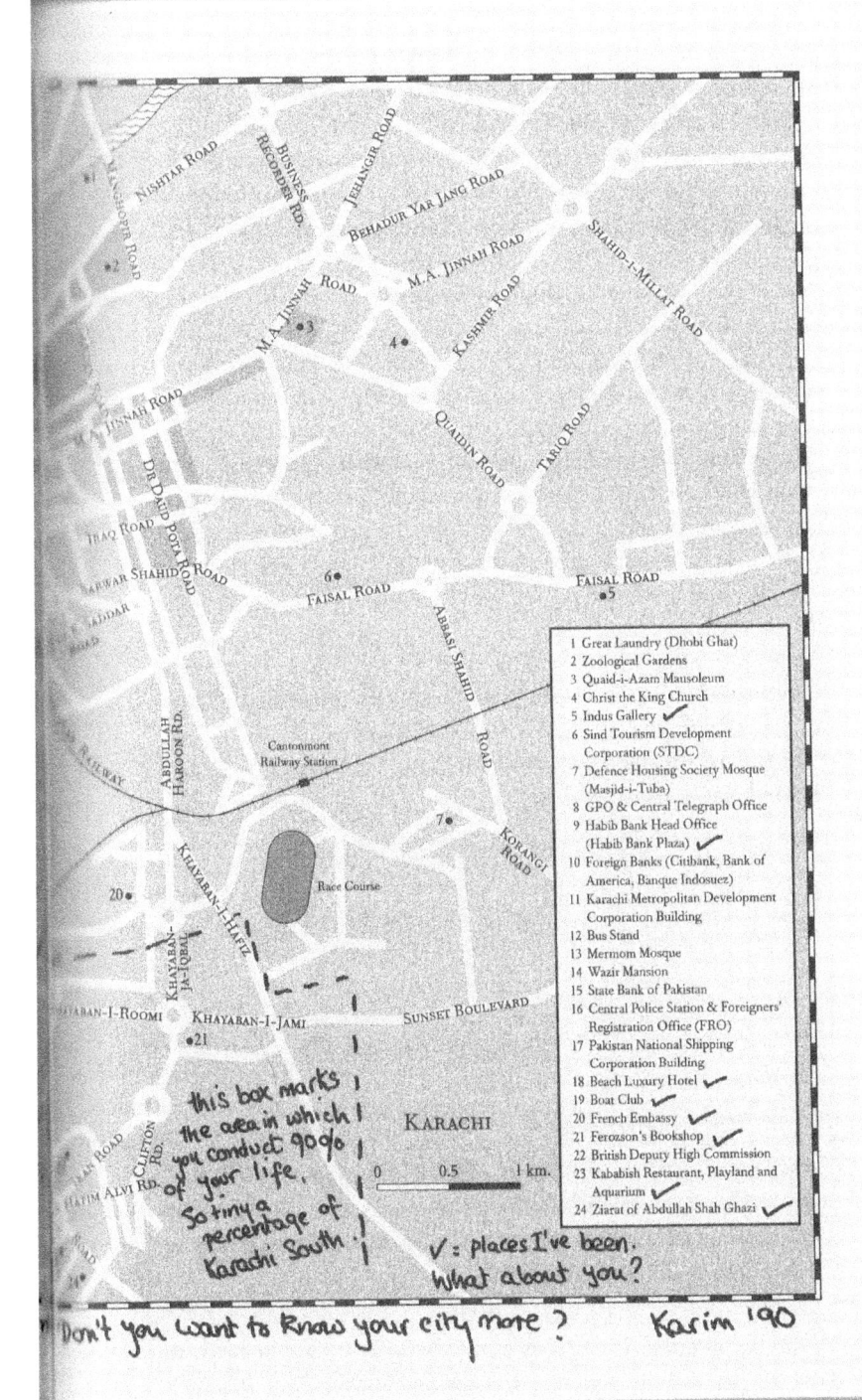

1 Great Laundry (Dhobi Ghat)
2 Zoological Gardens
3 Quaid-i-Azam Mausoleum
4 Christ the King Church
5 Indus Gallery ✓
6 Sind Tourism Development Corporation (STDC)
7 Defence Housing Society Mosque (Masjid-i-Tuba)
8 GPO & Central Telegraph Office
9 Habib Bank Head Office (Habib Bank Plaza) ✓
10 Foreign Banks (Citibank, Bank of America, Banque Indosuez)
11 Karachi Metropolitan Development Corporation Building
12 Bus Stand
13 Mermom Mosque
14 Wazir Mansion
15 State Bank of Pakistan
16 Central Police Station & Foreigners' Registration Office (FRO)
17 Pakistan National Shipping Corporation Building
18 Beach Luxury Hotel ✓
19 Boat Club ✓
20 French Embassy ✓
21 Ferozson's Bookshop ✓
22 British Deputy High Commission
23 Kababish Restaurant, Playland and Aquarium ✓
24 Ziarat of Abdullah Shah Ghazi ✓

this box marks the area in which you conduct 90% of your life. So tiny a percentage of Karachi South.

✓ = places I've been. What about you?

Don't you want to know your city more?   *Karim '90*

Plutarch's paradox that gives *Ship of Theseus* its title includes the ontological question, if you alter all the component parts of a ship, does it fundamentally remain the same? In the narrative, the paradox is literalized as S. travels aboard a ship that is wrecked and rebuilt with the same crew of sailors. The ship's status also reflects the subjectivity of the protagonist. Is S. the same person throughout the narrative? For the actual readers, this paradox posits a phenomenological question: can the actual readers experience Straka's *Ship of Theseus* after Eric's and Jen's commentaries have turned it into S.? This seems unlikely given that Eric and Jen have left their maps and footprints within the book, in the form of objects and annotations that also transform the visual-tactile layout of the text.

Kartography is more restrictive than *S.* when it comes to visual and conceptual layering, partly because, unlike *S.*, it does not comprise as many extensively developed ontological levels. The Karachi of Raheen's stories and experiences is partially built on the foundations of Italo Calvino's *Invisible Cities*. Shamsie embeds a very short story that is supposed to be a pastiche of Calvino's book in a letter Raheen writes to Karim. The city described in this pastiche is the oasis of friendship that Raheen envisions the Karachi of her childhood to be, but the story remains an allegory and is not enlarged upon over the course of the narrative (115).

A fluid digital map Karim envisions is the most succinct expression of *Kartography*'s approach to spatial thinking and representation. Karim tells Raheen:

> We'll make an interactive map on the Internet. You start with a basic street map, OK, but everywhere there are links. Click here, you get sound files of Karachiites telling stories of what it's like to live in different parts of town. Click there, you get a visual of any particular street. Click again, the camera zooms in and you see a rock or a leaf or a billboard that means something to that street. Click, you see streets that exist seasonally, like your lunar street. Click, you see which sections are under curfew. Click, you hear a poem. Click, you see a painting. Choice of languages in which you can read the thing. Sound files in all kinds of dialects. Strong on graphics for people who are illiterate. Just wait, Raheen, this is going to be amazing. And don't tell me most people can't afford computers; you just wait a few years and an amazing number of people will have access to one even if they don't own it themselves. (300)

Karim is, of course, excessively enthusiastic about the inclusive possibilities of the internet, but the digital media ecology enables him to assume a more layered approach to spaces. He can imagine the confluence of pictorial signposts with stories, graphics with multiple dialects. In this context, Raheen's entire narration that makes up the novel could be one story among many stories located in a part of south Karachi—perhaps geotagged to a "basic" map such as the one Karim once sent her. Thus, what seemed competing and discrete about Raheen's and Karim's cognitive habits find a way to merge in this vision of a digital map that can overlay a variety of information.

Twenty-First Century Dilemmas

As my discussion of the novels has shown, mapping inflects the thematics and guides the presentation of subjective relations in *Kartography* and *S*. Mapping as an analog captures the situated and multisensory connections of individuals with their surroundings. Fauconnier's (1985) observations about maps being a more versatile, dynamic, and contextually attuned metaphor for cognition than the conflation of cognition with computation is embraced by both narratives.

Through their use of discursive and artifactual maps, *Kartography* and *S*. also challenge the understanding of "maps" as a disembodied or aperspectival representation of space. Whether drawn by Caldeira or Karim, artifactual maps reflect specific positions, conditions of knowledge, and states of mind in the novels. The visual representation of commonplace habits like underlining and annotation in *S*. also suggests that readers' semantic networking of storyworlds, their cognitive maps, is embodied and adaptive.

From the point of view of readers, how and why characters map their experiences in *S*. and *Kartography* are more significant than the information about narrative spaces the maps offer. The narratives take into account the epistemological uncertainty characterizing the understanding of cartography as a means of knowledge production since, at least, the late twentieth century when the sociocultural underpinnings of maps became increasingly apparent. Historically and culturally situated aspects of cartography are of particular significance in Shamsie's novel. The colonial history of mapping and postcolonial endeavors to resist the replication of colonial practices inform Karim's cartographic projects. Initially, the manner in which generations of colonizers moved through Karachi and mapped South Asia impact Karim's imagination. He aspires to standardize provincial knowledge for a global audience and emulate practices of political mapping. He complains to Raheen that when anyone asks for directions in Karachi people use known landmarks, including the sea, as reference points to direct them, but that is of no help to someone who does not know where the sea is. Karim at this point is busy imagining a foreign audience for his maps. However, *Kartography* remains cognizant of the postcolonial critiques of cartographic practices that enshrine colonial knowledge and viewpoint. The narrative thus delineates how Karim learns to think of mapping as a means for mediating and remembering local history rather than a tool for making provincial knowledge global, with Raheen serving as his guide. As Butt notes in her analysis, "maps juxtapose globalization and regionalism" in Shamsie's fiction, as Shamsie demonstrates their potential to both connect and disconnect people and places (2015, 178). The idiosyncratic homages to colonial landmarks Karim encounters while visiting Karachi as an adult are among the many situational factors that prompt his transformation. For instance, he spots billboards advertising "WESTMINSTER ABBEY—an upstart rival to the well-established BIG BEN underwear company" (149). The sign exudes reverence for colonial culture and landmarks while also parodying them. Through his cartographic practices, Karim eventually seeks to attend to these everyday contradictions by constituting the lived experience of Karachi rather than highlighting the city's well-known sites and monuments.

In the case of *S.*, the characters' experiences of moving through their immediate surroundings are transposed onto the spatial information they encounter through other means to reflect on twenty-first-century cognitive habits. The narrative attempts to represent how we are present here and elsewhere at once with media technologies multiplying the demands on our time and attention. The overlaid maps we encounter in *S.* in one sense manifest the "aesthetic of cognitive mapping" that Jameson envisioned as a response to the "historically original dilemma" of late twentieth-century postmodern culture—the suppression of distance and the insertion of "individual subjects into a multidimensional set of radically discontinuous realities" (1988, 351). According to Jameson, "the postmodern body—whether wandering through a postmodern hotel, locked into rock sound by means of headphones, or undergoing the multiple shocks and bombardments of the Vietnam War . . .—is now exposed to a perceptual barrage of immediacy" (1988, 351). He called for a new aesthetic to mediate the experiences of the postmodern body in opposition to the modernist depiction of subjectivities as a "closed world" (1988, 350). Jameson's rhetoric identifies multiplying sensory stimuli as violent without exception. However, the twenty-first-century subject—as Cole (2017) suggests—is at home with multiplying realities, not shocked but habitually immersed in different worlds, walking through a city while also browsing on Safari. As such, the twenty-first-century subjectivities imagined in the narratives are not sealed; rather, these subjectivities come unbound, become extended over networks that include biological agents and media technologies.

CHAPTER 4

Anti-Archival Minds

Collecting, Deleting, and Scaling Memories

It is a key aim of this book to develop and model an interpretive approach within narrative studies that acknowledges contemporary cognitive sciences' reliance on explanatory pluralism and along with it, the provisional nature of what is known about cognition. Such an approach affirms the view that literary forms semiautonomously co-emerge with interdisciplinary knowledge about cognition. Twenty-first-century narratives that are thematically concerned with cognitive habits and combine an array of modes and media to represent these habits motivate my analytical project. Since I identify multimodal narratives as participating in ongoing ideation about how minds work, the main chapters of this book remain dedicated to close readings of such narratives. My readings attend to the relations among modes and media deployed for representing thought within a narrative as well as the broader intellectual culture that produces novel analogs to explain mental activities. This chapter adopts a similar reading strategy, but the focus is on the dismantling rather than the production of an analogical model in the broader culture. The analogical model in question is that of the archive as a structural and functional equivalent of memory. I explore alternatives to the archival model inscribed in two narratives—Graham Rawle's *Woman's World* (2005) and Lance Olsen's *Theories of Forgetting* (2014)—that enunciate memory's fallibility through the construction and manipulation of personal media archives. Surveying alternatives to the archival metaphor for memory, I also discuss how these narratives depict shifts in the valuation of mnemonic habits and practices in the face of not only changing media culture but also other widespread present-day concerns like rapid climate change.

Characters with faulty memory abound in contemporary multimodal literature: Jonathan Safran Foer's *Everything Is Illuminated* (2002), Hall's *The Raw Shark Texts* (2007), Abrams and Dorst's *S.* (2013), Graham Rawle's *Woman's World* (2005), Lance Olsen's *Theories of Forgetting* (2014), and James Sie's *Still Life Las Vegas* (2015) feature characters whose ability to remember their own past has been severely compromised.[1] Failures and omissions in individual memory are connected with a wider social-cultural predicament in some of these fictions: in Olsen's *Theories of Forgetting*, degenerating biological memory and planetary degeneration are intertwined, while characters' amnesia in Foer's *Everything Is Illuminated* is traced back to the traumas of the Holocaust.

The aesthetic strategies used to construct amnesiac minds vary across these texts, and as strategies of representation vary, so do the effects and meanings of the representations. That is, the poetics of memory representation encode stances about what memory is. In *Raw Shark Texts,* for instance, as I have discussed, the visual arrangement of the words on the page lay emphasis on the material and bodily groundings of memory. Within the two narratives I take up in this chapter—*Woman's World* and *Theories of Forgetting*—characters generate self-narratives by gathering, extracting, and piecing together fragmentary texts and images. The fragments are samplings from the characters' vaster and more chaotic collection of records. The artifactual books that comprise the appropriated and found scraps constituting these characters' autobiographical accounts become archives in their own right. These are of course not ordered institutional collections; rather, to repurpose what Jared Gardner says of graphic novels adopting similar strategies, "these are archives in the loosest, messiest sense of the word—archives of the forgotten artifacts and ephemera" (2012, 150). In *Woman's World* and *Theories of Forgetting*, autobiographical accounts emerging through the archived fragments reconstruct characters' negative experiences in ways that attest to their forgetting of these experiences.

The inclusion of appropriated and altered materials in narratives preoccupied with the workings of memory recall the metaphoric association of archival or storage and retrieval mechanisms with biological memory both in commonsensical views and first-generation cognitive-scientific theories. How-

---

1. See Ghosal (2020) for a discussion of how Sie's *Still Life Las Vegas* depicts forgetting as a process involving interference and artifice rather than decay caused by the passage of time.

ever, *Woman's World* and *Theories of Forgetting* complicate this analogic equation. As my reading of the two narratives in this chapter will demonstrate, gathering, selecting, and organizing images, texts, and documents instead of salvaging characters' past experiences assist in their forgetting. On the one hand, the narratives insist on the reconstructive and generative dimensions of memory. On the other hand, they also foreground the distinctiveness of particular archival modes and media. Their treatment of memory insists on the pragmatic relations of embodied memory with archival technologies rather than a reductive equation between the two. Such literary representations, I argue, share in the reappraisal of memory operations in the twenty-first century.

Rawle's and Olsen's processes of accumulating text and image fragments from various sources to reflect on the nature of memory are in dialogue with the established conventions of artists' books. Artists' books have often memorialized significant—even traumatic—events by incorporating objects connected to either the site or the survivors. A host of Holocaust and 9/11 memoirs follow this strategy. For instance, Tatana Kellner's limited-edition books, *71125, Fifty Years of Silence: Eva Kellner's Story* (1992) and *B 11226, Fifty Years of Silence: Eugene Kellner's Story* (1992), contain handwritten testimonies and papier-mâché hand casts of her parents, who were Holocaust survivors. Robbin Ami Silverberg's series of books labelled *Detritus* (2002) is composed of paper made from the pulp of detritus and dust that covered the trees around Ground Zero after the 9/11 terrorist attacks. Within memory discourses connected to the Holocaust in particular, the status of art is fiercely debated, and artistic works related to traumatic chapters of individual and collective history confront ethical questions about whether such episodes can or should be represented.[2] By assembling objects indexically connected with the traumatic event, books like *Fifty Years* seek to impress upon viewers that the past has been made present "un-mediated" without the touch of representational artifice.[3] Curation rather than authorship gives these books their affective power and authority. Such memorial practices and memory culture influence the narratives I analyze in this chapter, though *Woman's World* and *Theories of Forgetting* are fictions disseminated through mass-produced books. Characters turn into amateur archivists in the storyworlds of *Woman's World*

---

2. A variety of responses is available to these ethical dilemmas, ranging from Adorno's oft-quoted remark on the barbarism of writing poetry after Auschwitz to Agamben's argument for listening to what is absent in survivors' testimonies (Adorno 1981, 34; 2007, 362–63; Agamben 1999).

3. See Young (1990, 174; 1993) about how Holocaust memorials seek to make the past feel present.

and *Theories of Forgetting* with an initial understanding that the fragments they are piecing together will enable them to preserve their experiences. However, the mnemonic practices turn out to be generative and distortive rather than restorative.

The workings of memory, its cultural and historical significance, have been at the forefront of a prolific interdisciplinary body of research following what has been called the 1990s "memory boom" (see Huyssen 2003). Contemporary scholarship on memory focuses on how experiences are remembered and recovered, the ways in which literature and other arts portray the phenomenon of remembering, and also how experiential memory comes into play during a range of activities including writing and reading. The focus on remembering the past with some degree of accuracy in a host of interdisciplinary studies is a response to fears of political and cultural amnesia. French historian Pierre Nora, one of the pioneers of the "memory boom," observed that "we speak so much of memory because there is so little of it left" (1989, 7). Societies create memorials and monuments to elicit collective modes of remembering, because we believe that the passage of time will automatically contribute to forgetting. In other words, a commonplace assumption is that the past and the present will fade out and vanish unless preserved in durable form.

Durable media consequently supply the terms and concepts with which we reflect on embodied memories (see Draaisma 2000, 3). Twentieth-century cognitive-scientific language joined in the longer tradition of explicating and restating aspects of biological memory in terms of external media meant to record and retain information. First-generation cognitive-scientific approaches conceptualized biological memory as a data storage and retrieval technology, structurally and functionally similar to computer memory. Forgetting would mean an involuntary error or fault in the storage-retrieval system. This mechanistic conceptualization of biological memory is compatible with the idea that the brain has storage limits, as though it were a hard drive, and depends on external media and transactive or group memory systems for cognitive offloading. Second-generation cognitive-scientific studies of memory, as I will discuss shortly, challenge the dominant understanding of remembering as retrieval and forgetting, whether individual or social, as involuntary and passive.

Rawle's *Woman's World* and Olsen's *Theories of Forgetting* creatively participate in the reconsiderations of biological memory's relation with storage-retrieval mechanisms and archiving practices. Rawle cut and pasted 40,000 scraps from vintage women's magazines to compose *Woman's World*. Roy, the novel's character narrator, is devastated by his sister's death in an accident and seeks to preserve her as an embodied agent in his world. To memorialize her, he reimagines her. He begins to follow fashion tips in women's magazines to live *as* his deceased sister, thereby manufacturing an alternate subjectivity for himself. In addition, he collages scraps from the magazines to construct his sister's narrative voice and compose her self-narrative. Scrapbooking, as Benoît Crucifix notes, is "a mode of preservation at the margins of institutional archives" (2016, n. pag.). Roy's imaginative constitution and enactment of his sister's subjectivity through the practice of scrapbooking distorts the experiences he may have shared with her before her death and his experience of the accident that killed her. The novel thus presents scrapbooking, a practice of personal media assemblage and archiving, as a means for forgetting past experiences.

Olsen's *Theories of Forgetting* uses collage and erasure techniques to narrate three interlinked stories: the first, told in the first person, concerns an experimental filmmaker—Alana—who is losing control over her body-mind to a planetary pandemic called the Frost; the second, told in the third person, follows her husband Hugh who is trying to voluntarily forget his past and obliterate the traces of his own identity in the aftermath of Alana's illness and death; and the third concerns their daughter Aila's attempts at preserving the writings and ephemera—the "remains"—of her absent parents. Alana's journals, Hugh's self-narrative in the third person, and Aila's marginal notes appended to her parents' personal records have been supposedly collected and put together in the book form by Aila's estranged brother Lance, a self-reflexive reference to the author, Lance Olsen. Photographs and documents included in the book are connected to the family members' clashing approaches to remembering and forgetting. At the time of her death, Alana was making a film about the American sculptor Robert Smithson's earthwork, *Spiral Jetty*, and photographs of the earthwork are enclosed in the book. Alana's and Hugh's mnemonic habits and conceptualizations of memory are in dialogue with Smithson's aesthetic. As such my analysis of Olsen's novel will trace how the *Spiral Jetty* competes with the artifactual and archival affordances of the book as an analog for the structure and functions of embodied memory. As in *Woman's World*, the curated images and documents in *Theories of Forgetting* seem to function as aids to recollection and preservation but turn out to be accomplices of forgetting. Thereby forgetting becomes conceptualized as equally dynamic and deliberate as recollection, requiring laborious collection and manipulation of artifacts. By according pivotal importance to forgetting, both *Woman's World* and *Theories of Forgetting* develop a portrait of the mind as necessarily "anti-archival" and unsettle commonplace views equating technological records with embodied recall.

The Limits of Archives and Memory
in the Twenty-First Century

William J. T. Mitchell and Mark B. Hansen observe that

> Memory, which is usually understood as an interiorized and innate psychological faculty, has, from the standpoint of media studies, been understood as a crossroads of aesthetics, technology, and society since ancient times . . . Interior memory technologies, then, were understood as constellations of external media: words and images, tastes and sounds, cabinets and retrieval systems, marks on objects and bodies, buildings and statues, computers and clocks, coins and credit lines. (2010, xvii)

Common analogs for memory include media technologies invented to record, store, and reproduce information. When we understand embodied recall as similar to accessing "constellations of external media," we are thinking of memory as an archive where records of the past are waiting to be accessed. The description of memory as essentially a storage and retrieval system, analogous to archives, surfaces in both everyday conversations and specialized discourses of disciplines like the cognitive sciences and media studies. Douwe Draaisma notes that that there is "an almost irresistible tendency to represent the act of remembering as a person who enters the memory and starts searching there" (2000, 217). This person is a "restless archivist" or other "industrious employee" who is "busy recording, developing, and filing sensory information" (2000, 217). The equation of retention and archivation with memory accounts for the commonplace anxiety that innovations in recording and storage technologies will lead to the weakening of the human cognitive capacity to remember. This apprehension is voiced as early as Plato's *Phaedrus*, when Socrates recounts how the king Thamus rebuked Theuth for inventing alphabets, as he believed that writing would foster the conditions for forgetting. It is worth noting here that this concern seems to be especially high for what is commonly called semantic memory—memory of learned information—rather than episodic memory—memory of one's personal experiences (see Vargha-Khadem et al. 1997 and Elward and Vargha-Khadem 2018 for the relation of semantic and episodic memory). William James (1890) developed a multitiered model of memory to account for the differences in the longevity of various sorts of information in our minds.[4] Philosopher Bernard Stiegler

---

4. James's understanding aligns closely with contemporary embodied, enactive theories, as he observes that memory is "the feeling of belief in a peculiar complex object; but all the elements of this object may be known to other states of belief" (1918 [1890], 652).

articulates a tripartite model that is similar to James' but with greater emphasis on the functional equivalences of embodied and artificial memory: primary retention for Stiegler concerns perception and working memory; secondary retention refers to cognitive storage of information in a more long-term manner; and Stiegler equates tertiary retention with technological recording. In Stiegler's formulation, storage-retrieval media are components of embodied memory, and the logic and function of these media, what Stiegler calls mnemotechnological apparatus, essentially define and configure human memory. Thus, Stiegler notes, "We are in constant relation with mnemotechnological apparatuses of all kinds, from televisions and telephones to computers and GPS navigation systems. These cognitive technologies, to which we consign a greater and greater part of our memory, cause us to lose ever-greater parts of our knowledge" (2010, 68). At present, not only the memory drives of computers but also the internet is thought to be weakening our capacity to recall information. Betsy Sparrow, J. Liu, and D. M. Wegner (2011) note that the habitual use of search engines like Google causes people to remember where to access information rather than to retain the information. Empirical studies undertaken by Xiaoyue Liu et al. (2018) similarly suggest that the habit of searching the internet for information changes regional activities in the brain associated with "memory retrieval."

Even though the archival metaphor for memory can be discerned in various periods of the Western culture, as Naohisa Mori notes, "after the enthusiasm of classical cognitive psychology (cognitivism) sustained by computer analogy to humans, the archive metaphor started explicitly to rule psychology" (2011, 12). The cognitivist version of the archival metaphor assumes that experiences of the past are encoded and stored in the mind which is a computer and can be retrieved as and when needed. An isomorphic stance with regards to storage-retrieval technologies and biological memory undermines the extent to which acts of both recall and forgetting are adaptive and generative.

In the literary cultural sphere, fictions such as Philip K. Dick's "We Can Remember It for You Wholesale" (1987 [1966]) present memories as purchasable data stored on chips implanted in one's brain. The treatment of memories as stored data, retrievable and erasable using digital technologies, in the story reflects on mid-twentieth-century cognitive theories' enthusiastic equation of the mind with a computer. However, the characterization of human memory as essentially equivalent to computational memory in the cognitive sciences is especially incongruous given that artificial intelligence researchers sought to overcome the fallibility of human memory through AI. Daniel L. Schacter, Scott A. Guerin, and Peggy L. St. Jacques note that artificial intelligence researchers were apprehensive about the prospects of using human memory as a model: "Invariably, the remark is made [in AI research communities], 'Well, of course, we would not want our system to have something so unreliable as human memory.'" (Schacter et al. 2011, 468; Anderson and Milson 1989, 703)

Perfect, reliable recall approaching the promise of artificial intelligence is featured as a pathology in literature, or at least, an atypicality that isolates a character with such a capacity. A now canonical and influential example of an entity with perfect recall is the titular character of Jorge Luis Borges's "Funes, the Memorious" (1962 [1942]). Even though present-day debates between computational Theory of Mind and other embodied, enactive models of cognition may not have been available to Borges, he would have been aware of other versions of the archival metaphor for memory, and that may have prompted him to speculate about its possible affordances and limitations. Ireneo Funes has a prodigious memory and is incapable of forgetting. The narrator in Borges's story characterizes Funes as "eccentric," and the symptoms of his eccentricity would conform to contemporary stereotypical constructions of autism. For instance, Funes is not skilled at communicating with people but has an augmented sensory interface with the world. For Funes, the present moment is "so rich and bright" as to become "almost intolerable" (112). These traits are reminiscent of Christopher in Haddon's *Curious Incident*, who is also in heightened perceptual contact with his environment. Borges's narrator is in awe of Funes but also pathologizes him. He says that he does not doubt that "Funes was a precursor of the superman" and wonders why "no one should have experimented on Funes" (108, 113). It is the narrator's belief that Funes is not capable of thought, which the narrator equates with abstractions. Neuroscientist Rodrigo Quian Quiroga observes that Borges's story presents an interpretation of what modern neuroscience is learning about the brain, though Borges was able to construct this portrait "guided only by his reasoning and prodigious imagination" (2012, 4). Quian Quiroga argues that Borges's Funes lacks two essential memory functions of humans: to abstract and to synthesize. Funes interpreted in such a way seems more like a personified machine than a biological agent. However, in Borges's narrative, Funes's perfect memory is not data that can be stripped from its environmental and perceptual contexts. Funes's present perceptions entangle with his past perceptions of objects and people, and so, his recollections "were not simple; each visual image was linked to muscular sensations, thermal sensations" (112). Thus, Borges's story locates Funes's memoriousness in the character's unique perceptual abilities rather than in his mind's unique storage capacities. Such a representation finds its resonances in contemporary embodied and enacted theories of cognition.

The second generation of cognitive-scientific research questions the prevalent view of memory as a storage and retrieval technology. Jens Brockmeier observes that

> the notion of memory—the very idea that there is a particular capacity that enables us to remember, to store, and to recall experiences and knowledge and, in doing so, constitutes an essential part of our existence—is in the midst of dissolving. This dissolution of memory as a specific epistemological and scientific subject—which had come into being, as Hacking (1995, 1996) pointed out, only in the late 19th century—is itself a relatively recent process. What makes this process specially interesting is that it takes place in a broad spectrum of scientific and scholarly developments and, moreover, in literary, artistic, and public discourses. (2010, 7)

Today a wide range of empirical and theoretical cognitive-scientific studies recognizes memory as a process—constitutive of actions—rather than as an entity or data localized and inscribed in some corner of the human brain. Noting that there are no biological indicators that distinguish acts of remembering the past from acts of perceiving the present in any sensory mode, Brockmeier argues that human memory is best understood as the narrativization of autobiographical experiences (2015, 20, 311).

Other contemporary psychologists, cognitive scientists, and philosophers of mind like Stanley Klein (2015), Daniel D. Hutto and Anco Peeters (2018) agree with Brockmeier that remembering is not the retrieval of past experiences but do not share Brockmeier's narrative approach to memory. They understand remembering episodic and semantic knowledge as a reconstructive activity that depends on imagination and reenactment that need not exclusively take narrative form. Klein defines remembering as a distinct, qualitative mode of perceiving the world and explains that memory is not content but "the manner in which content is given to awareness" (2015, 16).

While studying autobiographical memory, Daniel M. Bernstein and Elizabeth Loftus explain that acts of recall generate and reconstruct rather than retrieve past experiences. Distortions are integral to recall, and "all memory is false to some degree. Memory is inherently a reconstructive process, whereby we piece together the past to form a coherent narrative that becomes our autobiography. In the process of reconstructing the past, we color and shape our life's experiences based on what we know about the world" (2009, 373). Loftus has been involved in several groundbreaking studies that contest popular views (perpetuated by Freud's notion of repression) about the possible suppression of memories and methods of memory recovery (Loftus, Garry, and Hayne 2007).[5] She observes that the prevalent beliefs about memory as a storage and retrieval system can mislead individuals into thinking that their motivated reconstruction of the past is an experience of accurate memory recovery. I will refer more specifically to some of the cognitive experiments Loftus has conducted in collaboration with Maryanne Garry and Ayanna Thomas, among others, when I begin to analyze the narratives in the following sections of this chapter (Loftus, Garry, and Hayne 2007; Garry et al. 1996; Thomas et al. 2003). Here I would like to note that it is not as if contemporary cognitive sciences have uniquely recognized memory's fallibility, just as contemporary literary narratives are not the first to exploit memory's unreliability for aesthetic purposes. However, what is noteworthy about both the cognitive-scientific research and the narratives is their exploration of *what* prevents us from experiencing the past as accurately and vividly as Funes.

Woman's World and *Theories of Forgetting* exemplify the questioning of the storage-retrieval model of memory in twenty-first-century literary and artistic undertakings. The novels underscore the plasticity of both technological archives and biological memory and in doing so, contest the standard assumptions of the archive metaphor for memory in early cognitive sciences and everyday parlance. Rawle's *Woman's World* dramatizes a character's creative uses of a personal media archive to construct and sustain a counterfactual view of negative experiences. Scrapbooking involves the collection and appropriation of source texts and the scrapbook owner's deliberate sequencing of those texts for self-expression. Through the character narrator's process of scrapbooking, Rawle explores the creative and manipulative dimensions of remembering and forgetting. Following my discussion of Rawle's novel, I will consider how Olsen's *Theories of Forgetting* presents plural attitudes to both remembering and forgetting as characters grapple with the limits of human understanding and imagination, on the one hand, and the ethics of archivation, on the other. The characters' memory practices in both novels relate to their histories, and in certain cases respond to their personal traumas, but my analysis intends to underscore how Rawle and Olsen explore the nature of cognition in general while depicting the distinctive predicament of their characters. I maintain that the forgetful minds of characters are not exceptions against which norms are defined in these narratives. Instead, the characters exemplify, albeit in an exaggerated manner, commonplace cognitive habits.

---

5. See Ciccoricco (2015, 161–93) for a discussion of how digital fiction lends itself to a more nuanced interpretation through a reconstructive view of memory rather than the Freudian notion of repression.

Scrapbooking to Forget in Graham Rawle's *Woman's World*

In 2004, a year before Rawle's *Woman's World* was published, a number of social media platforms like Orkut, Facebook, and Scrap Girls brought the possibilities of personal archiving afforded by analog scrapbooks to digital environments. Google's now obsolete platform Orkut named their message board "scrapbook" to emphasize the connections between the old media habit of scrapbooking and the practices of social media expression and self-documentation. Noting the similarities between analog scrapbooks and social media sites, Katie Day Good observes, "in addition to providing a setting in which users can creatively assemble content, both scrapbooks and Facebook also serve as reservoirs for that content . . . both are *personal media archives,* or sites that house personal media assemblages within a bounded setting, with options for both private viewing and public display" (2013, 559). The practice of self-presentation through archived and appropriated content thus is a tradition of long standing. However, the dominance of a mode of self-presentation may familiarize it to such an extent that its artifices start to go unnoticed. *Woman's World*'s highly stylized appearance, resulting from Rawle's method of composing it in the tradition of the analog scrapbook against a backdrop of rising social media platforms, calls attention to the contrivances of self-presentation through personal media archives. Moreover, *Woman's World* takes self-expression through scraps as powerfully instancing the habits of selection and omission integral to assembling autobiographical accounts. The treatment of memory in the novel as eliciting acts of strategic construction and reconstruction rather than the retrieval of saved content results from its mapping the habits and biases associated with scrapbooking onto the notion of embodied recall.

Rawle cut and pasted 40,000 scraps from his voluminous personal collection of 1960s British women's magazines to compose *Woman's World*. For fifteen years (1990–2005) Rawle published a comic collage column called "Lost Consonants" in *The Guardian*. The series put a found image beside a sentence from which a consonant had been removed and demonstrated Rawle's knack for discovering the absurd in the mundane by imposing procedural constraints. When he set out to create *Woman's World,* he drafted a version of the narrative and looked for suitable phrases to replace his own wording within a database comprising digitized version of his magazine collection. As he found relevant matches, he cut them up and pasted them to reconstruct the narrative discourse. The published book reproduces the collaged pages. The chaotic visual-tactile surface of the pages shares world-building responsibilities with language. Indeed, what sets Rawle's multimodal narrative apart from earlier collaged novels like William Burroughs' *Naked Lunch* (1959) or Kathy Acker's *Empire of the Senseless* (1988) is the extent to which the materiality of the scraps, how they look and feel, contributes to the narrative's progression and meaning.

The scrapbook form of *Woman's World* reflects on the dynamic interplay of individual and collective memory, embodied and media memory. In a statement placed at the end of *Woman's World*, Rawle says that the "voice of the original 1960s woman's world" came to remain in the novel through the scraps (439). He seems to interpret his task as a medium who detects and transmits voices inscribed in media records, and, indeed, the scrapbook form appears to relay something of the past. As Kiene Brillenburg Wurth puts it, the collaged scraps end up "stubbornly retaining a visible connection to an anterior site and time. *Woman's World* is never 'its own'; it is a prosthetic text" (2011a, 128). The handmade collage form of the pages in *Woman's World* affirms the role of the authorial hands at work. As if to shine a light on the authorial presence, Rawle places a photo showing two hands clipping magazines alongside the statement explaining his composition process (438). But this authorial hand is not composing alone. Rawle's practice locates authorial invention at the intersection of individual memory, imagination, and media collection. Hence, Brillenburg Wurth reads the novel's aesthetic as "personal and impersonal, authorial and procedural at the same time" (2011a, 130).

Both the collection of magazines and the clipping of scraps are attributed to the character narrator Norma in *Woman's World*. The narrative is set in the 1960s and Norma is an avid reader of women's magazines of the time. She considers herself an authority on women's fashion and housekeeping. The narrative opens with her asking, "What is your idea of a perfect home? Do you long for a gracious way of living that provides comfort without clutter and an atmosphere of charming elegance throughout the whole house?" (3; see Figure 4.1). The questions, especially the second one, sound as though they belong in commercials. The fonts and textures of the scraps assembled to create Norma's narrative voice intensify such an effect, as Alison Gibbons confirms following a short empirical study on the novel's reception (2012a, 188–92). Gibbons notes that "readers' perceptions of character voice and the visual world of the narrative become inflected by both the original collage novel they are reading and the contexts, perhaps numerous, that the source texts signify" (2012b, 431). While analyzing *Raw Shark Texts*, I had mentioned that even though as readers we understand that artifice is involved in the composition and presentation of any literary narrative, some narratives come across as more "synthetic" than others, taking my cue from James Phelan (2007). Phelan's argument is that readers typically develop interests and responses in relation

What

IS YOUR IDEA of a perfect home? Do you long for a gracious way of living that provides comfort without clutter and an atmosphere of charming elegance throughout the whole house?

I like things to be just so in my home. Mary, my housekeeper, never stops teasing me about it— though I'm sure that deep down she understands.

A richly coloured carpet that gathers the whole room together in a warm glow of friendliness. A cheerful kitchen warmed by a fire that never dreams of going out. *The* brilliant shine on new furniture, in five lovely wipe-clean **DEEP GLOSS** colours that invitingly wink the warmest of welcomes. It's what any woman wants when she loves her **HOME**. And I'm really not much different from other women.

When, like today, my brother, *Roy*, is 'on vacation' (as the Americans call it), my entire day is filled with womanly pursuits and the house is alive with feminine appeal. **NO** shirts tossed over the chair; no muddy brogues

3

FIGURE 4.1. Opening page of *Woman's World*

to three components of the narrative: mimetic, thematic, and synthetic. He explains

> Responses to the mimetic component involve an audience's interest in the characters as possible people and in the narrative world as like our own, that is, hypothetically or conceptually possible . . . Responses to the thematic component involve an interest in the ideational function of the characters and in the cultural, ideological, philosophical, or ethical issues being addressed by the narrative. Responses to the synthetic component involve an audience's interest in and attention to the characters and to the larger narrative as artificial constructs. (2007, 5–6)

The collaged appearance of *Woman's World*'s pages elicits responses to the characters as artificial constructs at the most obvious level. In other words, the synthetic component dominates, challenging readers' possible predilection for mimetic readings.[6]

Norma's narration insinuates that she usually remains confined at home because her housekeeper Mary does not let her step out. Her brother Roy is unemployed and is away on a vacation. Norma spends most of her day dressing up, reading women's magazines, and looking out of the window. On the few occasions she ventures out despite Mary's warnings or opens the door of the house to strangers, Mary admonishes her. The meaning of everything Norma says is recontextualized when we gather through the narration that it is Roy who cross-dresses and narrates as Norma. Roy's sister died in an accident when they were children. After her death, Mary, who is Roy's and Norma's mother (and not their housekeeper), asked him to donate his sister's clothes, but he saved them. He started cross-dressing as Norma and began to fabricate an autobiographical narrative for her through scraps. Scrapbooking thus features as an adaptive process for an emotionally disturbed character, enabling him to revise the negative experiences of his past. The narrative voice attributed to Norma keeps intact a degree of ambiguity about Roy's level of awareness regarding his sister's death as he becomes more and more immersed in playing and being Norma. The narrating voice resorts to various euphemisms when referring to the incident. The euphemisms, along with Roy's endeavors

---

6. Phelan observes that realistic narratives prompt readers to respond more readily to mimetic and thematic components, while metafiction draws attention to the synthetic component (2007,6). Also see Phelan's note about readers' possible impulse to preserve the mimetic (2005, 2). Fludernik's (1996) notion of experientiality operates with the assumption that readers are inclined to "naturalize" narrative utterances.

of scrapbooking and cross-dressing, indicate that he is actively constructing and reconstructing his experiences to disremember the accident.

Roy's fabrication of Norma's subjectivity is an action anticipated within the storyworld, as the narrating voice says:

> I really must think about starting a scrapbook. My dressing room is piled high with all the women's magazines I have saved over the years. Wouldn't it be wonderful to collect together my favorite fashion features, all the hints and tips on glamour and etiquette that I have found especially useful... And through them I could tell my own personal story. If published, it would be a guide to womanhood, dealing with all the things that matter to the average woman. Something to get into and feel part of. (429)

Roy imagines Norma as belonging to the category of the "average woman," a figure he has abstracted from reading the magazines. The average woman is normative, as the pun on Norma implies. The final sentence in the quoted extract captures the experiential and sentimental import of the process for Roy. He wants "something to get into," an expression that discloses his desire to enter the "women's world" evoked in the magazines as well as to slip into women's clothes. These declarations confirm that Norma's self-narrative is a multimodal fiction imagined and embodied by Roy. Roy adopts a third-person perspective toward himself in his fiction. The statements also denaturalize the notion of womanhood, and stress that gender is a manufactured commodity that is instrumentalized to buy and sell products. The denaturalization of gender becomes a necessary condition for Roy to articulate his aspiration for a world where his gender variant voice and subjectivity can belong without being told by strangers that "there's something wrong with you... very seriously wrong"—that is, a more trans-inclusive world (77).

Norma, the subjectivity Roy both imagines and embodies, is the novel's homodiegetic narrator—she is the first-person narrator of the events in which she is also a participant. According to Gerard Genette (1988 [1972]), the selection and presentation of narrative information is determined by who perceives—the focal character. The narrator—who speaks—may or may not always function as the focal character. The relation and distance between who perceives and who speaks can vary across narrative situations, depending on the style of narration. In *Woman's World*, the narrating voice, at least at the most overt level, is always Norma's. As a homodiegetic narrator, she relates her experiences and motivations. She also reports events and occurrences as she perceives them, functioning as the primary perceptual agent for large chunks of the discourse. However, Norma also pushes against the constraints of homodiegetic narration. As Mikko Keskinen observes, Norma "has the priority of narrating the whole story, even the happenings which she does not actually witness, as well as the minds of other characters" (2016, 88). Among the other minds she narrates, it is still understandable that Roy's experiences and beliefs would receive attention, because after all Norma has been constructed by Roy. So, the narrating voice and also the perceptual world are his as well. In fact, once we know that Norma is Roy, Gibbons argues, "from a reader's perspective, the focalization of the narrative shifts between Roy and Norma" (2012a, 182). So, for instance, when Norma finds Mary sobbing one evening, the narrating voice says, "I sometimes think she privately mourns the loss of her little Norma. However lovely a woman I am now, it must be hard for her to see me as her little girl" (80). Although the "I" is ostensibly Norma, there is a degree of self-awareness here about the "loss" of "little Norma" that is uncharacteristic of the voice in general. When the narrator says, "it must be hard for her to see *me* as her little girl," it seems as though Roy is the one assessing the situation and momentarily acknowledging that his sister is dead (italics mine). The narrative does not offer any more clarification about who speaks versus who perceives in this situation, but in the subsequent chapter we are told that Roy has "got back" after having been away for a week (83). The narrating voice begins to follow Roy and mostly reports his movements from the vantage point of an observer in that chapter.

While analyzing *Lazarus Project* and *Book of Portraiture* (chapter 2), I discussed how the narratives' multimodal features aid in the presentation of interpersonal experiences and the sociality of the self. The multimodal scraps of *Woman's World* similarly contribute to the dynamic emergence of Norma's subjectivity as always already shared with others. At the same time, the representation of shared subjectivities in *Woman's World* is not exactly identical to that in Hemon's and Tomasula's novels, given that unlike say, Brik and Rora, Norma and Roy even share bodies. Moreover, as Brillenburg Wurth observes, "Norma/Roy carries with her/him a multiplicity of found voices cut and reassembled from the magazines. This multiplicity makes it impossible to discover Norma/Roy's 'own' voice . . . There is an interiority that is at once alterity here—indeed, an artificiality (textual prosthesis) that undoes distinctions between interiority and exteriority" (2011a, 135). Thus, Norma is also able to narrate the thoughts of others to whom she/Roy[7] has no direct perceptual access and events neither she nor Roy witnesses. Some of these minds are her imaginative projections. She imagines an extended encounter with the actor

---

7. I use Norma/Roy for discussing scenes or moments in which the focalization is especially ambiguous.

COLLECTING, DELETING, AND SCALING MEMORIES • 161

Diana Dors in which she believes the actor is envying her appearance (70–71). However, Norma's speculations about others' thoughts follow more complicated logics in other instances.

Soon after "returning" from vacation, Roy (no longer cross-dressed as Norma) slips out of the house without confronting Mary, but the narrating voice recounts,

> Mary would have heard the gate slam and footsteps on the path but, assuming it was the milkman, thought nothing of it until later in the morning when she found Roy's comb in the washbasin, along with his little selection of men's grooming products . . . she quickly put two and two together and realized he was back. There was no real need to feel so jaunty, but a sudden lightening of the heart robbed her face, for the moment, of its usual severity, and she afforded herself the faintest flash of her old smile. (85)

The passage opens on the subjunctive mood, suggesting possibility as Norma says, "Mary would have." The narrating voice admits, as it were, that this is an instance of what Herman (2002) calls "hypothetical focalization"; that is, it is framed as what might have been or what Norma (or Roy) might have seen if she/he was around Mary. However, the voice grows in conviction about knowing Mary's thoughts and committing to her perspective. By the end of the paragraph, the focal character, that is, the character whose point of view and thoughts regulate the presentation of information, seems to be Mary (who may be looking at her own face in the wash basin mirror) rather than either Norma or Roy. Similarly, toward the end of the narrative, where Roy dressed as Norma has met with an accident,[8] the narrating voice anticipates, "Back at the little flat above the post office, Eve would be waiting eagerly for her beloved Roy, brimming with compassion and forgiveness, and wearing her attention-winning negligee set, frivolous and bridal" (435; Eve is Roy's girlfriend). The varied perspectival positions the narrating voice negotiates underscore the collage mechanics programming the narration.

Herman has observed that "the logic of narrative perspective intersects with the constraining and enabling properties of particular modes (=semiotic channels viewed as a means for the construction or design of a representation) and media (=semiotic channels viewed as a means for the dissemination or production of a given representation)" (2009, 134). In *Woman's World,* the abrupt switches in perspective thus intersect with and are indeed supported

---

8. The accident replicates the conditions in which the "real" Norma died. The narrative does not clarify whether Roy dressed as Norma dies in this second accident. After Mary finds him on the tarmac, the narrating voice primarily uses modal verbs and future tense.

by the effects of the visual-tactile fragments collaged to construct the narrative. In the words of Donald Kuspit, collage "is a demonstration of the many becoming the one, with the one never fully resolved because of the many that continue to impinge upon it" (1983, 127). The collaged appearance of the pages serves as a reminder that Roy assembled Norma from scraps—she is a singular creation comprising and representing plurality. As must have become clear, Norma's voice ensures that readers remain attuned to the synthetic nature of Norma's mind and subjectivity. The verbal-haptic surface of the text repeatedly reinforces how Norma was engineered out of commercial ephemera. I am dwelling on the text's surface that is made out of repurposed texts and images at length because it is fundamental to Rawle's presentation of remembering and recording experiences as reconstructive: the concern central to this chapter.

By heightening and highlighting the contrived status of the narrating voice, *Woman's World* reflects on the contrivances involved in mnemonic practices, including narrativization of experiences and scrapbooking. Scrapbooks (both analog and digital) seem to function as memory aids in a number of ways. According to Barbara J. Phillips, scrapbooks cue "anecdotes of the events and social relationships depicted in the photographs and journaling . . . hold implicit autobiographical memories of the creative personality of the maker, which can be cued by the album's style and techniques . . . preserve autobiographical memories of the social networks used to construct the album" (2016, 335). In short, the understanding is that scrapbooks can stimulate one to reexperience the past. The way Roy composes his scrapbook though is distinctive—he uses scraps to produce and preserve counterfactual views of the past (his sister's accident) and partially experiences the outcome of what he imagines by living as his sister. Rawle's presentation of a negative experience from Roy's childhood as the driving force behind the contrivances implies that the contrivances are directed and purposeful. Roy intends to forget the painful experience by envisioning and embodying an alternate series of events and actions.

In the actual world, though people generally produce counterfactual imaginings (i.e., daydreams and fantasies) without confusing them with their lived experiences, contemporary cognitive-scientific research on autobiographical memories recognizes certain phenomena in which individuals' vivid imagination of an event leads them to believe that they are remembering it (Schacter el. 2011; Garry and Polaschek 2000; Garry et al. 1996). Researchers such as Loftus, Schacter, and Maryanne Garry, who have significantly contributed to the understanding of the distortive aspects of episodic recollection and false memories, call this phenomenon "imagination inflation effect" and study them as one of many forms of memory distortion. Roy's scrapbooking and cross-dressing closely correspond to and illustrate the imagination inflation effect. In the next section I trace the points of correspondence between Roy's actions and the tendencies integral to this form of memory distortion. My aim in noting these correspondences is not to suggest that *Woman's World* plants clues to help readers "naturalize" the narrated situation in terms of an actual world cognitive experience, conceding to readers' supposed predilection for mimetic readings. Rather, I am suggesting that the pronounced artificiality of Rawle's narrative design encodes stances about what memory is, just as it encodes stances about what gender is.

Enacting Imagination Inflation in *Woman's World*

Schacter, Guerin, and St. Jacques point out that "Imagination inflation occurs when imagining a novel event leads people to i) increase their confidence or belief that the event actually occurred in their personal pasts; ii) claim that they performed an action or perceived an object that they only imagined; or iii) develop a full-blown false recollection of an experience that did not occur" (2011, n. pag.). Cognitive experiments studying the imagination inflation effect frequently focus on the individual's processes of recollecting events from their childhood. Garry et al. (1996) pretested participants on how confident they were that a number of childhood events had occurred, asked them to imagine the events in some detail, and then gathered new confidence measures. They noted that imagining increased the participants' confidence about the occurrence of the childhood event. In other words, the act of imagining can strengthen convictions about the veracity of what is imagined. To use Loftus, Garry, and Hayne's expression, under certain conditions, "false beliefs can morph into memory" (2007, 188).

Woman's World's narrating voice enacts the gradual increase of confidence in hypothetical and counterfactual imaginings when switching focal characters. As I discussed, Norma/Roy begins on a hesitant note while narrating other minds, but as the narration progresses the voice becomes more fully convinced of knowing the focal characters' thoughts. The key experience of the past that Roy is attempting to modify through the scrapbook is, of course, Norma's death. The narrating voice recalls the accident that killed Norma but adopts a distortive view of its outcome. The voice says, "as a young girl I was knocked down by a motor vehicle . . . If it hadn't been for my brother, I wouldn't be here today. I still bear the scars, but . . . they are emotional scars which go little deeper than skin deep" (52). The voice attributes the emotional scar to a subjectivity constructed by Roy instead of Roy's psyche. In another instance, the narrating voice says, Mary "thought I was buried six feet under in a field somewhere in the countryside" (430). The narrating voice is aware of what Mary thinks and identifies Mary rather than Roy as the one holding a delusional view of Norma's life and death. The process of scrapbooking, thus, enables Roy to develop and sustain false beliefs about the fatal accident.

Cross-dressing further helps him morph the false beliefs into memories. While relatively simple processes can result in the creation of counterfactual memories (Loftus, Garry, and Hayne 2007, 186), my discussion is trying to show how Roy engages in a detailed, multisensory performance to authenticate his counterfactual view of the past. There is a distinct haptic quality to how Roy attempts to embody his sister: making a scrapbook and touching and wearing women's clothes. By touching the clothes and the magazines that he associates with the "average woman," he attempts to be in touch with his deceased sister. The interplay of sensory modalities in Roy's memorial practice recalls Laura Marks's observation that we hold "memory in our senses" (2000, xiii). Drawing on phenomenological approaches to perception, Marks argues that objects and representations can awaken memory in the senses. The belief that a living body's contact with objects can indexically imprint objects with memories guides artists' books such as Kellner's where the papier-mâché hand casts of her parents—Holocaust survivors—seem to relay traces of the past. Rawle's fictional narrative, by contrast, explores how the sensory modalities that seem to transmit and mediate past experiences can be implicated in counterfactual imaginings. As a child when Roy wore the deceased Norma's clothes, disobeying his mother, who had asked him to donate them to the Salvation Army, he was appropriating Norma's things. But Norma died as a child, and so the women's clothes that the 29-year-old Roy wears in her memory do not bear her touch or trace as such. The clothes he wears, following the fashion tips in magazines, are generic. Nonetheless, they help him ground his imagination in sensory realities. It is his bodily interactions with novel objects—the clothes he buys and the scrapbook—that enable him to sustain an alternate and impossible view of the past and also the present.

The strength of perceptual details aids in the elaboration of the imagination inflation effect represented in the narrative. Thomas et al. (2003) observe that the quality of perceptual information significantly influences one's belief in imagined scenarios as having occurred. Roy's performed actions in this respect are crucial to the continuance of his false memories. The narrative representation of Roy's actions underscores the extent to which experiences of remembering, imagining, and forgetting replicate one another, and rely on embodied action. Rawle's narrative suggests that painful memories may not become automatically repressed but are perhaps actively revised or falsified through the repeated reconstruction of past experiences and their outcomes.

Along with the magazines and clothes, a broader media ecology comprising films and TV shows become integrated into the counterfactual thinking presented in Rawle's narrative. An entire sequence of events around Roy's desire to be photographed dressed as Norma is indebted to films from the '50s and '60s. Roy's acute dependence on women's clothes and the scrapbook to constitute and sustain false memories of his sister, imagine her back to life, is partly related to the absence of her photographs in the storyworld. After Norma died as a child, their mother Mary burnt all her photographs (365). When Roy cross-dresses as Norma, Mary refuses to take his photograph. Given Roy's desire to have Norma photographed, he becomes an easy target for a predatory photographer called Mr. Hands. Hands tries to sexually assault Norma/Roy and Norma/Roy hits him with slippers (225). That day Norma/Roy leaves the "crime scene" with the impression that she/he has murdered Hands. The narrating voice remains paranoid for days and expects the cops to arrest Roy for murder. However, Hands turns up at a movie theater where Roy goes on a date and starts blackmailing him. The episodes involving Hands rehash tropes from Alfred Hitchcock's films like *Murder!* (1930), *Psycho* (1960), and other '60s horror and slasher films, like William Castle's *Homicidal* (1961). Notably, *Psycho* also features a cross-dressing murderer, Norman, who adopts the identity of his mother, Norma. That Rawle's character Roy cross-dresses as Norma further consolidates *Woman's World*'s relation with *Psycho*, though in this case it is the deceased sister rather than the deceased mother who is kept "alive" through an imagination fed on films. The cross-dresser in such films is often a sinister figure, always the outsider and the antagonist. Inundated with such stereotypes, Roy misperceives the outcome of his encounter with Hands.

By showing the different ways in which media transform Roy's perceptions of the past and present, *Woman's World* underlines the complex entanglements of agents and environments that prompt and enrich imagination inflation. The narrative construes forgetting as an active process involving embodied, multisensory actions. Roy's forgetting the "facts" of his sister's death is not an outcome of gradual temporal distance from the experience nor is it related to his inability to retrieve stored information. Instead, it is his embodied performance as Norma that enables his amnesia and ensures its continuance. Ullrich K. H. Ecker and Stephan Lewandowsky adopt a computationalist view to study how individuals possibly distinguish between "actual" and "false" memories, and advance interference-based accounts of forgetting. They suggest that "because items are associated to overlapping context markers, they tend to over-write each other during encoding into the common associative network"

(2012, n. pag.). They attempt to explain biological cognition by extrapolating from digital neural networks, and their conception of "overwriting" assumes that accurate memories can be stored somewhere in the first place. However, Roy's manner of reconstituting the past, the instances in which the narrating voice almost but not quite admits what happened to Norma, emphasizes the deliberate and purposeful ways in which the past is always reconstructed in moments of recollection. The narrative undermines the impression that experiences of the past are data encoded in some corner of Roy's mind that can be accurately recovered or erased. Indeed, the collaged surface of *Woman's World* plays up the understanding that any experience of recollection and preservation involves selection, excision, and deliberate organization, and thus is necessarily generative and distortive.

Degenerative Memory in Lance Olsen's *Theories of Forgetting*

While the scrapbook form uniquely manifests the habits of selection and omission that *Woman's World* takes to be integral to memory, the treatment of memory in Olsen's *Theories of Forgetting* has two conceptual foundations: the book, a handheld artifact that gives a seemingly permanent form to thought, an ancient storage-retrieval technology; and Robert Smithson's *Spiral Jetty*, a basalt-rock earthwork sculpture built on the northeastern shore of the Great Salt Lake in Utah that has been slowly but visibly deforming since its creation in 1970. The *Spiral Jetty* appears and disappears based on the water levels of the Great Salt Lake. These two conceptual foundations are not in agreement with each other. In fact, the tension between the two forms and their epistemological ramifications informs the thematics of Olsen's novel. As my discussion will show, *Theories of Forgetting* is a book that wants to become an earthwork sculpture by undoing its own building blocks (page layout, legible writing, and linearity). Olsen is committed to what he calls "innovative writing," where art articulates theory and performs the theory it articulates (see Olsen and Dodge 2012). The subjects of theorization in this instance are personal and cultural memory practices and their ethics. The ethics of producing archives as a defense against loss are explored within the broader context of planetary change.

Theories of Forgetting's storyworld is ordered around a disintegrating family whose traces have been provisionally put together by the family's estranged son, Lance. This character shares his name with the book's author, but in the narrative, the fragments Lance has put together are supposed to have been collected by his sister Aila. Lance's and Aila's sorting and sharing of family memorabilia in book form shines a light on the connections of embodied memory with the recording and archiving functions of books. However, the habits and ethics of Lance's parents challenge the presumed rapport of embodied recall with storage-retrieval technologies. A mix of volition and pathology has caused Alana, an experimental filmmaker, and Hugh, a bookseller, to embrace forgetting as a vital, creative process. Since the family archive—the book—Lance creates centers the voices of Alana and Hugh, voices that question the values and logics of permanence, the artifact (the book) expresses misgivings about itself. The book's design augments the feeling that the characters—entities of the storyworld as well as the letters—compiled within it are fighting against its limits and would rather move beyond its confines.[9]

The book has two back covers with paratextual information like author bio, synopsis, and blurb. Inside the book, Alana's and Hugh's writings run in opposite directions: one runs on the top of the page and another, on the bottom. Like Mark Danielewski's *Only Revolutions* (2006), as a physical book *Theories of Forgetting* needs to be flipped 180 degrees in its orientation for readers to move from one narrative to the other. There are no visual, linguistic, or paratextual cues to direct readers as to which of the two narratives should be read first. One of the two main narratives opens with an epigraph from Robert Smithson that says, "Nature is never finished." Alana's diary entries organized by date follow this epigraph. The diary chronicles her everyday life and her experience of completing a documentary about Smithson's *Spiral Jetty*, while she becomes infected by a planetary pandemic called the Frost. Newspaper clips about the pandemic outbreak and the number of active cases, images and maps related to both the pandemic and the *Spiral Jetty* accompany Alana's writing. Her diary is a personal media assemblage and archive—a scrapbook (see Figure 4.2). It manifests her gradual loss of control over her mind and body. Pictures of human anatomy as well as increasing typographical errors in her writing make her degenerative condition visually palpable for readers, and her readers include both us—the actual readers of *Theories*—and also her own children, who survive her. Phillips has pointed out that scrapbooks can cue memory reconstruction not only for the individual who created it but also for those who outlive the individual (2016, 340). Thus, one purpose of Alana's scrapbook, that she may or may not have anticipated, is to aid in her children's reconstruction of their past experiences with her.

---

9. Olsen has acted upon this aspect of the narrative. In collaboration with his wife, Andi Olsen, he created a multimodal installation dedicated to the career of Alana. The installation is exhibited as though it was curated by Aila and includes a fictional catalogue. Both the installation and the catalogue are titled *there's no place like time*. See the accompanying website: http://www.zweifelundzweifel.org/#introduction.

The narrative that is laid out opposite to Alana's diary entries is focalized through an unnamed man. The man can be identified as Alana's husband Hugh due to the overlapping events reminisced in their narratives. Based on Alana and Hugh's daughter's comments in the margins, it seems that Hugh himself wrote this narrative but refused to adopt a first-person perspective. Autobiographical narration typically evokes at least two subject positions: the subject experiencing the events and the subject narrating them at a later time, even as these two subjects share the same social identity. The multiple subject positions are nonetheless usually bound together by a first-person pronoun. The third-person pronoun mediates a wider, more palpable breach between the experiencing and the narrating subjects. Philippe Lejeune observes that third-person pronouns can be used in autobiographical writings "for internal distancing and for expressing personal confrontation" and as a result, the strategy "brings both relief and tension to the text" (1977, 28, 29). Hugh's use of third-person pronouns illustrates his attempts at distancing himself from his own experiences. He is trying to write himself out of his self-narrative. Characters and places in his manuscript often remain anonymous since, we are told, "the man" has been forgetting names and words. On several occasions through the narrative, a sentence will include the phrase "what is the word": for example, "he becomes aware that the light surrounding him is resolving toward what is the word legibility" (26–27).[10] In another instance, he does not recall the name of the place he is in (195).

Whereas Alana is forgetting because of a disease, Hugh is represented as eliciting amnesia by revising his relationship with language. We are told, "What he is in the process of doing is becoming untraceable, disappearing from former venues and situations" (296). In order to disappear, he begins to compose a self-narrative that effaces nouns and pronouns, thereby embarking upon a journey toward anonymity. Hugh's narration performs language attrition, actively avoids certain words, expressions, and linguistic habits, and charts the impact of this avoidance on his motivations and beliefs.

His journey toward anonymity does not remain a solely linguistic performance for long. Like Roy from *Woman's World*, Hugh enacts what he imagines and narrativizes. He abandons his former life as a bookstore owner and starts to travel, following a cult that worships barbiturates. His narrative ends with him vanishing in Jordan. Thus, Hugh's revised relationship with language is entangled with his broader project of revising his relationship with his social and perceptual world. As Brockmeier (2015) and Loftus, Garry, and Hayne

---

10. Page numbers run on both the top and bottom corners of *Theories of Forgetting*, ascending in opposing directions. I am using the numbers that correspond with Alana's side when quoting her and Hugh's when quoting him and Aila.

(2007) have pointed out, experiences are reconstructed rather than recovered during autobiographical narration. The pervasive tendency of distorting past experiences that is integral to autobiography is augmented in Hugh's case. He willfully constructs an unnamed individual to whom he can ascribe events and beliefs in order to distance himself from his own experiences. For Hugh, as with Roy, this is an adaptive mechanism. He adopts this to cope with Alana's degenerative transformation and the degeneration of their relationship in the face of the pandemic. Hugh's narrative reflects on how the couple gradually became strangers while living under the same roof. As he watches his wife suffer, he is startled by "how little any two people on earth really have in common" (142). However, unlike Roy, Hugh is not invested in implanting and inflating a counterfactual view of painful experiences; rather he is interested in morphing his own experiences into those of someone else.

Conceptualizing forgetting as an embodied and enactive process, Marta Caravà (2020) argues that it may occur when certain paths of imaginative reenactment of past experiences are blocked or certain paths of imaginative reenactment become more relevant than others through practice. Her use of the term reenactment implies that recollection is first and foremost a form of action, requiring the same sensorimotor mechanisms as perception. She notes that individuals may be motivated to block channels of imaginative reenactments "to reduce or impair the accessibility of negative memories" (2020, n. pag.). Caravà, like Ecker and Lewandowsky (2012), does not fully abandon the understanding of memory as involving some form of storage. However, Caravà complicates the understanding of retrieval by pointing out that the paths and possibilities of access are contingent on an individual's present circumstances, habits, and motivations. In this light, Hugh's use of third-person pronoun can be understood as an attempt to block his recognition and imaginative reenactment of his own past experiences.

Pronouns can significantly influence the affective import of narratives. Through an empirical test, Franziska Hartung et al. (2016) find that first-person pronouns lead to higher immersion among readers. The experiment understands immersion as higher emotional engagement and sense of identification with subjects in the text. Third-person pronouns prompt higher arousal, that is, higher alertness and responsiveness. The relation of identification/immersion and arousal with first- and third-person pronouns as identified here is overly simple and dichotomous for the complex narrative situations we routinely encounter in literature. Other textual features inflect and reorient readers' relation with pronominal reference, as Hartung et al. (2016) note in the conclusion of their study. Herman thus proposed a scalar model for understanding the readers' dynamics of contextual anchoring in narratives (2002, 353). Within the narrative context of *Theories,* what is certain is that Hugh believes that the third-person pronoun will prevent him from latching on to his own narrated experiences. If the purpose of autobiographical writing is to cue one's own memories when the writing is read at a future time, then in such a situation too the third-person pronoun may potentially restrict Hugh's imaginative identification with his own experiences. I say Hugh believes because his actions replicate to some extent what he witnessed happening to his grandfather. He recalls that his grandfather had begun to stumble on nouns (221) and then "his sentences started letting him down. Parts of them flaking off, going into hiding" (325). The same observations can be made about Hugh's narration, though whereas his grandfather's condition was related to aging, Hugh's situation involves volition.

While Hugh's avoidance of nouns and pronouns in his narration communicates his diminishing recognition of the objects and people around him, the syntax of his sentences indicates his reduced fluency in other ordinary actions. His statements and phrases often default to a pattern. They open with interrogative pronouns, seemingly buying him time to recall the precise terms to articulate his actions, as in, "What he is in the process of doing is" (296). He actively reduces his fluency in language and other ordinary actions in order to prevent episodic recollection. For example, the narrative says, "it must be morning—four, four thirty: that's what he would guess. The cereal bowl, black, black or grey, is full of granola and the man realizes there is something in his left hand and something in his right" (13). The "somethings" turn out to be strawberry yoghurt and a spoon. The section ends with "To the best of his knowledge, he is making breakfast" (13). Processes of thinking and remembering are protracted and described in a step-by-step manner in Hugh's narration, bordering on the formulaic and mechanical descriptions of thought we also come across in *Curious Incident*'s narration.

Hugh's voluntary replication of his grandfather's condition raises questions similar to those raised by the Turing test. If machines, through the manipulation of abstract, amodal, arbitrary symbols, solve the same problems as biological agents, then is the machine thinking?[11] Similarly, if Hugh manipulates language and replicates his grandfather's language attrition, is he really forgetting? Will his style of narration *really* thwart his attempts at reconstructing and reenacting his past experiences? The narrative does not offer easy answers to these questions. However, it does stress that his imitation of his grandfather's condition is motivated by the deeply personal and painful experience of

---

11. John Searle's Chinese Room thought experiment debunks Turing's and other computationalists' more affirmative answer to the question. See "Artificial Intelligence and the Chinese Room: An Exchange" (Motzkin and Searle 1989).

being his wife's sole caregiver during the final days of her life, when she would, among other things, fail to recognize him.[12] Besides, given that Alana's disease manifests itself in her use of language—a point I will develop further in the next section—language is construed as anything but amodal or disembodied in *Theories*.

Hugh, like several other characters discussed in *Out of Mind*, theorizes about how minds work. He considers the possibility of artificial intelligence approaching, duplicating, and superseding biological cognition (228). When confronting new, seemingly difficult information, Hugh says, "the human psyche just tends to sort of shut down, block out the menace, squeeze shut its metaphorical eyes while clapping its metaphorical hands" (230). He uses "glitch"—a word that originated in the 1960s to refer to malfunctioning equipment—when referring to his forgetful and distracted mind (105). During his travel, he asks an interlocutor to give him directions as though he has an "information processing disorder" (87). In other words, notwithstanding the embodied and dynamic ways in which Olsen's novel shows Hugh to be enacting his amnesia, Hugh depends on a computationalist framework to think about his mind and memory. His dependence on such a framework may be related to his desire to forget the emotional import of witnessing Alana's degeneration. He notes that only in the near future artificial intelligence will "blink into self-awareness" (228). The implication is that present-day AI is devoid of consciousness, even as it accomplishes tasks, and if Hugh can emulate artificial intelligence, he would not have to reflect on his own painful experiences.

As the title of the novel suggests, Hugh's is one among plural theories of remembering and forgetting articulated and enacted in the narrative. His manuscript reaches his daughter Aila a year after his disappearance in Jordan. She does not recognize his voice or handwriting (37)—so, Hugh has succeeded in effacing himself to a certain degree. Then again, Aila recognizes specific spaces and moments described in the manuscript (see 26–27). Aila's commentaries on the margins of Hugh's manuscript express bewilderment and recognition by turns, and the notes she addresses to her brother tend to succinctly reconstruct experiences from their past when they were "an airtight box called Family" (65).

Hugh's performance of forgetting, as I have already mentioned, is prompted by the degenerative condition of his wife, Alana. When Alana began losing control over her body and mind to the planetary pandemic, she sur-

---

12. In *there's no place like time*, Aila confirms that Hugh alone held Alana's hands as she wasted away. The children—Aila and Lance—were not with their parents at the time.

rendered her filming and writing to this degeneration. Hugh notes that "she became scared and then slowly less scared, and then writing trailed off into some sort of asemic scribble among a welter of taped-in photographs" (106). After Alana's death, what remains of her creative projects bear the mark of her bodily and cognitive collapse. Since Alana's journal entries are gradually drained of semantic content, the writings that her children find are not always records of experiences Alana was predetermined to save but were produced by chance through her ailing body's contact with recording technologies. The journal entries, photographs, and other ephemera Alana leaves behind are full of errors—misspelled words, struck-through sentences, still photographs from an unfinished documentary—and in this sense, much of what is in this archive that her daughter and son assemble existed at the limits of Alana's knowledge and consciousness.

Notably, neither Alana nor Hugh makes many attempts to reconstruct experiences from the time before the pandemic ruptured their family life, the period when in Aila's words, they were "an airtight box called Family." Instead, Alana and Hugh not only reckon with the inevitability of degeneration but also embrace it as necessity. Alana remarks, "It is what it is" (223). Their self-effacing actions stand in opposition to Aila's and Lance's archival impulses. Aila does recognize that Alana and Hugh are advocating for an "aesthetics of obscurity"—she refers to her mother's artistic career in these terms in *there's no place like time* (2018), the (fictional) exhibition catalog that reflects on Alana's career as a filmmaker.[13] Despite recognizing their parents' desire to forget and be forgotten, both brother and sister remain invested in processes of collection, selection, and display of family memorabilia. Still, they fail to salvage their family. As Gibbons observes, "three [Alana's, Hugh's, and Aila's] narratives come together in *Theories of Forgetting* to produce a whole, and that whole can be read as a kind of complex system—in this case, a family—but through the course of the novel that system becomes more dispersed, disintegrating" (2019, 287). It is the experience of dispersal that is quite paradoxically represented by the memorabilia archived in the book. The book though a storage-retrieval and mnemotechnological apparatus cannot restore the broken family.

The family members' irreconcilable approaches to memory have to do with their attitudes to life's impermanence. The siblings possibly find the idea of obscurity or insignificance disturbing, as Aila's marginal comments suggest.

---

13. In *there's no place like time,* Aila recalls Alana's life and work and "wonders what an aesthetics of obscurity looks like" (2018, 2).

In one instance she says, "[[imagine: you & i, dear bro, exist as 4 words in the hem of this narrative. Remarkable how noisy silence can be]]" (59). By "this narrative," Aila means the narrative Hugh has composed. In another instance, Aila notes that their parents "were simply committed to living their lives, of which we were simply a very small part, a fact simply impossible for us to take in" (191). Olsen's novel thus connects the compulsion to remember and be remembered with the desire for significance. This desire is exposed to be fraught through Alana's and Hugh's meditations on how the human species' self-centering, the assumption of self-importance, and exercise of agency have contributed to planetary destruction.

Scaling Memory in *Theories of Forgetting*

Alana's and Hugh's narration and action urge their children (and us) to consider whether the preservation of human footprints and accomplishments are an essential good, given that human actions have had irreversible, catastrophic impact on the planet. Historically, human beings have resorted to archival practices to document individual as well as social and planetary conditions. Ursula K. Heise points out that writers and artists have composed lists and catalogs in verbal and visual forms to mourn and memorialize endangered species (2016, 55). However, Olsen's novel calls for a reevaluation of memorial processes. Activating clashing attitudes to storage and dispersal through the different family members, the novel assumes an ambivalent stance toward commemoration.

Lucy Bond, Ben De Bruyn, and Jessica Rapson argue that "familiar forms of orthodox memorial culture (memorials, archives, monuments, etc.)" do not always "join macro-, meso- and microscopic perspectives" necessary for addressing the "complex imbrication of personal and planetary experience" (2017, 859). Inscribing and commemorating in the context of climate change requires "us to consider other traces of human history, such as carbon dioxide levels in the atmosphere and the chemical composition of our seas and soils" (2017, 860). Uncritical and compulsive archivation of human traces need not be a productive undertaking. Landscapes that have indexed human presence have also registered the violence of human activities. Besides, the possibilities and consequences of planetary destruction are so sweeping that they obviate the need for archives. Claire Colebrook, thus, speculates, "the archive could remain, materially, but that its conditions for sense destroyed. (In some ways this condition is already being approached today: the twenty-first century may be the beginning of an epoch in which texts exist in the material form alone but are no longer accompanied by readers). What if, centuries from now, another species were to discover the human archive but not be blessed with human language?" (2014, 23–24). The inadequacy of established paradigms of personal and collective memory is a key concern of Olsen's novel. The narrative dwells on how commemorative structures shape our understanding of the past and also formalize what can be said of the past and the present in the future. Alana quotes and underlines Robert Smithson saying, "Instead of causing us to remember the past like the old monuments, the new monuments seem to cause us to forget the future" (119; see Figure 4.2). In this light, she takes on a project to remedy the failure of orthodox commemorative structures to configure our relationship to both the past—what has been done to the planet—and the future.

As an alternative to the orthodox memorial culture that *Theories of Forgetting* problematizes through Alana's reflections, it offers the ethics and aesthetics of Smithson's *Spiral Jetty*. When compared to the principles undergirding archival technologies, including those of the artifactual book, an earthwork's impermanence becomes particularly evident. Smithson created the *Spiral Jetty* during a temporary drought in 1970. In a couple of years, the sculpture was completely submerged and it remained under the waters of the Great Salt Lake in Utah for about thirty years. During this period, an audience could experience the sculpture through photographs taken before it was submerged. Around 2000, the earthwork reemerged as the lake receded more permanently, due to the megadrought affecting the Western US, caused by global warming as well as the upstream demand for the water that would earlier flow to the Salt Lake's terminal basin. Thus, Smithson's earthwork has a rather complicated relationship with archives: on the one hand, ephemerality is fundamental to the sculpture's conceptualization and aesthetic. As Alana in the novel recognizes, the *Spiral Jetty* is "in the perpetual process of misremembering itself" (260), and so, in this sense, it is anti-archival. On the other hand, one of the ways the sculpture can be experienced is through its photographs. Dia Art Foundation photographs the earthwork to record any changes to it. Alana keeps photographs of the sculpture in her scrapbook and thus, she too participates in a mode of archiving.

Representing the irresolvable conflict between permanence and impermanence, the *Spiral Jetty* as a disintegrating earthwork and the book as an archival technology juxtapose multiple temporal and spatial scales. As records of the past transcending the limits of a human lifetime, books can potentially link human experiential scales and non-human spatio-temporalities. Smithson's earthwork too can outlive a generation or so, but not by much. There are

18 July

Robert Smithson: <u>Instead of causing us to remember the past like the old monuments, the new monuments seem to cause us to forget the future.</u>

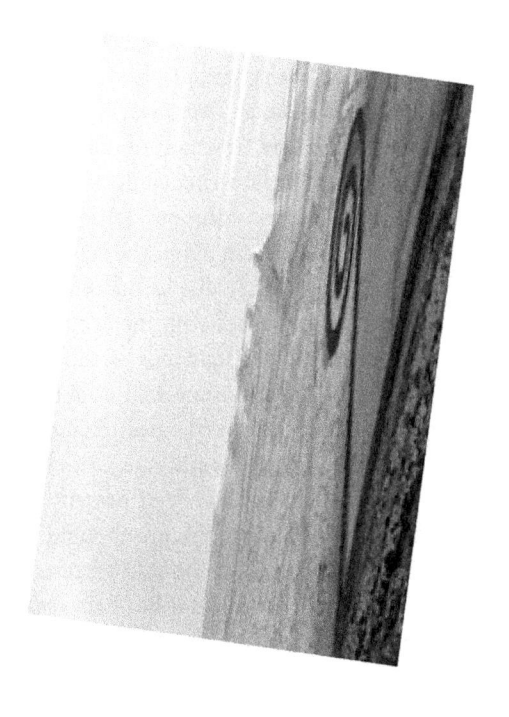

Honestly, dude, he says, you look awful. You want to sit down and talk about this? I'm sure we

THEORIES OF FORGETTING | 119

FIGURE 4.2. Photograph of the *Spiral Jetty* enclosed within Alana's scrapbook. Image courtesy Lance Olsen.

also discrepancies in how long it takes to experience a book and an earthwork. Alana mentions that the *Spiral Jetty* requires observers to acknowledge "time's process in the perceiving act," and time in this context refers to both the duration of viewing the sculpture and historical time, given that the earthwork is impermanent (205). Furthermore, there are also discrepancies in size: whereas a standard book is approximately six by nine inches, the *Spiral Jetty* is fifteen feet by fifteen hundred feet. These scalar misalignments between the book and the earthwork serve as a metonym for the misalignment of embodied human memory and the environmental history that Olsen's novel seeks to capture (though the narrative does not suggest that there is a clear one-on-one correspondence between book and human mind, earthwork and environmental conditions).

Olsen utilizes the misalignment of the book form with the *Spiral Jetty* to convey an understanding of the limitations of conventional memory practices in the context of climate change. Amitav Ghosh has observed that climate change-related phenomena are "resistant to the customary frames that literature has applied to 'Nature,'" and writers must find new ways of imagining the "unthinkable beings and events of this era" (2016, 33). Heise (2016) and Timothy Clark (2015) agree with Ghosh about the representational challenges that climate change poses, particularly due to the misalignments of the phenomenological scales of time and space with the ecological. The problem of scale has thus emerged as central to discussions of climate change. Environmental crisis often defies legibility within our well-established models of cognition and knowledge production since ecological phenomena "are difficult to see or describe [. . .] are at odds with basic categories like emotion, narrative, or even language" (Bond et al. 2017, 857). At present, the cognitive and behavioral limitations of the human species are thought to be hindering climate-related action. Olsen's novel reflects on and represents these limitations. For instance, in one scene, Hugh is asked if he "believes" in deforestation, which leads Hugh to retort, "Is deforestation a category of belief?" (221). When he is told, "Everything is a category of belief," he acknowledges that he "believes" in deforestation.

Environmental and social psychologist Robert Gifford (2011) notes that psychological barriers hinder the behavioral choices that would facilitate mitigation, adaptation, and environmental sustainability and argues that removing these barriers is as crucial as changing the climate-averse infrastructure. Authors concerned with communicating the climate crisis are thus compelled to innovate narrative forms to represent a phenomenon that defies frames of comprehension. Marco Caracciolo writes about the renewed emphasis on analogical relations at micro and macro levels of narrative form as a means "to bring down abstract concepts into human-scale experience" (2019, 277). *Theories of Forgetting*'s structural design is an attempt to find a narrative form that can bridge the limitations in human thinking and reasoning.

The scalar misalignment of the book and the *Spiral Jetty* as a metonym for the misalignment between degenerative human memory and planetary degeneration resists easy projective equations. Nonetheless, the planetary condition and weather supply Olsen with key terminologies and images for representing Alana's amnesiac but creative mind. The pandemic affecting Alana is "The Frost" and "sleet" is said to be migrating up her arms. Her body and mind in this sense realize and manifest the degenerative possibilities of anthropogenic global warming and the accompanying extreme weather phenomena. Common metaphors conceptualize forgetting as absence or death, associate it with water-related images, owing to the mythological connection of oblivion with the river Lethe, and as a fault or error (see Gudmundsdottir 2016). These metaphors imply that forgetting is a gradual, involuntary process of decay. By contrast, the weather metaphors for Alana's amnesiac condition carry connotations of randomness and abruptness. Alana's cycles of sudden remembering and misremembering of semantic and episodic information after contracting the Frost resemble the cycles of the *Spiral Jetty*'s emergence and submergence. In the long term though, Alana's condition remains degenerative, just as the *Spiral Jetty* wastes away.

Photographs showing the emergence and submergence of the *Spiral Jetty* that Alana collects and keeps within her scrapbook (presented in *Theories of Forgetting*) function as effective climate imagery as they make visible a gradual process that challenges human-scale perception and cognition. In one instance, Alana writes and then strikes out, "When you're well, even if you've only been well a little while, your body can't remember what it was like being unwell" (21). She understands that individuals are inclined to falsely reconstruct an experience that no longer matches their immediate bodily and perceptual situations. Imagination is context-dependent, wherein context includes current bodily states and the perceivable state of the environment in which the body is embedded. Alana seems to share Lawrence Barsalou, Leo Dutriaux, and Christoph Scheepers's theoretical position on how a concept is "typically coupled with its referents in the body and the world" (2018, 1). To be able to conceptualize climate change, one needs to perceive its referents. Alana's multimodal attempts at making slow degeneration visible through photographs, thus, carry ethical significance.

Identifying climate change as an urgent cultural and science communication problem, Betsy Lehman, Jessica Thompson, Shawn Davis and Joshua M. Carlson (2019) argue that the cognitive processes related to experiencing climate change imagery may aid in mobilizing climate adaptation and resilience efforts. Following an empirical study in which Lehman et al. exposed participants to climate change-related imagery, they concluded that "images that were rated as highly relevant to climate change also tended to be rated as exciting and negative" (2019, n. pag.).¹⁴ Beside the photographs of the *Spiral Jetty*, Alana includes photos showing the carcass of a bird lying in snow and an oil rig explosion—instances of the kind of "negative" climate imagery that Lehman et al. identify as evoking responses among observers (Olsen 2014, 149, 230; see Figure 4.3). Evidently, Alana as a filmmaker understands and acknowledges the affective power of visuals for cuing memory and imagination related to planetary degeneration. She notes that Smithson's art, including the films he made with the artist Nancy Holt, are "the act of "perfperception itself, about what constitutes determined noticing" (277). The same can be said of Alana's art—both her scrapbook and her films described in the narrative. They are about perception, or to build on her involuntary "error," they are about the act of perfecting perception.

Toward the end of her diary, Alana mentions that she is editing a close-up shot of "desiccated nearly colorless bardbird carcasses," and the shot prompts her to remark, "the very intensity of the environment in which they tried living murdered them" (309; see Figure 4.3). The joined homophones—bardbird—generate double-meaning. The environment that killed the birds, Alana's erroneous writing predicts, would also choke the bard, that is, the poet or artist—Alana. Alana's errors wherein she writes tempest in place of temper, plum in place of palm, or bardbird imagine and mediate new relations between the human and the non-human (289, 251, 309). This novelty is the residue of decay. Smithson was interested in the generative outcomes of degeneration. In his essays about the *Spiral Jetty*, Smithson discussed Claude Levi-Strauss's notion of "entropology." Lévi-Strauss blended "entropy" and "anthropology" to come up with the term to stand for the study of the disintegrative impacts of the human species (Levi-Strauss 2012 [1955]). The *Spiral Jetty* assumes novel forms even as it disintegrates. The earthwork thus showcases the simultaneity of creative and destructive processes.¹⁵ As an artist Alana seeks to emulate Smithson's aesthetic. Her daughter observes that her project of filming the *Spiral Jetty* "theorizes decay, not merely as a process of emptying and exhaustion, but also as one of relay and salvage" (99). Alana's philosophical position on decay is materialized through her amnesiac mind-body. Her bodily state, as her writing shows, is gradually resituating her in relation to the environment. The scrapbook recording the stream of her perceptual experiences becomes a rich milieu for her children and actual readers to study. In a way, via the scrapbook, she is offering her own body and mind as referents for conceptualizing climate phenomena that defy human-scale experience.

---

14. Lehman et al. (2019) also maintain a website repository of images for testing an audience's response to climate change imagery: https://affectiveclimateimages.weebly.com/about.html.

15. See Gibbons (2019) for a discussion of Olsen's entropological poetics.

COLLECTING, DELETING, AND SCALING MEMORIES • 179

> OLSEN | 149
>
> 11 September
>
> Robert Smithson: <u>Every object, if it is art, is charged with the rich rush of time.</u>
>
> kisses every leaf on the large rhododendron in the corner. She kisses a vast white wall, moves to the window flooded with white light, moves back to the wall. The video runs without dialogue, without music. There is no soundtrack except for the small raspings parts of her make as she traverses the apartment, her apartment, he would imagine, and sometimes her breathing, and sometimes the kisses themselves. Every so often the camera draws in for a close-up of her profile as her lips touch something and pulls back

FIGURE 4.3. Photograph of a bird enclosed within Alana's scrapbook. Image courtesy Lance Olsen.

Taking his cue from studies on distortive and false memories such as those conducted by Schacter and Loftus, among others, psychologist Simon Nørby (2015) explains that forgetting can be an adaptive mechanism not only for coping with painful and traumatic events, but also for context attunement and updating knowledge. Alana's amnesiac condition, while degenerative in many respects, also uniquely attunes her to her environmental surroundings. Olsen's novel hints that the kind of context attunement Alana undergoes may be necessary for remedying the current limitations in perception and reasoning that make large-scale environmental degeneration unthinkable. Changing minds about climate-related phenomena, *Theories of Forgetting* suggests, requires forgetting the earlier habits and behaviors that have contributed to rapid environmental change.

Smithson's *Spiral Jetty* has a fractal topological form—similar patterns recur at different scales to make up the sculpture (see Figure 4.2). The narrative thematics of *Theories of Forgetting* are similarly laid out; that is, patterns of disintegration and regeneration repeat at various scales throughout the text. Through Alana, alongside Hugh, *Theories of Forgetting* offers an opportunity to engage with the notion of what memory is without the automatic valuation of remembering and archival. As an aesthetic experience, Olsen's novel can potentially unsettle readers' assumptions about retaining information and its ethical as well as epistemological implications.

Changing Minds

While earlier cognitive-scientific conceptions of memory were limited to storage and retrieval models, more recently scientists and philosophers have construed memory as a reconstructive, dynamic, and situated process. Shifts in the understanding of remembering and forgetting in cognitive sciences and philosophy of mind attest to the broader changes in conceptualization of cognition. Instead of thinking about thought as founded on input-processing-output circuits, present-day cognitive theories recognize thought's embodied, embedded, enacted, and extended dimensions. The narratives analyzed in *Out of Mind* often explicitly and at times implicitly exploit emergent knowledge for creatively rendering minds and mental activities. Social, technological, and environmental developments of the present offer an impetus to literature's speculative and creative forays into cognitive theories. And narratives like Olsen's *Theories of Forgetting* offer resources for thinking about (and rethinking) these developments.

This chapter has traced how *Woman's World* and *Theories of Forgetting* redefine the relations of archive with memory through representations that are opposed to valuing perfect recall (if such recall were even possible), albeit for different reasons. Both novels incorporate and represent personal archival practices to showcase the motivated and creative aspects of remembering and forgetting. By doing so, the narratives emphasize the limitations of conceptualizing embodied memory as a storage and retrieval technology.

Theories of Forgetting, more explicitly than *Woman's World*, grounds its exploration of memory in the urgent concerns of the twenty-first century. The presentation of the pandemic in the narrative becomes especially poignant and relevant in the context of the worldwide COVID-19 outbreak. The plural approaches to remembering and forgetting imagined in the narrative stand for the plurality of possible relations with the past and the future. Particular members of the represented family not only adopt different attitudes to their shared past but also through that attitude embody different modes of future-thinking. Even amid dispersal and disintegration, through the character of Alana, Olsen's novel envisions possibilities of relay and salvage.

The aesthetic treatments of memory studied in this chapter and presentations of mind studied across the chapters in this book evince contemporary literature's divergent ways of thinking about thought. Acknowledging the divergent ways of thinking encapsulated in narratives creates conditions for accommodating divergent styles of thinking in our societies. Instead of simply reflecting the established norms and pathologies of the mind, thought representation in narratives, *Out of Mind* has sought to show, partake in generative thinking.

CODA

Binge Reading versus Picnoleptic Reading

> Reading can be freefall
> —Anne Carson, *Float* (2016)

Our thoughts and beliefs about how we think cohere into theories of reading, and theories of reading are conspicuously plural in the twenty-first century. Anne Carson distills an idealized, transhistorical attitude in the statement I quote here. Freefall denotes rapid downward motion under the force of gravity. To someone who has dropped three thousand feet in fifteen seconds under gravity—I skydived—freefall connotes a lapse, of not only judgement, but also consciousness. I remember tumbling and folding, snippets of canola fields stretching for miles underneath, the tug of wind, but above all, I recall the sensation that "a little of" my life "simply escaped" (Virilio 2009 [1980], 19). Such limit states of consciousness during which the familiar world seems to disappear before reappearing, quickly and suddenly again, are what the French cultural theorist Paul Virilio terms picnolepsy. Picnolepsy is "the epileptic state of consciousness produced by speed,"[1] as a subject invents moments of recess to cope with the fast pace. It feels like a break or speed bump; it is "missing time" (2009 [1980], 112, 19). Reading, as Carson says, can be freefall in the sense that it can come as a break from routine. This is the model of reading construed as an interruption in the course of everyday life.

When Virilio theorized "picnolepsy" in the 1970s, he was thinking about the quality of perception naturalized by contemporary media—in particular,

---

1. This definition of picnolepsy is from Virilio's book's dust jacket.

cinema and the illusion of continuity it constructs out of discrete still images. Virilio extrapolated from cinema's formal features to reflect on the homogeneity of time and the expectations of continuous productivity enforced in the twentieth century. Against this background, he attempted to de-pathologize breaks and pauses, and imagine a picnoleptic way of being. Some of the social-historical conditions Virilio was problematizing have only been augmented in the twenty-first-century media ecology.

We live in a time when rapid, almost compulsive, encounter with words, images, and other semiotic modes is a fact of everyday life. As we habitually scroll, skim, and browse, reading becomes one means of rapidly consuming information. In a 2015 article, Nikkitha Bakshani labelled the rate at which we consume words in the twenty-first century "binge reading disorder" (n. pag.). Bakshani approximated that the "typical American consumes more than 100,000 words a day and remembers none of them," based on studies of consumer habits conducted by Roger E. Bohn and James Short (2009), among others, and a Pew Research Center Report. This presents a much less flattering picture of reading, and as the title of Bakshani's article indicates, one way of construing online habits of reading is to think of them as a pathology. The spread of fake news and misinformation would be side-effects of this pathology and reduced attention spans and forgetfulness its symptoms. The identification of symptoms and side-effects reifies habits and aptitudes seemingly voided by the pathology. The habits endangered by binge reading disorder include the practice of reading as an interruption, that is, picnoleptic reading.

Essays, studies, and thought pieces that, along the lines of Bakshani's article, consign themselves to articulating the trouble with reading today paint a picture of readers' minds as irredeemably tainted (see for instance Beck 2018). Contemporary readers may as well be the kin of *Raw Shark Texts*' Ludovician, nothing but repositories of undigested textual material. Yet, the keen articulation of values, reflections on faculties and habits of consumption also offer up instances that seem to suggest we may have always failed the standards we reify when it comes to reading. Perhaps we habitually misperceive the value and skill of reading. Ian Crouch, a writer on the editorial staff for *The New Yorker*, for example, recaps his experience of purchasing a book and some five pages into it, coming upon a passage that reminds him of reading the same book three years earlier. He notes,

> I cannot recall forgetting another novel entirely—both the contents of the book and the act of reading it . . . But, looking at my bookshelves, I am aware of another kind of forgetting—the spines look familiar; the names and titles

bring to mind perhaps a character name, a turn of plot, often just a mood or feeling—but for the most part, the assembled books, and the hundreds of others that I've read and discarded, given away, or returned to libraries, represent a vast catalogue of forgetting. (2013, n. pag.)

This leads Crouch to wonder whether he enjoys reading, whether he has especially poor attention and therefore retains little, whether he is actually a poor reader. He associates these doubts with "a false sense of reading as conquest" when, in fact, "reading has many facets, one of which might be the rather indescribable, and naturally fleeting, mix of thought and emotion and sensory manipulations that happen in the moment and then fade" (2013, n. pag.). The mix of thoughts, perceptions, and emotions evoked during a reading session are ephemeral. If readerly practices are anything to go by, then readers seem to intuitively know that their minds are not reliable storage and retrieval units. That is why readers write in the margins of books, extract texts and paste them in scrapbooks or notetaking applications, post photos of books with discursive notes on Instagram.

The digital media ecology challenges the skills we regard as essential to literary reading in novel ways. The narratives studied in this book mediate various ideas and challenges we associate with reading and thinking at present, especially through their jostling multimodal features. Eric, Jen, Caldeira in *S.* and Aila in *Theories of Forgetting* are readers who track their own evolution through marginalia. Brik in *The Lazarus Project* and Roy in *Woman's World* repurpose what they read in historical and personal media archives to constitute fictions that simultaneously function as their self-narratives. It is because these narratives are committed to examining frameworks through which characters make sense of texts and by extension of the world that they speak to one another. The narratives' depictions of the characters' habits of mind also incorporate assumptions about the minds that will engage with the texts, though the relation between actual and fictional minds, as I have maintained throughout *Out of Mind,* need not result in a one-on-one correspondence (see chapter 1). If genres function as "conventionalized repositories of memory" in our cultures, as Astrid Erll and Ansgar Nünning have suggested, then the generic emergence of books with multimodal features archive contemporary beliefs about thinking and reading (2005, 273).

The tension between various theoretical positions on binge reading and picnoleptic reading in the wider culture has been generative for literature. The forms and thematics of the novels discussed in *Out of Mind* are informed by this tension. The mishmash of semiotic modes and artifacts included in these narratives can impede the speed of reading them. A minute recess opens for readers to interact with and puzzle over the included objects and images, allowing them to inhabit a state in-between moving forward and staying in place. *Raw Shark Texts*, *Theories of Forgetting*, and *S.* also have supplementary information available online. While not integral to the narratives, the additional text and images further saturate the storyworlds and can extend readers' engagement with them. The poetics of these narratives depend on twenty-first-century readers' habits of looking up information online and proclivity for multitasking.[2] In a media culture where "engaging" audiences is believed to be a difficult undertaking, the multimodal form of these books offers plural channels of sensory engagement and somatic interactivity. Multimodality in this sense is an attention-grabbing mechanism. In the introductory chapter, I mentioned Natalia Cooper et al.'s (2018) empirical study that found multimodality to be effective in immersing readers in virtual environments, though of course whether the same effect holds for print narratives is up for debate. Features that require readers to interact with enclosed objects or distribute attention among multiple micronarratives laid out on the same page also risk alienating readers. Through a series of cognitive experiments, Eyal Ophir, Clifford Nass, and Anthony D. Wagner (2009) concluded that "chronic media multitasking"[3] increases our susceptibility to irrelevant distractions. The multimodal form thus risks readers' not returning to the narrative that prompted them to interact with artifacts or look up information, even as the multimodality grabs their attention and slows down perusal.

Shalena Srna, Rom Y. Schrift, and Gal Zauberman (2018) considered the miscellaneous ways in which individuals deploy and perceive the term multitasking. Following thirty-two studies involving more than eight thousand participants, they inferred that individuals who perceived themselves to be multitasking were more engaged and performed better on the same task compared to those who construed the same activity as a single task. The findings of this cognitive experiment highlight the extent to which our metacognitive awareness, thinking about cognitive habits, impacts the way we behave. How we think of reading, then, influences how we read.

Multimodality as form cannot fully predetermine readers' level of engagement and interest in pursuing a narrative. What multimodal print narratives do is contain irreconcilable choices for readers. These choices are clearly encapsulated in the form of Jonathan Safran Foer's *Tree of Codes* (2010). *Tree*

---

2. The term multitasking was used in the 1960s to refer to the capabilities of an IBM system. Now a popular term for describing human behaviour, the term has its origin in computing technologies.

3. Ophir, Nass, and Wagner (2009) also note that though multitasking is becoming a societal tendency, human cognition is ill-suited for attending to multiple tasks at the same time.

of Codes is a narrative pitched on the tension of reading as forgetful consumption and reading as attentive memory work. I examine it here to anchor my summative remarks about multimodal narratives' conceptualization of our minds—the minds of twenty-first-century readers.

Readers' Anti-Archival Minds

Foer's *Tree of Codes* is a materially altered book that self-reflexively demonstrates the patterns of attention that constitute reading and shape our memories of texts. To compose *Tree of Codes,* Foer die-cut and rearranged pages of a translated edition of *Sklepy Cynamonowe* (1934),[4] a collection of short stories by the Polish-Jewish author Bruno Schulz. It is the sparest narrative and has the weakest narrativity of the texts considered in *Out of Mind.* To use Alexander Starre's term, it is a "book fiction" or a book about books (2015, 248). The elliptical narrative demands readers' familiarity with *Tree of Codes'* intertextual origins. In an extradiegetic note added to the book, Foer clarifies that he intends to memorialize Schulz, who was shot by a Gestapo officer in the Drohobycz ghetto in November 1942 (Foer 2010, 137–39). Schulz's two collections of short stories, *Street of Crocodiles* (1934) and *Sanatorium under the Sign of the Hourglass* (1937), had been published by then. However, the bulk of Schulz's manuscripts, including an unpublished novel called *The Messiah,* is believed to have been destroyed during the Holocaust, and this loss prompts Foer's memorial project.[5]

While Foer's strategy of writing through erasure in *Tree of Codes* is reminiscent of similar experiments by Tom Phillips and Mary Ruefle, unlike them, Foer altered a book he holds in high regard. Philips repurposed a lesser-known Victorian novel that he had found by chance to create *A Humument* (1970–2016). Ruefle, too, transformed a forgotten novella, self-published in the nineteenth century, to compose *A Little White Shadow* (2006). Foer, on the other hand, closely read and admired Schulz's collection of stories long before he conceived of his project. Foer's method of die-cutting is thus a slow and laborious process of rereading Schulz's fiction. His aesthetic stresses the

---

4. Foer uses Celina Wieniewska's English translation of Bruno Schulz's short stories.

5. Schulz's missing manuscripts have assumed a mythical stature. Critics now debate whether *The Messiah* ever existed; the only proof of its existence are references to it in surviving letters. David Grossman's *See Under: Love* (1989) weaves an elaborate fantasy around Schulz and *The Messiah.* In Cynthia Ozick's *The Messiah of Stockholm* (1987), the protagonist declares himself to be Schulz's son and *The Messiah* supposedly surfaces in Stockholm. Hemon's *Lazarus Project* also features a minor character named Bruno Schulz.

dynamic and creative dimensions of reading, celebrates it as a forgetful and unfaithful experience. Foer explains, "I have never read another book so intensely or so many times. I've never memorized so many phrases, or, as the act of erasure progressed, forgotten so many phrases" (2010, 139). Excision enacts and amplifies patterns of flickering attention constitutive of any reading experience. As Gérard Genette explains, excision is a strategy of rewriting which is "built upon (and in its turn reinforces) a practice of reading, in the strong sense: i.e., a choice of attention" (1997, 230). The uneven distribution of attention during reading entails a "spontaneous infidelity" to the text (1997, 230). Therefore, Genette argues, every text is more or less amputated from its "true birth: that is to say, from its first reading" (1997, 230). *Tree of Codes* is an exaggerated performance of the cognitive habits that make up the reading experience. Readers' minds, Foer's experiment suggests, are fundamentally anti-archival.

    The die-cut holes of *Tree of Codes* are rectangular in shape and frame what remains of Schulz's words; or put another way, the words that Foer's book has retained frame the absence of Schulz's. The narrative of *Tree of Codes,* if summarized in a few sentences, follows the perceptions of a bored young narrator who is witnessing his family's disintegration. The narrator anticipates that his father will disappear and holds his mother responsible for his father's condition. The world around the narrator is also changing: children play outside wearing masks and the city's other inhabitants are acutely lonely. Oblivion is a pervasive condition touching every aspect of the storyworld, taking the form of an epidemic, but is not without generative outcomes. Forgetting, like die-cutting, can produce novel configurations of sense. Thus, the narrator's father exclaims, "How beautiful is forgetting! What relief it would be for the world to lose some of its content" (Foer 2010, 48). A summary of *Tree of Codes* that leaves out an account of its material form could with some modifications also fit Foer's earlier novels, particularly, *Extremely Loud and Incredibly Close* (2005). Foer's representation of familial disintegration over the course of an epidemic is also similar to Olsen's *Theories.* Moreover, the gist reflects the major preoccupations of Schulz's *Street of Crocodiles.* In fact, N. Katherine Hayles proposes a mode of reading altered books that would detect in them narratives repressed in the source text. Hayles takes this rather Freudian approach to *Tree of Codes* when she notes that by doing away with several thematic strands from Schulz's text, Foer "brings to the fore the oedipal conflict that in Schulz is a subtext" (2013, 229). My reading diverges from Hayles' since I treat the textual surface with gaps as a representation of the ordinary cycles of remembering and forgetting (also explored in chapter 4) rather than as a representation of pathologies.

The verbal discourse of *Tree of Codes* is replete with descriptions of loss and disappearance. Descriptions like "sinking city" and "sleeping garden" evoke a benumbed state of mind that can be associated with the unnamed narrator as well as the other inhabitants of his city. The stupor of the represented world, though, contrasts with the effort a reader must put in to read *Tree of Codes,* given the altered state of the book. The first page of *Tree of Codes* has no words, only five quadrangular holes of different sizes. Kiene Brillenburg Wurth (2011b) observes that these holes give the pages the appearance of punch cards. Through the holes on the opening page, we see an array of letters and words:

ne bri | hoa[6]
ss |k
back rising and fall | the | mother and I | wanting to| | s.
over a keyboard | dless day. | the | normous || of || gr | paving stones
had their eyes half-closed
. Everyone
Clumsy gestur | . | whole generations
wore his
fallen asleep
the | children | greeted each other with | jar |masks | painted
on their faces | pain || witl | we pass | ; they smiled at each other's
secret of | The sleeping| smiles

The author, Foer, might be having a rich "keyboard/dless day," working as he is with scissors, but what does a reader do with this book? The concurrence of words from the different pages, that do not cohere to form meaningful units challenge readers. As with Borges's Funes, whose present seems sometimes too rich and bright because of everything he remembers, the reader of Foer's book must tackle multiple layers of stimuli, though in the case of *Tree of Codes* the perceptual field is crowded by glimpses of the future rather than the past. Through the die-cut holes on each page, words from the next ones appear. Separation of the pages necessary for following the narrative of *Tree of Codes* entails either placing blank sheets between them or training our eyes to skip the words peeping out of holes from a later page. With a white page placed between sheets, the first page *of Tree of Codes* becomes blank. The second page reads: "The passersby / had their eyes half-closed. / Everyone / wore his / mask. / children greeted each other with masks painted / on their faces; they

---

6. I am using "|" to mark different layers of pages.

smiled at each other's / smiles" (2010, 8; see Figure 5.1). The need to separate the layers of text to read them certainly slows down perusal.

Reading *Tree of Codes,* as must have become clear by now, is not akin to reading traditional books. At a cursory glance it even comes across as a book sculpture, what Garrett Stewart calls "bookworks." Bookworks are demediated books, where demediation implies "the process by which a transmissible text or image is blocked by the obtruded fact of its own neutralized medium" (2010, 413). Bookworks cannot be "binge read"—they are usually unreadable books. In other words, demediation obstructs the conventional use of the medium. Foer's book, though, can be read with some initiative on the readers' part.

Foer's note about *Tree of Codes*' connection with Schulz's work—his close reading of the content that the book has lost—becomes the context grounding the elliptical narrative. Readers are invited to recall and reflect on the intertext that the surface of Foer's book materially forgets. As Brillenburg Wurth puts it, "Foer has created a ruin in which the past, *The Street of Crocodiles,* remains palpably present as an index: the very physical features of *Tree of Codes,* the contours of its gaping holes, point to that older text. When we read *Tree of Codes,* our eyes skip these open spaces. They perform an act of overlooking, of forgetting . . . Yet, simultaneously, this is a skipping that takes time, the whites and holes halting our reading . . . constantly reminding us of an irreparable loss. What appeared to be a (physical) act of forgetting becomes a roundabout or peripheral mode of remembering" (2011b, 3). The die-cut, demediated form of Foer's book thus signifies the conflicting processes shaping the readers' memory of texts.

The readers' memory on which the self-reflexive dynamics of *Tree of Codes* depend resist generalization. Embodied and experiential memories of particular individuals come into play when they read. Marco Caracciolo, for instance, argues that reading a passage that mentions moving birds and objects "activates something akin to actual memories of seeing birds in flight and counting moving objects, not some abstract 'recipe' for carrying out these activities" (2014a, 46). Caracciolo's observation builds on cognitive-scientific studies such as Barsalou's (1999, 2008) that discuss how semiotic modes may prompt the perceptual faculties to simulate former embodied experiences. In addition, each reader approaches a text having read different texts before it, with their own textual archives. As Michael Burke (2011) notes, one reading experience is embedded within others and memories of earlier readings are reexperienced through the present one. What an individual reader remembers cannot be revealed through empirical experiments and can be self-reported only to an extent. The precise conditions of a particular reader's reading are not

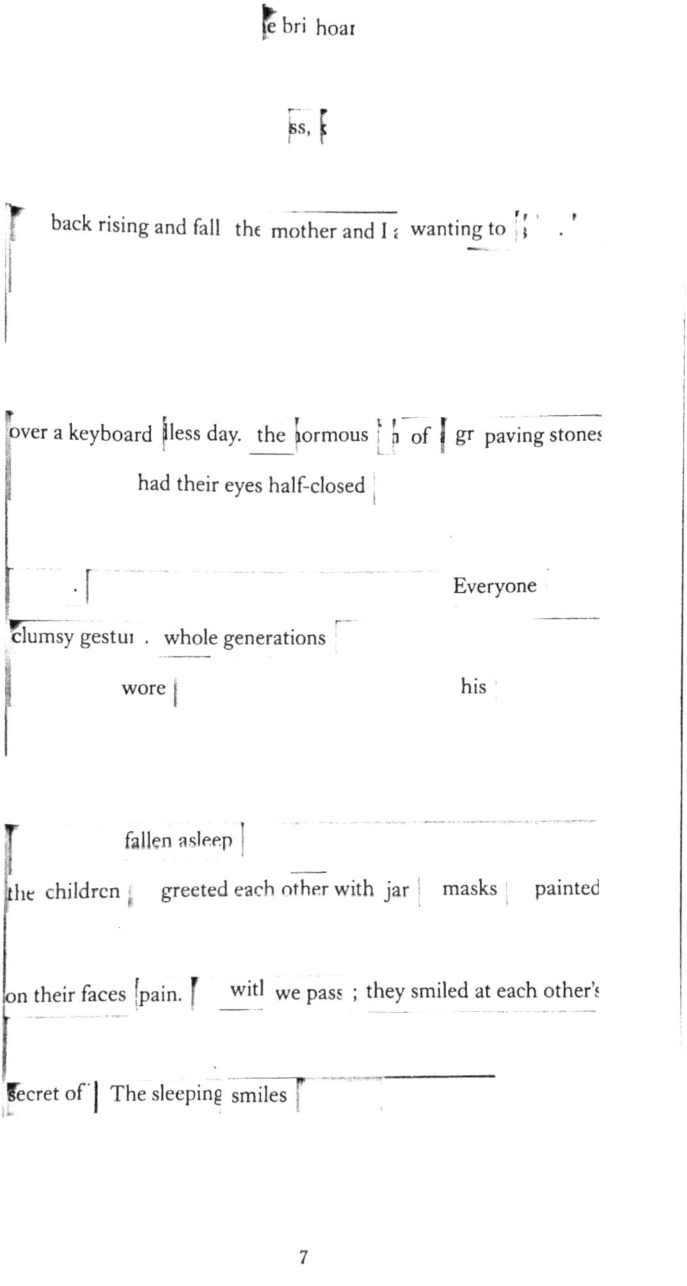

e bri hoar

ss,

back rising and fall the mother and I a wanting to

over a keyboard iless day. the ormous of gr paving stones
had their eyes half-closed

.   Everyone
clumsy gestur . whole generations
         wore   his

fallen asleep
the children   greeted each other with jar masks   painted

on their faces pain.   with we pass ; they smiled at each other's

secret of The sleeping smiles

FIGURE 5.1. *Tree of Codes* without a white sheet placed between pages (left). Reading *Tree of Codes* with a white sheet placed between pages (right).

had their eyes half-closed

. Everyone

wore his

children greeted each other with masks painted

on their faces ; they smiled at each other's

smiles

repeatable. Thus, the materiality of Foer's book cues a metacognitive awareness about the presence of an intertext (Schulz's manuscripts), though it cannot and does not demand a reader's verbatim retention of that text for its memorial effect.

It is intuitive to assume that the slower we read the more we attend to the textual details and the longer we remember what we read. Given that Foer has only retained 10% of the total words from *Street of Crocodiles* in *Tree of Codes* (3815 out of the original 37,843 words, according to Hayles [2013]), the implied author-figure of *Tree of Codes* seems to be a poor reader, deficient in attention and retention, perhaps engaged in a game with a more memorious reader, one who possibly recalls Schulz's text to a greater degree. The minimal retention of the surface structure of Schulz's writing, though, mirrors the findings of empirical studies on reading.

What readers remember of literary texts has been a subject of debate within cognitive sciences and psychology. The issue is often addressed through cognitive experiments that operate with a shell versus semantics binary, where shell refers to the surface—that is, the precise words and the authorial style—and semantics is the gist of the text. Empirical studies designed along these lines particularly from the 1970s to the 1990s operate on the assumption that "memory" is what can be retained and eventually reported at a later time. Such studies conclude that readers have poor retention of the shell or the surface of a text. In a more recent experiment that relies on the archival model of memory, Marisa Bortolussi and Peter Dixon (2013) altered words from Joyce's "Evelyn" in order to find out whether readers retained the semantic information better than the story's surface structure. They concluded that subjects have a fair memory for the semantics, but they barely retain the surface details or styles of texts. The semantic memory of texts of course involves the dynamic reconstruction of texts. Rolf Zwaan had undertaken experiments that juxtaposed two modes of narration that he identified as "news perspective" and "literary perspective" (1993, 41–60). The experiment showed that, relatively speaking, literary perspective compelled participants to read slower and they were able to recognize the surface structure better after reading texts that they believed to be "literary." It seems we believe the surface structure to hold more significance in aesthetic experiences and are more motivated to reconstruct them. A reader's retention of the material structure of texts, that is, texture and typography and not only language, features more prominently in empirical studies on rereading. Transferred typography and visual patterns have been used to test rereading proficiency among adults (see Kolers 1976; Kolers and Lochlan 1978). The results of these experiments reiterate that readers have poor retention for material surfaces, though rereading proficiency improves if the text is presented using the same typography, which implies that readers recognize some qualities of the shell when encountering it a second time (Levy 1993, 49–70). Based on these experiments that test retention—the supposed archiving functions of memory—readers' capacity for storage seems to be poor. However, poor retention need not imply inferior engagement with a text, as *Tree of Codes* suggests through its material design. Reading as an experience is complex and generative; it involves imagination and experientiality rather than the storage and retrieval of information.

Foer has previously tackled questions pertaining to the relationship of language and media with the mind. His first two multimodal novels *Everything Is Illuminated* (1999) and *Extremely Loud and Incredibly Close* (2005), like *Tree of Codes,* addressed questions such as, how do media objects record and organize memories? How do they prompt imagination and recall? Are particular media objects (read: books) better equipped to serve as memory aids than others? In the storyworlds of *Everything Is Illuminated* and *Extremely Loud,* books and libraries typically function as reliable mnemotechnological apparatus that outlive individuals, record and survive catastrophes, and mend breaches in communication across generations (see Starre 2015). In *Tree of Codes,* however, Foer adopts a different tactic. *Tree of Codes* not only celebrates what books retain and record but also what they cannot. Accentuating the fragility of the artifactual book, Foer extols creative destruction and distortion as crucial ways of engaging with texts, as central to the reading experience. Foer's aesthetic also registers a shift from metaphorically understanding memory in terms of bound books to approaching recollection as an embodied process that involves interactions with texts and media-objects.

Foer's source text—Schulz's *Street of Crocodiles*—mediated anxieties about old and new worlds. The Polish title of the book, literally translated to "Cinnamon Shops," refers to one of the short stories in the collection and an area of the fictional town Schulz creates. The Cinnamon Shops located at the center of the town represent an old, fast-disappearing world that exudes a deep sensorial charm for the young narrator. The narrator remarks, "These truly noble shops, open late at night, have always been the objects of my ardent interest. Dimly lit, their dark and solemn interiors were redolent of the smell of paint, varnish, and incense; of the aroma of distant countries and rare commodities. You could find in them Bengal lights, magic boxes, the stamps of long-forgotten countries, Chinese decals, indigo . . ." (61–62). The Street of Crocodiles, on the other hand, is a "pseudo-American," "commercial" district with houses that appear to be one-dimensional, and according to the narrator, the "grey" locality resembles the monochrome photographs or cheap illustrations found in catalogs (70–71). Schulz's rich synesthetic accounts of the Cinnamon Shops give way to epithets such as "colorlessness," "whiteness," or "greyness" when describing the Street of Crocodiles. Cinnamon Shops and Street of Crocodiles signify an opposition between two cultures. In *Tree of Codes,* the opposition at the heart of Schulz's fictional town is modified to stand for old and new media ecologies.

In Foer's book, "tree of codes" is an "empty and unexplored" terrain appearing on the map of the town. It typifies a quality of existence in which "a screen / [is] placed to hide the true / meaning of things" (91). Whereas in Schulz's stories, the inhabitants of the old town manage to stay away from the Street of Crocodiles, despite its "tawdry charm," the entire town in Foer's text has become part of the "tree of codes" (Schulz 1988, 73; Foer 2010, 94). By cutting out several descriptive paragraphs from Schulz's story, Foer turns the conflict between old and new worlds, Cinnamon Shops and Street of Crocodiles, into a conflict between a virtual world, which is the world of codes and screens, and the world of paper, the "real" world that barely endures. One cannot help but note the fragile state of the paper on which these words appear. The opposition between the actual and the virtual in Foer's text serves as a eulogy for the "Book" which, it is anticipated, is in the process of "dying." If everything is reduced to "codes," then like the old town of Schulz's stories, the old media platform of the book will become an object of the past, available only through memory and saved in institutional archives. This apprehension was highlighted during the book's marketing campaign. In an interview given after the publication of *Tree of Codes,* Foer said, "On the brink of the end of paper, I was attracted to the idea of a book that can't forget it has a body" (Heller 2010). The publishing house Visual Editions released a video about *Tree of Codes*'s making and explained that both Foer and the publishing team were "exploring the idea of the pages' physical relationship to one another and how this could somehow be developed to work with a meaningful narrative" (Visual Editions 2010, n. pag.). Thus, Foer's experiments with the book-form are prompted by speculations about what would be lost when we read on the book's other—the electronic screen.

Andrea Ballatore and Simone Natale observe, in media history, change is often perceived "as a process in which innovation is inseparable from loss" (2016, 2390), and this perception is a driving force behind the multimodal experiments in books including Foer's *Tree of Codes.* The vanishing sensory world of cinnamon shops offers Foer an analog for the deep, sensorial reading with which books are routinely associated in the twenty-first century. The retro-projection of sensory appeal onto books is prototypical of ways in which we understand the relation between old and new media. What is remarkable about *Tree of Codes* is thus not how it affirms a popular binary opposition between the page and the screen but the fact that it pays homage to the page by tearing it.[7] A reader might even question how sincere Foer is about his professed goals of eulogizing Schulz's writing, which for him supposedly even encapsulates the very idea of the Book (in the singular, definitive sense). Namwali Serpell aptly answers this question while examining *Tree of Codes*—she notes, "contemporary fiction's material experiments are often as earnest as they are self-conscious . . . Even the high-low seriousness of Susan Sontag's *camp* doesn't quite fit the affective mash-up of sentimentality and irony evident in this fondling of the form" (2014, 285). Whereas the binary set up within the textual world and underscored by the marketing campaign fetishizes the book-form, Foer undoes the book-form to reengage the readers' cognitive and perceptual faculties. When a reader opens *Tree of Codes,* its most striking feature is the gaping holes. The narrative form, with its barely formed sentences and multilayered, fragmented structure, is indebted to electronic literature as much as it is indebted to avant-garde and procedural texts printed throughout the twentieth century.

Rethinking

This book opened with the question of how we think about thinking in the twenty-first century. The bulk of the book remained devoted to studying the mechanics of consciousness representation in contemporary Anglophone narratives and examining the assumptions about thinking underwritten in such representation, guided by that opening question. The malleability of narrative forms makes them amenable to speculative and projective metacognitive exercises. I discussed cognitive theories to identify co-emergent trajectories and instances of cross-pollination across aesthetic practices and other contemporary modes of knowledge production. The presence of multimodal features in narratives, I argued, both informs and is informed by the reconceptualization of thought across disciplinary lines, the questioning of seemingly higher-order mental activities like reading as distinct from lower-level perceptual processes.

Through my opening question and narrative analyses, I have attempted to underscore the provisional nature of cognitive theories and models. These models tend to be provisional not because they are later proven to be incorrect but because they are developed in response to rather specific questions particular cognitive-scientific studies ask about minds. My approach advocates for

---

7. See Ghosal (2015) for an analysis of texts such as Chris Ware's *Building Stories* (2012) that pay homage to print culture and the codex by breaking the book's body.

self-consciousness—metacognitive awareness—within literary studies about how we engage with cognitive theories. I urge us to consider whether we are refracting contingent models through our analysis to stand for the universal and transhistorical, entrenching problematic theories or enshrining provisional meta-concepts (like computationalism or Theory of Mind) by reading narrative representations as attesting to their veracity and irrefutability.

Sciences of the mind turn to literature and other arts to find case studies or evidence for postulations in ways that do not acknowledge issues of aesthetic complexity or literary history. In fact, even long before the development of contemporary cognitive sciences, Charles Bell (1806) referred to paintings and Charles Darwin (1998 [1899]) cited Shakespeare in order to assess what the artists may have gotten wrong or right about human minds and emotions. That is one method of linking emergent knowledge about minds to aesthetic treatments, but cognitive literary criticism is not obliged to replicate it. As cognitive literary critics such as Sue J. Kim and H. Porter Abbott have shown, literary narratives can venture into territories that are yet to be theorized or may never be fully theorized in the cognitive sciences, create conditions for us to experience our ignorance about how minds work (Kim 2013, 153–54; Abbott 2013).

Out of Mind's salient concern has been narrative's conceptualization of thinking. I have examined narratives that are preoccupied with cognition in theme and form, and identified the manifold analogs and modes rendering the characters' minds in them. In some of the fictions I have analyzed, like *Raw Shark Texts* and *Theories of Forgetting*, multiple hypotheses about cognition are embodied by characters and played out within the same storyworld. My aim has been to demonstrate the dialogic relationship between these imaginative and speculative literary constructions and cognitive-scientific projects of the twenty-first century. Rather than borrow a particular heuristic framework from the cognitive sciences to analyze literature, I have attempted to engage with and acknowledge multiple, coexisting heuristic frameworks, following the formal insights of the multimodal narratives I study. Literary narratives are significant contributors in ongoing conversations about how minds work, and as *Out of Mind* reveals, by examining literature we can not only grasp but also question the beliefs integral to the dominant models of cognition.

WORKS CITED

Abbott, H. Porter. 2008. *The Cambridge Introduction to Narrative*. New York: Cambridge University Press.

———. 2013. *Real Mysteries: Narrative and the Unknowable*. Columbus: The Ohio State University Press.

Abrams, J. J. and Doug Dorst. *S*. 2013. New York: Mulholland Books.

Acker, Kathy. 1988. *Empire of the Senseless*. New York: Grove Press.

Adorno, Theodor W. 1981. *Prisms*. Translated by Samuel Weber and Shierry Weber. Cambridge, MA: MIT Press.

———. *Negative Dialectics*. 2007 [1973]. Translated by E. B. Ashton. New York: Continuum.

"Advertisement for Mince Text Editor." 1981. *Byte Magazine* 6, no. 12 (December), 123.

Agamben, Giorgio. 1999. *Remnants of Auschwitz: The Witness and the Archive*. Translated by Daniel Heller-Roazen. New York: Zone Books.

Alber, Jan, Stefan Iversen, Henrik Skov Nielsen, and Brian Richardson. 2010. "Unnatural Narratives, Unnatural Narratology: Beyond Mimetic Models." *Narrative* 18, no. 2: 113–36.

Aldama, Frederick Luis. 2010. *Toward a Cognitive Theory of Narrative Acts*. Austin: University of Texas Press.

Andersen, Hanne, Peter Barker, and Xiang Chen. 2006. *The Cognitive Structure of Scientific Revolutions*. New York: Cambridge University Press.

Anderson, John R. and Robert Milson. 1989. "Human Memory: An Adaptive Perspective." *Psychological Review* 96, no. 4:703–19.

Aristotle. *De Anima*. 2008 [c. 350 B.C]. Translated by R. D. Hicks. New York: Cosimo Classics.

Armstrong, Nancy. 1999. *Fiction in the Age of Photography: The Legacy of British Realism*. Cambridge, MA: Harvard University Press.

Atkins, Kim. 2010. *Narrative Identity and Moral Identity: A Practical Perspective.* New York: Routledge.

Bakshani, Nikkitha. 2015. "Binge Reading Disorder." *The Morning News,* April 16, 2015. https://themorningnews.org/article/binge-reading-disorder.

Ballatore, A. and S. Natale. 2016. "E-readers and the Death of the Book: Or, New Media and the Myth of the Disappearing Medium." *New Media & Society* 18, no. 10: 2379–94.

Banfield, Ann. 1982. *Unspeakable Sentences: Narration and Representation in the Language of Fiction.* New York: Routledge.

Baron-Cohen, Simon. 1995. *Mindblindness: An Essay on Autism and Theory of Mind.* Cambridge, MA: MIT Press.

Barrett, Paul H, Donald J. Weinshank, Timothy T. Gottleber, and Charles Darwin. 1981. *A Concordance to Darwin's Origin of Species.* Ithaca: Cornell University Press.

Barsalou, Lawrence W. 1999. "Perceptual Symbol Systems." *Behavioral and Brain Sciences* 22, no. 4: 577–609.

———. 2008. "Grounded Cognition." *Annual Review of Psychology* 59, no. 1 (January): 617–45.

———. 2009. "Simulation, Situated Conceptualization, and Prediction." *Philosophical Transactions. Biological Sciences* 364, no. 1521 (May): 1281–89.

———. 2020. "Challenges and Opportunities for Grounding Cognition." *Journal of Cognition* 3, no. 1, art. 31 (September): 1–24.

Barsalou, Lawrence W., W. Kyle Simmons, Aron K. Barbey, and Christine D Wilson. 2003. "Grounding Conceptual Knowledge in Modality-Specific Systems." *Trends in Cognitive Sciences* 7, no. 2 (February): 84–91.

Barsalou Lawrence W., L. Dutriaux, and C. Scheepers. 2018. "Moving beyond the Distinction between Concrete and Abstract Concepts." *Philosophical Transactions. Royal Society. B* 373, no. 1752 (June): 20170144.

Barthes, Roland. 1977. *Roland Barthes.* Translated by Richard Howard. New York: Hill and Wang.

———. 1981. *Camera Lucida: Reflections on Photography.* Translated by Richard Howard. New York: Hill and Wang.

Bateman, John A. and Janina Wildfeuer. 2014. "A Multimodal Discourse Theory of Visual Narrative." *Journal of Pragmatics* 74 (December): 180–208.

Beaujour, Michel. 1981. "Some Paradoxes of Description." *Yale French Studies,* no. 61: 27–59.

Beck, Julia. 2018. "Why We Forget Most of the Books We Read." *The Atlantic,* January 26, 2018. https://www.theatlantic.com/science/archive/2018/01/what-was-this-article-about-again/551603/.

Bell, Charles. 1806. "Essays on the Anatomy of Expressions in Painting." https://www.bible.ca/psychiatry/essays-on-the-anatomy-of-expression-in-painting-sir-charles-bell-1806ad.htm.

Bergson, Henri. 1959. *Matter and Memory.* Translated by Nancy M. Paul and W. Scott Palmer. New York: Doubleday & Company, Inc.

Bernstein, D. M. and Elizabeth Loftus. 2009. "How to Tell If a Particular Memory Is True or False." *Perspectives on Psychological Science* 4: 370–74.

Bil'ak, Peter. 1999–2015. *Typotheque.* Web. https://www.typotheque.com/authors/peter_bilak.

Boden, Margaret A. 2006. *Mind as Machine: A History of Cognitive Science.* 2 vols. Oxford: Oxford University Press.

Bogost, Ian and Nick Montfort. 2009. "Platform Studies: Frequently Questioned Answers." *Plenaries: After Media—Embodiment and Context. Proceedings of the Digital Arts and Culture Conference,* UC Irvine. https://nickm.com/if/bogost_montfort_dac_2009.pdf.

Bohn, Roger E. and James E. Short. 2009. "How Much Information? 2009 Report on American Consumers." San Diego: Global Information Center, UC San Diego.

Bolter, Jay David. 1991. *Writing Space: The Computer, Hypertext, and the History of Writing.* Hillsdale, NJ: Lawrence Erlbaum Associates.

Bond, Lucy, Ben De Bruyn, and Jessica Rapson. 2017. "Planetary Memory in Contemporary American Fiction." *Textual Practice* 31, no. 5: 853–66.

Borges, Jorge Luis. 1962. "Funes, the Memorious." In *Ficciones,* 107–1942. Translated by Anthony Kerrigan. Buenos Aires: Emecé Editores.

Bortolussi, Marisa and Peter Dixon. 2013. "Minding the Text: Memory for Literary Narrative." In *Stories and Minds: Cognitive Approaches to Literary Narrative,* edited by Bart Vervaeck, Lars Bernaerts, Dirk de Geest, and Luc Herman, 23–37. Lincoln: University of Nebraska Press.

Boyagoda, Randy. 2012. "Benjy's Red-Letter Days." *The New York Times,* September 15, 2012. https://nyti.ms/Ub2LJ5.

Brillenburg Wurth, Kiene. 2011a. "Posthumanities and Post-Textualities: Reading *The Raw Shark Texts* and *Woman's World.*" *Comparative Literature* 63, no. 2: 119–41.

———. 2011b. "Old and New Medialities in Foer's *Tree of Codes.*" *Clcweb: Comparative Literature and Culture* 13, no. 3. https://doi.org/10.7771/1481-4374.1800.

Brillenburg Wurth, Kiene, Kári Driscoll, and Jessica Pressman, eds. 2018. *Book Presence in a Digital Age.* New York: Bloomsbury Academic.

Bringhurst, Robert. 1996. *The Elements of Typographic Style.* Vancouver: Hartley & Marks.

Brockmeier, Jens. 2010. "After the Archive: Remapping Memory." *Culture & Psychology* 16, no. 1: 5–35.

———. 2015. *Beyond the Archive: Memory, Narrative, and the Autobiographical Process.* Oxford: Oxford University Press.

Bruner, Jerome. 2003. "Self-Making Narratives." In *Autobiographical Memory and the Construction of a Narrative Self: Developmental and Cultural Perspectives,* edited by R. Fivush and C. A. Haden, 209–25. Mahwah, NJ: Lawrence Erlbaum Associates.

Buccino, Giovanni, Ivan Colagè, Nicola Gobbi, and Giorgio Bonaccorso. 2016. "Grounding Meaning in Experience: A Broad Perspective on Embodied Language." *Neuroscience & Biobehavioral Reviews* 69, no. 6: 69–78.

Bueno, Claudio Celis. 2017. *The Attention Economy.* London: Rowman and Littlefield.

Burke, Michael. 2011. *Literary Reading, Cognition and Emotion: An Exploration of the Oceanic Mind.* New York: Routledge.

Burroughs, William S. 1992 [1959]. *Naked Lunch.* New York: Grove Weidenfeld.

Burrows, Stuart. 2008. *A Familiar Strangeness: American Fiction and the Language of Photography, 1839–1945.* Athens: University of Georgia Press.

Butt, Nadia. 2015. *Transcultural Memory and Globalised Modernity in Contemporary Indo-English Novels.* Berlin: De Gruyter.

Cadava, Eduardo. 1997. *Words of Light: Theses on the Photography of History.* Princeton: Princeton University Press.

Calvino, Italo. 1981. *If on a Winter's Night a Traveler.* Translated by William Weaver. New York: Harcourt Brace Jovanovich.

Caquard, Sébastien. 2015. "Cartography III: A Post-Representational Perspective on Cognitive Cartography." *Progress in Human Geography* 39, no. 2: 225–35.

Caracciolo, Marco. 2011. "The Reader's Virtual Body: Narrative Space and Its Reconstruction." *Storyworlds* 3, no. 1: 117–38.

———. 2013. "Narrative Space and Readers' Responses to Stories: A Phenomenological Account." *Style* 47, no. 4: 425–44.

———. 2014a. *The Experientiality of Narrative: An Enactivist Approach.* Boston: De Gruyter.

———. 2014b. "Two Child Narrators: Defamiliarization, Empathy, and Reader-Response in Mark Haddon's *The Curious Incident* and Emma Donoghue's *Room*." *Semiotica* 202: 183–205.

———. 2019. "Form, Science, and Narrative in the Anthropocene." *Narrative* 27, no. 3: 270–89.

Caravà, Marta. 2020. "An Exploration into Enactive Forms of Forgetting." *Phenomenology and the Cognitive Sciences,* April 3, 2020. https://doi.org/10.1007/s11097-020-09670-6.

Carter, James Bucky. 2007. "Imagetext in *The Curious Incident of the Dog in the Night-Time*." *ImageTexT: Interdisciplinary Comics Studies* 3, no. 3. http://imagetext.english.ufl.edu/archives/v3_3/carter/.

Chakraborty, Anya and Bhismadev Chakrabarti. 2018. "Looking at My Own Face: Visual Processing Strategies in Self–Other Face Recognition." *Frontiers in Psychology* 9, no. 121. https://doi.org/10.3389/fpsyg.2018.00121.

Chemero, Anthony. 2009. *Radical Embodied Cognitive Science.* Cambridge, MA: MIT Press.

Chen, Fang, Jianlong Zhou, Yang Wang, Kun Yu, Syed Z. Arshad, Ahmad Khawaji, and Dan Conway. 2016. *Robust Multimodal Cognitive Load Measurement.* Berlin: Springer.

Chevaillier, Flore. 2015. "Literary Archaeologies in Steve Tomasula's *The Book of Portraiture*." In *Steve Tomasula: The Art and Science of New Media Fiction,* edited by David Banash, 117–32. New York: Bloomsbury Academic.

———. 2019. "Experiment with Textual Materiality: Page, Author, and Medium in the Works of Steve Tomasula, Michael Martone, and Eduardo Kac." *College Literature* 46, no. 1: 179–203.

Chomsky, Noam. 1965. *Aspects of the Theory of Syntax.* Cambridge, MA: M. I. T. Press.

Churchland, Patricia S., Vilaynur S. Ramachandran, and Terrence J. Sejnowski. 1994. "A Critique of Pure Vision." In *Large-Scale Neuronal Theories of the Brain,* edited by C. Koch and J. L. Davis, 23–60. Cambridge, MA: MIT Press.

Ciccoricco, David. 2007. *Reading Network Fiction.* Tuscaloosa: University of Alabama Press.

———. 2015. *Refiguring Minds in Narrative Media.* Lincoln: University of Nebraska Press.

Clark, Andy. 1998. *Being There: Putting Brain, Body, and World Together Again.* Cambridge, MA: MIT Press.

———. 1999. "An Embodied Cognitive Science?" *Trends in Cognitive Sciences* 3, no. 9: 345–51.

———. 2016. *Surfing Uncertainty. Prediction, Action, and the Embodied Mind.* Oxford: Oxford University Press.

Clark, Andy and D. Chalmers. 1998. "The Extended Mind." *Analysis (Oxford)* 58, no. 1: 7–19.

Clark, Timothy. 2015. *Ecocriticism on the Edge: The Anthropocene as a Threshold Concept.* London: Bloomsbury Academic.

Clemmons, Zinzi. 2017. *What We Lose.* New York: Viking.

Cohn, Dorrit. 1978. *Transparent Minds: Narrative Modes for Presenting Consciousness in Fiction.* Princeton.: Princeton University Press.

———. 2012. "Metalepsis and Mise en Abyme." Translated by Lewis S Gleich. *Narrative* 20, no. 1: 105–14.

Cole, Teju. 2014. *Every Day Is for the Thief.* Random House.

———. 2017. *Blind Spot.* New York: Random House.

Colebrook, Claire. 2014. "Archiviolithic: The Anthropocene and the Hetero-Archive." *Derrida Today* 7, no. 1: 21–43.

Cooper, Natalia et al. 2018. "The Effects of Substitute Multisensory Feedback on Task Performance and the Sense of Presence in a Virtual Reality Environment." *PloS One* 13, no. 2 (February): e0191846. https://doi.org/10.1371/journal.pone.0191846.

Cosgrove, Denis. 1999."Introduction: Mapping Meaning." In *Mappings*, 1–23. London: Reaktion Books.

Costall, Alan and Ivan Leudar, eds. 2009. *Against Theory of Mind*. New York: Palgrave Macmillan.

Crick, Francis. 1995. *The Astonishing Hypothesis: The Scientific Search for the Soul*. New York: Simon & Schuster.

Crouch, Ian. 2013. "The Curse of Reading and Forgetting." *The New Yorker,* May 22, 2013. https://www.newyorker.com/books/page-turner/the-curse-of-reading-and-forgetting.

Crucifix, B. 2016. "Witnessing Fukushima Secondhand: Collage, Archive and Travelling Memory in Jacques Ristorcelli's *Les Écrans*." *The Comics Grid: Journal of Comics Scholarship* 6, no. 4. https://www.comicsgrid.com/articles/10.16995/cg.73/.

Cuddy-Keane, Melba. 2020. "Distributed Cognition, Porous Qualia, and Modernist Narrative." In *Distributed Cognition from Victorian Culture to Modernism,* edited by Miranda Anderson, Peter Garratt, and Mark Sprevak, 189–208. Edinburgh: Edinburgh University Press.

Dale, Rick, Eric Dietrich, and Anthony Chemero. 2009. "Explanatory Pluralism in Cognitive Science." *Cognitive Science* 33, no. 5: 739–42.

Danielewski, Mark Z. 2000. *House of Leaves*. New York: Pantheon Books.

———. 2006. *Only Revolutions*. New York: Pantheon Books.

———. 2015. *The Familiar, Volume 1: One Rainy Day in May*. New York: Knopf Doubleday.

Darwin, Charles. 1998 [1899]. *The Expression of Emotion in Man and Animals*. Project Gutenberg ebook.

De Jaegher, Hanne. 2013. "Embodiment and Sense-Making in Autism." *Frontiers in Integrative Neuroscience* 7, no. 15: 1–19.

de Souza e Silva, Adriana. 2013. "Mobile Narratives: Reading and Writing Urban Space with Location-Based Technologies." In *Comparative Textual Media,* edited by N. Katherine Hayles and Jessica Pressman, 33–52. Minneapolis: University of Minnesota Press.

de Vreese, Leen, Erik Weber, and Jeroen Van Bouwel. 2010. "Explanatory Pluralism in the Medical Sciences: Theory and Practice." *Theoretical Medicine and Bioethics* 31, no. 5: 371–90.

Dennett, Daniel C. 1991. *Consciousness Explained*. Boston: Little, Brown and Co.

Descartes, Rene. 1916 [1637]. *A Discourse on Method*. Translated by John Veitch. New York: E. P. Dutton & Co.

Dick, Philip K. 1987. *We Can Remember It for You Wholesale: And Other Classic Stories*. New York: Citadel Press.

Didi-Huberman, Georges. 2004. *Invention of Hysteria: Charcot and the Photographic Iconography of the Salpêtrière*. Cambridge, MA: MIT Press.

Dodson, Zachary Thomas. 2015. *Bats of the Republic: An Illuminated Novel*. New York: Knopf Doubleday.

Doloughan, Fiona. 2011. *Contemporary Narrative: Textual Production, Multimodality and Multiliteracies*. New York: Continuum.

Draaisma, Douwe. 2000. *Metaphors of Memory: A History of Ideas about the Mind*. Cambridge: Cambridge University Press.

Driscoll, Kári and Inge van de Ven. 2018. "Book Presence and Feline Absence: A Conversation with Mark Danielewski." In *Book Presence in a Digital Age,* edited by Kiene Brillenburg Wurth, Kári Driscoll, and Jessica Pressman, 145–60. New York: Bloomsbury Academic.

Drucker, Johanna and Brad Freeman. 1992. *Otherspace: Martian Ty/opography.* Atlanta: Nexus and Interplanetary Productions.

Du Bois, W. E. B. 2011. *The Sociological Souls of Black Folk: Essays.* Lanham, MD: Lexington Books.

Ecker, Ullrich K. H. and Stephan Lewandowsky. 2012. "Computational Constraints in Cognitive Theories of Forgetting." *Frontiers in Psychology* 3, no. 400. https://doi.org/10.3389/fpsyg.2012.00400.

Edelman, Gerald. 1987. *Neural Darwinism: The Theory of Neuronal Group Selection.* New York: Basic Books.

———. 2003. "Naturalizing Consciousness: A Theoretical Framework." *Proceedings of the National Academy of Sciences—PNAS* 100, no. 9: 5520–24.

Elward, Rachael L. and Faraneh Vargha-Khadem. 2018. "Semantic Memory in Developmental Amnesia." *Neuroscience Letters* 680: 23–30.

Emmott, Catherine. 1997. *Narrative Comprehension: A Discourse Perspective.* Oxford: Oxford University Press.

Entin, Joseph B. 2012. *Sensational Modernism: Experimental Fiction and Photography in Thirties America.* Chapel Hill: University of North Carolina Press.

Erll, Astrid and Ansgar Nünning. 2005. "Where Literature and Memory Meet." In *Literature, Literary History, and Cultural Memory,* edited by Herbert Grabes, 261–94. Gottingen: Hubert and Co.

Etzler, Melissa Starre. 2014. *Writing from the Periphery: W. G. Sebald and Outsider Art.* Ph.D. dissertation, University of California, Berkeley.

———. 2019. "Peripheral Writing: Psychosis and Prose from Ernst Herbeck to W. G. Sebald." In *Literature and Psychology: Writing, Trauma, and the Self,* edited by Önder Çakirtaş, 18–48. Newcastle upon Tyne: Cambridge Scholars Publishing.

Fauconnier, Gilles. 1985. *Mental Spaces: Aspects of Meaning Construction in Natural Language.* Cambridge, MA: MIT Press.

———. 1997. *Mappings in Thought and Language.* Cambridge: Cambridge University Press.

Fee, Dwight. 2000. *Pathology and the Postmodern: Mental Illness as Discourse and Experience.* London: SAGE Publications.

Firth, Joseph et al. 2019. "The "Online Brain": How the Internet May Be Changing Our Cognition." *World Psychiatry: Official Journal of the World Psychiatric Association (WPA)* 18, no. 2: 119–29. https://doi.org/10.1002/wps.20617.

Fjellestad, Danuta. 2015. "Nesting—Braiding—Weaving: Photographic Interventions in Three Contemporary American Novels." In *Handbook of Intermediality: Image—Sound—Music,* edited by Gabriele Rippl, 193–218. Berlin: De Gruyter.

Fludernik, Monika. 1993. *The Fictions of Language and the Languages of Fiction: The Linguistic Representation of Speech and Consciousness.* London: Routledge.

———. 1996. *Towards a 'Natural' Narratology.* London: Routledge.

———. 2018. "*Towards a 'Natural' Narratology* Twenty Years After." *Partial Answers: Journal of Literature and the History of Ideas* 16, no. 2: 329–47.

Fodor, Jerry A. 1980. *The Language of Thought.* Cambridge, MA: Harvard University Press.

———. 1983. *The Modularity of Mind.* Cambridge, MA: MIT Press.

———. 2001. *The Mind Doesn't Work That Way: The Scope and Limits of Computational Psychology*. Cambridge, MA: MIT Press.

———. 2008. *LOT 2: The Language of Thought Revisited*. Oxford: Oxford University Press.

Foer, Jonathan Safran. 2002. *Everything Is Illuminated: A Novel*. Boston: Houghton Mifflin.

———. 2005. *Extremely Loud & Incredibly Close*. Boston: Mariner Books.

———. 2010. *Tree of Codes*. London: Visual Editions.

Forceville, Charles. 2009. "Non-Verbal and Multimodal Metaphor in a Cognitivist Framework: Agendas for Research." In *Multimodal Metaphor*, edited by Charles Forceville and Eduardo Urios-Aparisi, 19–42. Berlin: Mouton de Gruyter.

Fowler, Roger. 1977. *Linguistics and the Novel*. London: Methuen.

Frank, Joseph. 1991. *The Idea of Spatial Form*. New Brunswick: Rutgers University Press.

Freedberg, D. and V. Gallese. 2007. "Motion, Emotion and Empathy in Esthetic Experience." *Trends in Cognitive Sciences* 11, no. 5: 197–203.

Frelik, Pawel. 2014. "Reading the Background: The Textual and the Visual in Steve Tomasula's *The Book of Portraiture*." *Sillages Critiques* 17. https://doi.org/10.4000/sillagescritiques.3582.

Fuchs, E. and G. Flügge. 2014. "Adult Neuroplasticity: More Than 40 Years of Research." *Neural Plasticity 2014*, n. pag. https://doi.org/10.1155/2014/541870.

Fuller, Matthew. 2005. *Media Ecologies: Materialist Energies in Art and Technoculture*. Cambridge, MA: MIT Press.

Gallup, G. G. 1970. "Chimpanzees: Self-Recognition." *Science* 167: 86–87.

Gardner, Jared. 2012. *Projections: Comics and the History of Twenty-First-Century Storytelling*. Stanford: Stanford University Press.

Garry, Maryanne and Devon L. L. Polaschek. 2000. "Imagination and Memory." *Current Directions in Psychological Science* 9, no. 1: 6–10.

Garry, Maryanne, Charles G. Manning, Elizabeth F. Loftus, and Steven J. Sherman. 1996. "Imagination Inflation: Imagining a Childhood Event Inflates Confidence that it Occurred." *Psychonomic Bulletin and Review* 3, no. 2: 208–14.

Gavins, Joanna. 2005. "Mental Mapping of Narrative." In *The Routledge Encyclopedia of Narrative Theory*, edited by David Herman, Manfred Jahn, and Marie-Laure Ryan, 300. New York: Routledge.

Gehlawat, Monika. 2020. "Sharing Inwardness in Teju Cole's *Blind Spot*." *Word & Image* 36, no. 2: 211–24.

Genette, Gérard. 1988 [1972]. *Narrative Discourse*. Translated by Jane E. Lewin. Ithaca: Cornell University Press.

———. 1997. *Palimpsests: Literature in the Second Degree*. Translated by Channa Newman and Claude Doubinsky. Lincoln: University of Nebraska Press.

Gergen, Kenneth J. and Mary M. Gergen. 1988. "Narrative and the Self as Relationship." *Advances in Experimental Social Psychology* 21: 17–56.

Gerrig, Richard. 1993. *Experiencing Narrative Worlds: On the Psychological Activities of Reading*. New Haven: Yale University Press.

Ghosal, Torsa. 2015. "Books with Bodies: Narrative Progression in Chris Ware's *Building Stories*." *Storyworlds* 7, no. 1: 75–99.

———. 2019a. "At Hand: Handwriting as a Device for Spatial Orientation in J. J. Abrams and Doug Dorst's *S*." *Poetics Today* 40, no. 2: 189–213.

———. 2019b. "Shapes of Cognition in Typographical Fictions." *Studies in the Novel* 51, no. 2: 276–96.

———. 2020. "Forgetting at the Intersection of Comics and the Multimodal Novel. James Sie's *Still Life Las Vegas*." In *The Oxford Handbook of Comic Book Studies,* edited by Frederick Luis Aldama, 473–89. New York: Oxford University Press.

Ghosh, Amitav. 2016. *The Great Derangement: Climate Change and the Unthinkable.* Chicago: University of Chicago Press.

Gibbons, Alison. 2012a. *Multimodality, Cognition, and Experimental Literature.* London: Routledge.

———. 2012b. "Multimodal Literature and Experimentation." In *The Routledge Companion to Experimental Literature,* edited by Joe Bray, Alison Gibbons, and Brian McHale, 420–34. London: Routledge.

———. 2019. "Entropology and the End of Nature in Lance Olsen's *Theories of Forgetting.*" *Textual Practice* 33, no. 2: 280–99.

Gibbs, Raymond W. 2005. *Embodiment and Cognitive Science.* Cambridge: Cambridge University Press.

Gifford, Robert. 2011. "The Dragons of Inaction." *American Psychologist* 66, no. 4: 290–302.

Goddard, Michael. 2014. "Media Ecology." In *The Johns Hopkins Guide to Digital Media,* edited by Marie-Laure Ryan, Lori Emerson, and Benjamin J. Robertson, 331–33. Baltimore: Johns Hopkins University Press.

Goldman, Alvin I. 2006. *Simulating Minds: The Philosophy, Psychology, and Neuroscience of Mindreading.* Oxford: Oxford University Press.

González, Christopher. 2017. *Permissible Narratives: The Promise of Latino/a Literature.* Columbus: The Ohio State University Press.

Good, Katie Day. 2013. "From Scrapbook to Facebook: A History of Personal Media Assemblage and Archives." *New Media & Society* 15, no. 4: 557–73.

Grossman, David. 1989. *See Under: Love.* Translated by Betsy Rosenberg. New York: Farrar, Straus and Giroux.

Gudmundsdottir, Gunnthorunn. 2016. *Representations of Forgetting in Life Writing and Fiction.* London: Palgrave Macmillan UK.

Gumbrecht, Hans U. 2004. *Production of Presence: What Meaning Cannot Convey.* Stanford: Stanford University Press.

Gutjahar, Paul C. and Megan L. Benton. 2001. "Introduction: Reading the Invisible." In *Illuminating Letters: Typography and Literary Interpretation,* edited by Paul C. Gutjahar and Megan L. Benton, 1–15. Boston: University of Massachusetts Press.

Hacking, I. 1995. *Rewriting the Soul: Multiple Personality and the Sciences of Memory.* Princeton: Princeton University Press.

———. 1996. "Memory Science, Memory Politics." In *Tense Past: Cultural Essays in Trauma and Memory,* edited by P. Antze and M. Lambek, 76–88. New York: Routledge.

Haddon, Mark. 2003. *The Curious Incident of the Dog in the Night-Time.* New York: Doubleday.

———. 2009. "Asperger's & Autism." MarkHaddon.com. 16 July. http://www.markhaddon.com/blog/aspergers-autism.

Hall, Steven. 2007. *The Raw Shark Texts.* Edinburgh: Canongate.

Hallet, Wolfgang. 2009. "The Multimodal Novel: The Integration of Modes and Media in Novelistic Narration." In *Narratology in the Age of Cross-Disciplinary Narrative Research,* edited by Sandra Heinen and Roy Sommer, 129–53. Berlin: De Gruyter.

Harnad, Stevan. 1990. "The Symbol Grounding Problem." *Physica D: Nonlinear Phenomena* 42, no. 1–3: 335–46.

———. 2009. Annotation on "Computing, Machinery, and Intelligence." In *Parsing the Turing Test: Philosophical and Methodological Issues in the Quest for the Thinking Computer,* edited by Robert Epstein and Grace Peters, 23–66. Berlin: Springer.

Hartung, Franziska, Michael Burke, Peter Hagoort, and Role M. Willems. 2016. "Taking Perspective: Personal Pronouns Affect Experiential Aspects of Literary Reading." *PloS One* 11, no. 5: e0154732. https://doi.org/10.1371/journal.pone.0157285.

Hayles, N. Katherine. 1999. *How We Became Posthuman.* Chicago: University of Chicago Press.

———. 2011. "Material Entanglements: Steven Hall's *The Raw Shark Texts* as Slipstream Novel." *Science Fiction Studies* 38, no.1: 115–33.

———. 2012. *How We Think: Digital Media and Contemporary Technogenesis.* Chicago: University of Chicago Press.

———. 2013. "Combining Close and Distant Reading: Jonathan Safran Foer's *Tree of Codes* and the Aesthetic of Bookishness." *PMLA* 128, no. 1: 226–31.

———. 2015. "Beyond Human Scale." *Steve Tomasula: The Art and Science of New Media Fiction,* edited by David Banash, 133–46. London: Bloomsbury Academic.

Hecht, David, Miriam Reiner, and Gad Halevy. 2006. *Multimodal Virtual Environments: Response Times, Attention, and Presence.* Cambridge, MA: MIT Press.

Heise, Ursula K. 2016. *Imagining Extinction: The Cultural Meanings of Endangered Species.* Chicago: University of Chicago Press.

Heller, Steven. 2010. "Jonathan Safran Foer's Book as Art Object." *Arts Beat, The New York Times,* November 24, 2010. https://artsbeat.blogs.nytimes.com/2010/11/24/jonathan-safran-foers-book-as-art-object/.

Hemon, Aleksandar. 2008. *The Lazarus Project.* New York: Riverhead Books.

Herbert, Caroline. 2014. "Postcolonial Cities." In *The Cambridge Companion to the City in Literature,* edited by Kevin R. McNamara, 200–215. Cambridge: Cambridge University Press.

Herman, David. 2000. "Narratology as a Cognitive Science." *Image & Narrative* 1, no. 1. http://www.imageandnarrative.be/inarchive/narratology/davidherman.htm.

———. 2002. *Story Logic: Problems and Possibilities of Narrative.* Lincoln: University of Nebraska Press.

———. 2009. "Beyond Voice and Vision: Cognitive Grammar and Focalization Theory." In *Point of View, Perspective, and Focalization: Modeling Mediacy in Narrative,* edited by P. Hühn et al., 119–42. Berlin: De Gruyter.

———. 2011. *The Emergence of Mind: Representations of Consciousness in Narrative Discourse in English.* Lincoln: University of Nebraska Press.

Hustvedt, Siri. 2017. "Foreword." *Blind Spot* by Teju Cole. New York: Random House.

Hutchins, Edwin. 1995. *Cognition in the Wild.* Cambridge, MA: MIT Press.

Hutto, Daniel D. 2008. *Folk Psychological Narratives: The Sociocultural Basis of Understanding Reasons.* Cambridge, MA: MIT Press.

Hutto, Daniel D. and Anco Peters. 2018. "The Roots of Remembering." In *New Directions in the Philosophy of Memory,* edited by Kourken Michaelian et al., 97–118. New York: Routledge.

Huyssen, Andreas. 2003. *Present Pasts: Urban Palimpsests and the Politics of Memory: Cultural Memory in the Present.* Stanford: Stanford University Press.

Iacoboni, M., I. Molnar-Szakacs, V. Gallese, G. Buccino, J. C. Mazziotta, and G. Rizzolatti. 2005. "Grasping the Intentions of Others with One's Own Mirror Neuron System." *Plos Biology* 3, no. 3. https://doi.org/10.1371/journal.pbio.0030079.

Jackson, H. J. 2001. *Marginalia: Readers Writing in Books*. New Haven: Yale University Press.

Jackson, Shelley. 1995. *Patchwork Girl*. Watertown, MA: Eastgate Systems.

———. 1997. *My Body & A Wunderkammer*. http://www.altx.com/thebody/.

Jahn, Manfred. 1997. "Frames, Preferences, and the Reading of Third-Person Narratives: Towards a Cognitive Narratology." *Poetics Today* 18, no. 4: 441–68.

James, William. 1918 [1890]. *The Principles of Psychology*. Vol. 1. New York: H. Holt.

———. 1904. "Does 'Consciousness' Exist?" *The Journal of Philosophy, Psychology and Scientific Methods* 1, no. 18: 477–91.

Jameson, Fredric. 1988. "Cognitive Mapping." In *Marxism and the Interpretation of Culture*, edited by C. Nelson and L. Grossberg, 347–60. Urbana: University of Illinois Press.

Jani, Pranav. 2010. *Decentering Rushdie: Cosmopolitanism and the Indian Novel in English*. Columbus: The Ohio State University Press.

Jewitt, Carey. 2005. "Multimodality, 'Reading,' and 'Writing' for the 21st Century." *Discourse: Studies in the Cultural Politics of Education* 26, no. 3: 315–31.

———. 2009. *The Routledge Handbook of Multimodal Analysis*. London: Routledge.

Johnson, Geoffrey. 2009. "The Lost Boy." *Chicago Magazine*, May 2009. https://www.chicagomag.com/Chicago-Magazine/May-2009/Lost-Boy/The-Lost-Boy/.

Kandel, Sonia, Jean-Pierre Orliaguet, and Paolo Viviani. 2000. "Perceptual Anticipation in Handwriting: The Role of Implicit Motor Competence." *Perception & Psychophysics* 62: 706–16.

Keenan, Julian. 2004. *The Face in the Mirror: How We Know Who We Are*. New York: HarperCollins.

Kellner, Tatana. 1992a. *71125, Fifty Years of Silence: Eva Kellner's Story*. Rosendale, NY: Women's Studio Workshop.

———. 1992b. *B 11226, Fifty Years of Silence: Eugene Kellner's Story*. Rosendale, NY: Women's Studio Workshop.

Keskinen, Mikko. 2016. "Facsimile: The Makings of the Similar in Graham Rawle's Collage Novel *Woman's World*." *Image & Narrative* 17, no 1. http://www.imageandnarrative.be/index.php/imagenarrative/article/view/1102/889.

Kim, Sue J. 2013. *On Anger: Race, Cognition, Narrative*. Columbus: The Ohio State University Press.

Kittler, Friedrich A. 1990. "The Mechanized Philosopher." In *Looking after Nietzsche*, edited by Laurence A. Rickels, 195–208. Albany: State University of New York.

———. 1999. *Gramophone, Film, Typewriter*. Translated by Geoffrey Winthrop-Young and Michael Wutz. Stanford: Stanford University Press.

———. 2006. "Thinking Colours and/or Machines." *Theory, Culture, & Society* 23, no. 7: 39–50.

Klein, Stanley B. 2015. "What Memory Is." *Wiley Interdisciplinary Reviews: Cognitive Science* 6, no. 1: 1–38.

Kolers, Paul A. 1976. "Reading a Year Later." *Journal of Experimental Psychology: Human Learning and Memory* 2, no. 5: 554–65.

Kolers, Paul A. and Magee E. Lochlan. 1978. "Specificity of Pattern-Analyzing Skills in Reading." *Canadian Journal of Psychology/Revue Canadienne de Psychologie* 32, no. 1: 43–51.

Kosslyn, Stephen Michael. 1994. *Image and Brain: The Resolution of the Imagery Debate*. Cambridge, MA: MIT Press.

Kress, Gunther R. 2010. *Multimodality: A Social Semiotic Approach to Contemporary Communication*. London: Routledge.

Kress, Gunther R. and Theo van Leeuwen. 1996. *Reading Images: The Grammar of Visual Design*. London: Routledge.

———. 2001. *Multimodal Discourse: The Modes and Media of Contemporary Communication*. London: Arnold.

Kukkonen, Karin. 2020. *Probability Designs: Literature and Predictive Processing*. Oxford: Oxford University Press.

Kukkonen, Karin and Marco Caracciolo. 2014. "Introduction: What Is the 'Second Generation?'" *Style* 48, no. 3: 261–74.

Kumar, Amitava. 2018. *Immigrant, Montana*. New York: Alfred A. Knopf.

Kuspit, Donald B. 1983. "Collage: The Organizing Principle of Art in the Age of the Relativity of Art." In *Relativism in the Arts,* edited by Betty Jean Craige, 123–47. Athens: University of George Press.

Lacan, Jacques. 2018 [1973]. *The Four Fundamental Concepts of Psycho-Analysis*. Translated by Alan Sheridan. London: Taylor & Francis.

Lakoff, George. 1993. "Contemporary Theory of Metaphor." In *Metaphor and Thought*, edited by Andrew Ortony, 202–51. Cambridge: Cambridge University Press.

Lakoff, George and Mark Johnson. 1980. *Metaphors We Live By*. Chicago: University of Chicago Press.

———. 1999. *Philosophy in the Flesh: The Embodied Mind and Its Challenge to Western Thought*. New York: Basic Books.

Larsen, Reif. 2009. *The Selected Works of T. S. Spivet*. New York: Penguin.

Lawson, Mark. 2013. Review of "S. by Doug Dorst and JJ Abrams," *The Guardian,* November 13, 2013. https://www.theguardian.com/books/2013/nov/13/s-jj-abrams-doug-dorst-review.

Laszlo, Ervin, Ignazio Masulli, Robert Artigiani, and Vilmos Csnáyi, eds. 1993. *The Evolution of Cognitive Maps: New Paradigms for the Twenty-First Century*. Amsterdam: Gordon and Breach Science Publishers.

Lehman, Betsy, Jessica Thompson, Shawn Davis, and Joshua M. Carlson. 2019. "Affective Images of Climate Change." *Frontiers in Psychology* 10, no. 960 (May 15, 2019). https://doi.org/10.3389/fpsyg.2019.00960.

Lejeune, Philippe. 1977. "Autobiography in the Third Person." *New Literary History* 9, no. 1: 27–50.

Levi-Strauss, Claude. 2012. *Tristes Tropiques*. Translated by Patrick Wilcken and Doreen Weightman. New York: Penguin.

Levy, Betty Ann. 1993. "Fluent Rereading: An Implicit Indicator of Reading Skill Development." In *Implicit Memory: New Directions in Cognition, Development, and Neuropsychology,* edited by Peter Graf and Michael E. J. Masson, 49–73. Mahwah, NJ: Lawrence Erlbaum Associates.

Linde, C. and W. Labov. 1975. "Spatial Networks as a Site for the Study of Language and Thought." *Language* 51, no. 4: 924–39.

Linkis, Sara T. 2019. *Memory, Intermediality, and Literature: Something to Hold On To*. London: Routledge.

Liu, X., X. Lin, M. Zheng, Y. Hu, Y. Wang, L. Wang, X. Du, and G. Dong. 2018. "Internet Search Alters Intra- and Inter-regional Synchronization in the Temporal Gyrus." *Frontiers in Psychology* 9: 260. https://doi.org/10.3389/fpsyg.2018.00260.

Ljungberg, Christina. 2010. "Dynamic Instances of Interaction: The Performative Function of Iconicity in Literary Texts." *Sign Systems Studies* 38(1/4): 270–97.

Locke, John. 1836. *An Essay Concerning Human Understanding*. 27th ed. London: T. Tegg and Son.

Loftis, Sonya Freeman. 2015. *Imagining Autism: Fiction and Stereotypes on the Spectrum*. Bloomington: Indiana University Press.

Loftus, E. F., M. Garry, and H. Hayne. 2007. "Repressed and Recovered Memory." In *Beyond Common Sense: Psychological Science in the Courtroom,* edited by E. Borgida and S. T. Fiske, 177-94. Hoboken: Blackwell Publishing.

Lombroso, Cesare. 2006 [1876]. *Criminal Man*. Translated by Mary Gibson and Nicole Hahn Rafter. Durham: Duke University Press.

Lombrozo, Tania. 2010. "Causal-Explanatory Pluralism: How Intentions, Functions, and Mechanisms Influence Causal Ascriptions." *Cognitive Psychology* 61, no. 4: 303-32.

Longcamp, M., Y. Hlushchuk, and R. Hari. 2011. "What Differs in Visual Recognition of Handwritten vs. Printed Letters?" *Human Brain Mapping* 32, no. 8: 1250-59.

Luiselli, Valeria. 2019. *Lost Children Archive: A Novel*. New York: Alfred A. Knopf.

Lynch, Kevin A. 1960. *The Image of the City*. Cambridge, MA: MIT Press.

Magnée, M. J., B. de Gelder, H. van Engeland, and C. Kemner. 2011. "Multisensory Integration and Attention in Autism Spectrum Disorder: Evidence from Event-Related Potentials." *Plos One* 6, no. 8. https://doi.org/10.1371/journal.pone.0024196.

Maguire, E. A., N. Burgess, and J. O'Keefe. 1999. "Human Spatial Navigation: Cognitive Maps, Sexual Dimorphism, and Neural Substrates." *Current Opinion in Neurobiology* 9: 171-77. https://pubmed.ncbi.nlm.nih.gov/10322179/.

Mäkelä, Maria. 2006. "Possible Minds. Constructing—and Reading—Another Consciousness as Fiction." In *Free Language, Indirect Translation, Discourse Narratology: Linguistic, Translatological and Literary-Theoretical Encounters,* edited by Pekka Tammi and Hannu Tommola, 231-60. Tampere: Tampere University Press. https://trepo.tuni.fi/handle/10024/95968.

———. 2018a. "Toward the Non-Natural: Diachronicity and the Trained Reader in Fludernik's Natural Narratology." *Partial Answers: Journal of Literature and the History of Ideas* 16, no. 2: 271-77.

———. 2018b. "Exceptionality or Exemplarity?: The Emergence of the Schematized Mind in the Seventeenth- and Eighteenth-Century Novel." *Poetics Today* 39, no. 1: 17-39.

Mantzavinos, Chrysostomos. 2016. *Explanatory Pluralism*. Cambridge. Cambridge University Press.

Marks, Laura U. 2000. *The Skin of the Film: Intercultural Cinema, Embodiment, and the Senses*. Durham, NC: Duke University Press.

Matsuo, Kayako, Chikako Kato, Chika Sumiyoshi, Keiichiro Toma, Dinh Ha Duy Thuy, Tetsuo Moriya, Hidenao Fukuyama, and Toshiharu Nakai. 2003. "Discrimination of Exner's Area and the Frontal Eye Field in Humans—Functional Magnetic Resonance Imaging during Language and Saccade Tasks." *Neuroscience Letters* 340, no. 1: 13-16.

McCarthy, Tom. *Remainder*. 2005. New York: Random House.

———. 2007. "Straight to the Multiplex [Review of Steven Hall's *The Raw Shark Texts*]." *London Review of Books,* November 1, 2007. https://www.lrb.co.uk/the-paper/v29/n21/tom-mccarthy/straight-to-the-multiplex.

McCulloch, Warren S. 2016. *Embodiments of Mind*. Cambridge, MA: MIT Press.

McCulloch, Warren S. and Walter H. Pitts. 1990 [1943]. "A Logical Calculus of the Ideas Immanent in Nervous Activity." *Bulletin of Mathematical Biology* 52: 99-115.

McHale, Brian. 1987. *Postmodernist Fiction*. New York: Methuen.

———. 2012. "*Transparent Minds* Revisited." *Narrative* 20, no. 1: 115–24. https://doi.org/10.1353/nar.2012.0004.

Merleau-Ponty, Maurice. 2003. *The Phenomenology of Perception*. Translated by Colin Smith. London: Routledge.

Metelmann, J. and Thomas Telios. 2018. "Putting Oneself Out There: The "Selfie" and the Alter-Rithmic Transformations of Subjectivity." In *Transparency, Society and Subjectivity*, edited by E. Alloa and D. Thomä, 323–41. London: Palgrave Macmillan.

Metzinger, Thomas. 2003. *Being No One: The Self-Model Theory of Subjectivity*. Cambridge, MA: MIT Press.

Mihăilescu, Dana. 2014. "Negotiating Traumas via Cross-Cultural Urban Identity Configurations out of Grief: Aleksandar Hemon's *The Lazarus Project*." In *Mapping Generations of Traumatic Memory in American Narratives,* edited by Dana Mihăilescu, Mihaela Precup, and Roxana Oltean, 31–53. Newcastle upon Tyne: Cambridge Scholars Publishing.

Miłkowski, Marcin. 2013. *Explaining the Computational Mind*. Cambridge, MA: MIT Press.

Minsky, Marvin. 1977 [1975]. "A Framework for Representing Knowledge." In *Thinking: Readings in Cognitive Science,* edited by P. N. Johnson-Laird and P. C. Wason, 355–76. Cambridge: Cambridge University Press.

Mitchell, W. J. T. 1994. *Picture Theory: Essays on Verbal and Visual Representation*. Chicago: University of Chicago Press.

Mitchell, William. J. T. and Mark B. Hansen. 2010. "Introduction." In *Critical Terms for Media Studies,* edited by William J. T. Mitchell and Mark B. Hansen, vii–xxii. Chicago: University of Chicago Press.

Montfort, Nick and Ian Bogost. 2009. *Racing the Beam: The Atari Video Computer System*. MIT Press.

Mori, Naohisa. 2011. "Where Are We Going beyond the Archive Metaphor?" *Culture & Psychology* 17, no. 1: 11–19.

Moser, E. I., E. Kropff, and M. B. Moser. 2008. "Place Cells, Grid Cells, and the Brain's Spatial Representation System." *Annual Review of Neuroscience*. 31: 69–89. https://doi.org/10.1146/annurev.neuro.31.061307.090723.

Motzkin, Elhanan and John R. Searle. 1989. "Artificial Intelligence and the Chinese Room: An Exchange." *New York Review of Books* 36, no. 2.

Moulthrop, Stuart. 1993. *Victory Garden*. Cambridge: Eastgate Systems.

Muller, Vivienne. 2006. "Constituting Christopher: Disability Theory and Mark Haddon's *The Curious Incident of the Dog in the Night-Time*." *Papers: Explorations into Children's Literature* 16, no. 2: 118–25.

Murray, Stuart. 2008. *Representing Autism*. Liverpool: Liverpool University Press.

Nabokov, Vladimir. 1962. *Pale Fire: A Novel*. New York: G. P. Putnam and Sons.

Nadesan, Majia H. 2005. *Constructing Autism*. London: Routledge.

Nagel, Thomas. 1974. "What Is It Like to Be a Bat?" *The Philosophical Review* 83, no. 4: 435–50.

Nietzsche, Friedrich. 1981. *Briefwechsel. Kritische Gesamtausgabe III.I,* edited by Giorgio Colli and Mazzino Montinari. New York: De Gruyter.

Nora, Pierre. 1989. "Between Memory and History: Les Lieux de Mémoire." *Representations* no. 26: 7–24. https://doi-org.proxy.lib.csus.edu/10.2307/2928520.

Nørby, Simon. 2015. "Why Forget? On the Adaptive Value of Memory Loss." *Perspectives on Psychological Science* 10, no. 5: 551–78.

Nørgaard, Nina. 2003. *Systemic Functional Linguistics and Literary Analysis: A Hallidayan Approach to Joyce, a Joycean Approach to Halliday*. Odense: University Press of Southern Denmark.

———. 2018. *Multimodal Stylistics of the Novel: More Than Words*. New York: Routledge.

Nørgaard, Nina, Rocío Montoro, and Beatrix Busse. 2010. *Key Terms in Stylistics*. London: Continuum.

Novak, Daniel A. 2010. "Photographic Fictions: Nineteenth-Century Photography and the Novel Form." *NOVEL: A Forum on Fiction* 43, no. 1: 23–30.

O'Keefe, John. 1976. "Place Units in the Hippocampus of the Freely Moving Rat." *Experimental Neurology*. 51: 78–109. https://doi.org/10.1016/0014-4886(76)90055-8.

O'Keefe, John and J. Dostrovsky. 1971. "The Hippocampus as a Spatial Map. Preliminary Evidence from Unit Activity in the Freely-Moving Rat." *Brain Research*. 34: 171–75.

O'Keefe, John and Lynn Nadel. 1978. *The Hippocampus as a Cognitive Map*. Oxford: Oxford University Press.

Olive, Thierry and Jean-Michel Passerault. 2012. "The Visuospatial Dimension of Writing." *Written Communication* 29: 326–44.

Olsen, Lance. 2014. *Theories of Forgetting*. Tuscaloosa: University of Alabama Press.

———. 2018. *There's No Place Like Time*. Evanston: Northwestern University Press.

Olsen, Lance and Trevor Dodge. 2012. *Architectures of Possibility: After Innovative Writing*. Bowie, MD: Guide Dog Books.

Ophir, Eyal, Clifford Nass, and Anthony D. Wagner. 2009. "Cognitive Control in Media Multitaskers." *Proceedings of the National Academy of Sciences* 106, no. 37: 15583–87.

Ozick, Cynthia. 1987. *The Messiah of Stockholm: A Novel*. New York: A. A. Knopf.

Page, Ruth E., ed. 2010. *New Perspectives on Narrative and Multimodality*. New York: Routledge.

Palmer, Alan. 2010. *Social Minds in the Novel*. Columbus: The Ohio State University Press.

Patel, Shaista. 2014. "Racing Madness: The Terrorizing Madness of the Post-9/11 Terrorist Body." In *Disability Incarcerated: Imprisonment and Disability in the United States and Canada*, edited by L. Ben-Moshe, C. Chapman, and A. C. Carey, 201–15. London: Palgrave Macmillan.

Paulson, Steve. 2017. "Finding My Way into a New Form: An Interview with Teju Cole." *The Millions*, July 5, 2017. https://themillions.com/2017/07/finding-way-new-form-interview-teju-cole.html.

Peirce, Charles S. and James Hoopes. 1991. *Peirce on Signs: Writings on Semiotic*. Chapel Hill: University of North Carolina Press.

Phelan, James. 2005. *Living to Tell about It: A Rhetoric and Ethics of Character Narration*. Ithaca: Cornell University Press.

———. 2007. *Experiencing Fiction: Judgments, Progressions, and the Rhetorical Theory of Narrative*. Columbus: The Ohio State University Press.

Phillips, Barbara J. 2016. "The Scrapbook as an Autobiographical Memory Tool." *Marketing Theory* 16, no. 3: 325–46.

Phillips, Tom. 1970-2016. *A Humument: A Treated Victorian Novel*. 1970. London: Thames & Hudson.

Pier, John. 2016. "Metalepsis (revised version)." In *The Living Handbook of Narratology*, edited by Peter Hühn et al. Hamburg: Hamburg University. https://www.lhn.uni-hamburg.de/node/51.html.

Pinker, Steven. 1997. *How the Mind Works*. New York: Norton.

Piper, Andrew. 2012. "Reading's Refrain: From Bibliography to Topology." *English Literary History* 80, no. 2: 373–99.

Poulet, Georges. 1969. "Phenomenology of Reading." *New Literary History* 1, no. 1: 53–68.

Pressman, Jessica. 2009. "The Aesthetics of Bookishness in Twenty-First Century Literature." *Michigan Quarterly Review* 48, no. 4: 107–28.

———. 2020. *Bookishness: Loving Books in a Digital Age*. New York: Columbia University Press.

Proulx, Michael J. et al. 2016. "Where Am I? Who Am I? The Relation between Spatial Cognition, Social Cognition and Individual Differences in the Built Environment." *Frontiers in Psychology* 7, no. 64 (February 11, 2016). https://doi.org/10.3389/fpsyg.2016.00064.

Quian Quiroga, Rodrigo. 2012. *Borges and Memory: Encounters with the Human Brain*. Cambridge, MA: MIT Press.

Raisman, Geoffrey. 1969. "Neuronal Plasticity in the Septal Nuclei of the Adult Rat." *Brain Research* 14, no. 1: 25–48.

Rawle, Graham. 2008 [2005]. *Woman's World: A Novel*. Berkeley, CA: Counterpoint.

Rescher, Nicholas. 1979. "Ontology of the Possible." In *The Possible and the Actual*, edited by Michael J. Loux, 166–81. Ithaca: Cornell University Press.

Richardson, Alan. 2010. "Facial Expression Theory from Romanticism to the Present." In *Introduction to Cognitive Cultural Studies*, edited by Alan Richardson, 65–83. Baltimore: Johns Hopkins University Press.

Richardson, Brian. 2002. *Narrative Dynamics: Essays on Time, Plot, Closure, and Frames*. Columbus: The Ohio State University Press.

Roberts, Adam. 2013. Review of "*S*. by Doug Dorst and JJ Abrams," *Strange Horizons*, December 9, 2013. http://www.strangehorizons.com/non-fiction/reviews/s-by-j-j-abrams-and-doug-dorst.

Robinson, A. H. 1952. *The Look of Maps*. Madison: University of Wisconsin Press.

Rowlands, Mark. 2010. *The New Science of the Mind: From Extended Mind to Embodied Phenomenology*. Cambridge, MA: MIT Press.

Ruefle, Mary. 2006. *A Little White Shadow*. Seattle: Wave Books.

Ryan, Marie-Laure. 1991. *Possible Worlds, Artificial Intelligence, and Narrative Theory*. Bloomington: Indiana University Press.

———. 2001. *Narrative as Virtual Reality: Immersion and Interactivity in Literature and Electronic Media*. Baltimore: Johns Hopkins University Press.

———. 2003. "Cognitive Maps and the Construction of Narrative Space." In *Narrative Theory and the Cognitive Science*, edited by David Herman, 214–42. Stanford: CSLI.

———. 2006. *Avatars of Story*. Minneapolis: University of Minnesota Press.

———. 2015. *Narrative as Virtual Reality 2: Revisiting Immersion and Interactivity in Literature and Electronic Media*. Baltimore: Johns Hopkins University Press.

Ryan, Marie-Laure, Kenneth E. Foote, and Maoz Azaryahu. 2016. *Narrating Space/Spatializing Narrative: Where Narrative Theory and Geography Meet*. Columbus: The Ohio State University Press.

Sacks, Oliver. 2003. Cover Endorsement. *The Curious Incident of the Dog in the Night-Time* by Mark Haddon. London: Jonathan Cape.

Sartre, Jean-Paul. 2004. *The Imaginary: A Phenomenological Psychology of the Imagination*. Translated by Jonathan Webber. New York: Routledge.

Savarese, Ralph J. and Lisa Zunshine. 2014. "The Critic as Neurocosmopolite; Or, What Cognitive Approaches to Literature Can Learn from Disability Studies." *Narrative* 22, no. 1: 17–44.

Schacter, Daniel L., Scott A. Guerin, and Peggy L. St. Jacques. 2011. "Memory Distortion: An Adaptive Perspective." *Trends in Cognitive Sciences* 15, no. 10: 467–74.

Schulz, Bruno. 1988. *The Fictions of Bruno Schulz: The Street of Crocodiles and Sanatorium under the Sign of the Hourglass*. Translated by Celina Wieniewska. New York: Picador.

Searle, John R. 1992. *The Rediscovery of the Mind*. Cambridge, MA: MIT Press.

Sebald, W. G. 2018 [2000] *Austerlitz*. Translated by Anthea Bell. New York: Penguin.

Semino, Elena. 2003. "Possible Worlds and Mental Spaces in Hemingway's 'A Very Short Story.'" In *Cognitive Poetics in Practice*, edited by Joanna Gavins and Gerard Steens, 83–98. London: Routledge.

———. 2014. "Language, Mind and Autism in Mark Haddon's *The Curious Incident of the Dog in the Night-Time*." In *Linguistics and Literary Studies*, edited by Monika Fludernik and Daniel Jacob, 279–305. Boston: De Gruyter.

Serpell, C. Namwali. 2014. *Seven Modes of Uncertainty*. Cambridge, MA: Harvard University Press.

Seth, Anil K. 2013. "Interoceptive Inference, Emotion, and the Embodied Self." *Trends in Cognitive Sciences* 17, no. 11: 565–73.

Sforza A., I. Bufalari, P. Haggard, and S. M. Aglioti. 2010. "My Face in Yours: Visuo-tactile Facial Stimulation Influences Sense of Identity." *Social Neuroscience* 5, no. 2: 148–62. https://doi.org/10.1080/17470910903205503.

Shamsie, Kamila. 2002. *Kartography*. Orlando: Harcourt.

———. 2017. *Home Fire*. New York: Riverhead Books.

Sie, James. 2015. *Still Life Las Vegas*. New York: St. Martin's Press.

Siegel, Susanna. 2012. "Cognitive Penetrability and Perceptual Justification." *Noûs* 46, no. 2: 201–22.

Silverberg, Robbin A. 2002. *Detritus*. Brooklyn: Dobbin Books.

Silverman, Gillian. 2012. *Bodies and Books: Reading and the Fantasy of Communion in Nineteenth-Century America*. Philadelphia: University of Pennsylvania Press.

———. 2016. "Neurodiversity and the Revision of Book History." *PMLA* 131, no. 2: 307–23.

Small, Gary W., Teena D. Moody, Prabha Siddarth, and Susan Y. Bookheimer. 2009. "Your Brain on Google: Patterns of Cerebral Activation during Internet Searching." *The American Journal of Geriatric Psychiatry* 17, no. 2: 116–26.

Smith, Jonathan. 2006. *Charles Darwin and Victorian Visual Culture*. Cambridge: Cambridge University Press.

Smith, Shawn Michelle. 2000. "'Looking at One's Self through the Eyes of Others': W. E. B. Du Bois's Photographs for the 1900 Paris Exposition." *African American Review* 34, no. 4: 581–99.

Smith, Zadie. 2008. "Two Paths for the Novel." *The New York Review of Books*. November 20, 2008. https://www.nybooks.com/articles/2008/11/20/two-paths-for-the-novel/.

Sparrow, B., J. Liu, and D. M. Wegner. 2011. "Google Effects on Memory: Cognitive Consequences of Having Information at Our Fingertips." *Science (American Association for the Advancement of Science)* 333, no. 6043: 776–78.

Sperber, Dan. 2001. "In Defense of Massive Modularity." In *Language, Brain, and Cognitive Development: Essays in Honor of Jacques Mehler*, edited by E. Dupoux, 47–57. Cambridge, MA: MIT Press.

Sperduti, Marco, Marie Pieron, Marion Leboyer, and Tiziana Zalla. 2014. "Altered Pre-Reflective Sense of Agency in Autism Spectrum Disorders as Revealed by Reduced Intentional Binding." *Journal of Autism and Developmental Disorders* 44, no. 2: 343–52.

Srna, Shalena, Rom Y. Schrift, and Gal Zauberman. 2018. "The Illusion of Multitasking and Its Positive Effect on Performance." *Psychological Science* 29, no. 12: 1942–55.

Stafford, Thomas. 2015. "Radical Embodied Cognition: Interview with Andrew Wilson." *Mind Hacks,* March 5, 2015. https://mindhacks.com/2015/03/05/radical-embodied-cognition-an-interview-with-andrew-wilson/.

Starre, Alexander. 2015. *Metamedia: American Book Fictions and Literary Print Culture after Digitization.* Iowa City: University of Iowa Press.

Sterne, Laurence. 1940 [1759]. *The Life and Opinions of Tristram Shandy, Gentleman.* New York: Odyssey Press.

Stewart, Garrett. 2010. "Bookwork as Demediation." *Critical Inquiry* 36 (Spring): 410–57.

Stiegler, Bernard. 2010. "Memory." In *Critical Terms for Media Studies,* edited by William J. T. Mitchell and Mark B. Hansen, 66–84. Chicago: University of Chicago Press.

Stingelin, Martin. 1994. "Comments on a Ball: Nietzsche's Play on the Typewriter." In *Materialities of Communication,* edited by Hans Ulrich Gumbrecht and Karl Ludwig Pfeiffer, translated by William Whobrey, 70–82. Stanford: Stanford University Press.

Sweeney, Seamus. 2008. Review of *The Raw Shark Texts. nthposition Online Magazine.* http://www.nthposition.com/therawsharktexts.php/. https://seamussweeney.net/2018/12/03/review-of-the-raw-shark-texts-steven-hall/.

"The Curious Incident of the Dog in the Night-Time—Working on the Spectrum." 2012. *YouTube.* National Theater, October 2, 2012. https://www.youtube.com/watch?v=k2bV75ITXJw.

Thomas, Ayanna K., John B. Bulevich, and Elizabeth F. Loftus. 2003. "Exploring the Role of Repetition and Sensory Elaboration in the Imagination Inflation Effect." *Memory & Cognition* 31, no. 4: 630–40.

Tillman, Lynne. 2018. *Men and Apparitions.* New York: Soft Skull Press.

Tolman, Edward. 1948. "Cognitive Maps in Rats and Men." *Psychological Review* 55: 189–208.

Tomasula, Steve. 2006. *The Book of Portraiture.* Tuscaloosa: FC2.

———. 2018. "Our Tools Make Us (and Our Literature) Post." In *The Bloomsbury Handbook of Electronic Literature,* edited by Joseph Tabbi, 39–58. New York: Bloomsbury Academic.

Tooby, John and Leda Cosmides. 1995. "Foreword." *Mindblindness: An Essay on Autism and Theory of Mind* by Simon Baron-Cohen. Cambridge, MA: MIT Press.

Torgovnick, Marianna. 1985. *The Visual Arts, Pictorialism, and the Novel: James, Lawrence, and Woolf.* Princeton: Princeton University Press.

Trifonova, Temenuga. 2007. *The Image in French Philosophy.* Amsterdam: Rodopi.

Turing, Alan. 1950. "Computing Machinery and Intelligence." *Mind* 59, no. 236: 433–60.

Turner, Mark. 1996. *The Literary Mind.* New York: Oxford University Press.

Tye, Michael. 1991. *The Imagery Debate.* Cambridge, MA: MIT Press.

van Leeuwen, Theo. 2006. "Towards a Semiotics of Typography." *Information Design Journal* 14: 139–55.

Varela, Francisco J., Eleanor Rosch, and Evan Thompson. 2016 [1991] *The Embodied Mind: Cognitive Science and Human Experience.* Cambridge, MA: MIT Press.

Vargha-Khadem, F., D. G. Gadian, K. E. Watkins, A. Connelly, and W. Van Paesschen, and M. Mishkin. 1997. "Differential Effects of Early Hippocampal Pathology on Episodic and Semantic Memory." *Science (American Association for the Advancement of Science)* 277, no. 5324: 376–80.

Vega, Manuel, Arthur M. Glenberg, and Arthur C. Graesser. 2008. *Symbols and Embodiment: Debates on Meaning and Cognition.* Oxford: Oxford University Press.

Venkatesh Ghosh, Shoba. 2013. "The Archeology of Representation: Steve Tomasula's *The Book of Portraiture*." *Electronic Book Review*. https://electronicbookreview.com/essay/the-archeology-of-representation-steve-tomasulas-the-book-of-portraiture/.

Virilio, P. 2009 [1980]. *The Aesthetics of Disappearance*. Translated by Philip Beitchman. New York: Semiotext(e).

Visual Editions. 2010. *Tree of Codes*. https://2005.visual-editions.com/our-books/tree-of-codes.

von Neumann, John. 2000 [1958]. *The Computer and the Brain*. New Haven: Yale University Press.

Warde, Beatrice. 2009 [1930]. "The Crystal Goblet, or, Printing Should be Invisible." In *Graphic Design Theory: Readings from the Field*, edited by Helen Armstrong, 39–43. Princeton: Princeton Architectural Press.

Weiner, Sonia. 2014. "Double Visions and Aesthetics of the Migratory in Aleksandar Hemon's *The Lazarus Project*." *Studies in the Novel* 46, no. 2: 215–35.

Werth, Paul. 1999. *Text Worlds: Representing Conceptual Space in Discourse*. London: Longman.

White, Glyn. 2005. *Reading the Graphic Surface: The Presence of the Book in Prose Fiction*. Manchester: Manchester University Press.

Wildgust, Patrick. 2013. "The Emblem of My Work in Tristram Shandy." In *The Emblem of My Work*. London: Laurence Sterne Trust. https://www.laurencesternetrust.org.uk/exhibition.php?id=100.

Wilson, Andrew D. and Sabrina Golonka. 2013. "Embodied Cognition Is Not What You Think It Is." *Frontiers in Psychology* 4, no. 58: 1–13. https://doi.org/10.3389/fpsyg.2013.00058.

Wolf, Werner. 2006. "Introduction: Frames, Framings, and Framing Borders in Literature and Other Media." In *Framing Borders in Literature and Other Media*, edited by Werner Wolf and Walter Bernhart, 1–40. New York: Rodopi.

———. 2013. "Introduction: Aesthetic Illusion." In *Immersion and Distance: Aesthetic Illusion in Literature and Other Media*, edited by Werner Wolf, Walter Bernhart, and Andreas Mahler, 1–63. Amsterdam: Rodopi.

Yergeau, Melanie. 2013. "Clinically Significant Disturbance: On Theorists Who Theorize Theory of Mind." *Disability Studies Quarterly* 33, no. 4. https://dsq-sds.org/article/view/3876/3405.

Young, James E. 1990. *Writing and Rewriting the Holocaust: Narrative and the Consequences of Interpretation*. Bloomington: Indiana University Press.

———. 1993. *The Texture of Memory: Holocaust Memorials and Meaning*. New Haven: Yale University Press.

Zahavi, Dan. 2010. "A Distinction in Need of Refinement." In *The Embodied Self: Dimensions, Coherence, and Disorders*, edited by Thomas Fuchs, Heribert C. Sattel, and Peter Henningsen, 3–11. New York: Schattauer.

———. 2014. *Self and Other: Exploring Subjectivity, Empathy, and Shame*. Oxford: Oxford University Press.

Zahavi, Dan and Philippe Rochat. 2015. "Empathy≠Sharing: Perspectives from Phenomenology and Developmental Psychology." *Consciousness and Cognition* 36: 543–53.

Zelnick, Sharon. 2017. "Visual Resurrections: An Interview with Velibor Božović." *GUP Magazine*. July 20, 2017. https://gupmagazine.com/interview/visual-resurrections-an-interview-with-velibor-bozovic/.

Zilles, Karl. 1992. "Neuronal Plasticity as an Adaptive Property of the Central Nervous System." *Annals of Anatomy—Anatomischer Anzeiger* 174, no. 5: 383–91.

Zlatev, Jordan, Timothy P. Racine, Esa Itkonen, and Chris Sinha. 2008. *The Shared Mind: Perspectives on Intersubjectivity.* Amsterdam: John Benjamins Publishing.

Zunshine, Lisa. 2006. *Why We Read Fiction.* Columbus: The Ohio State University Press.

———. 2008. "Theory of Mind and Fictions of Embodied Transparency." *Narrative* 16, no. 1: 65–92.

Zwaan, Rolf A. 1993. *Aspects of Literary Comprehension.* Amsterdam: John Benjamins Publishing.

INDEX

Abbott, H. Porter, 19–20, 107, 196

Abrams, J. J., and Doug Dorst. See *S*.

abstract: and amodal, arbitrary representations or symbols (AAA), 15, 25, 29, 50–51, 59, 117, 170; concepts, 176; thinking and reasoning, 16, 21, 45, 48, 152, 189. *See also* abstraction; amodal

abstraction, 49–50, 54, 55–56, 117, 152

aesthetic: choice and possibilities, 37, 61; of cognitive mapping, 144; experience, 3, 17, 17n13, 20, 180, 192, 196; illusion, 130, 130n12, 139; multimodal, 7; norms, 84; and scientific and technological frameworks, 2, 68, 110, 195; treatment of thought or cognition, 2, 3, 4–5, 9, 10, 16, 20, 25, 105, 109, 146, 154, 181, 196

affect, 76, 92, 95, 102–3, 112, 121, 137, 147, 169, 178, 195

affordances: bodily or perceptual, 8, 124; of books, 128, 149; of mode, media, and technologies, 8, 31, 63, 93, 124, 152

Agamben, Giorgio, 147n2

Alber, Jan, 31

Aldama, Frederick Luis, 19

amnesia, 18, 26, 30n6, 46, 48, 51, 54, 119, 124, 146, 165, 168, 171, 177–79. *See also* forgetting; memory

amodal: definition of, 8; experience of language and literature, 8, 13, 21, 33, 34, 49, 171; representations or symbols, 10, 15, 25, 34, 39, 44, 51, 52, 62, 68, 70, 129. *See also* abstract; abstraction

anti-archival: mind, 22–23, 149; minds of readers, 186–95; and *Spiral Jetty*, 174. *See also* archive; forgetting; memory

archive, 3, 23, 80, 99, 166–67, 173–74, 184, 189, 194; as metaphor for or equivalent of memory, 22–23, 63, 145, 150–54, 155, 180. *See also* anti-archival; forgetting; memory

Aristotle, 1

Armstrong, Nancy, 75n12

art, 17, 73, 75n12, 82, 123, 147; digital, 108; frames in, 82, 89; transgenic, 93, 102. *See also* narrative; photography

artificial intelligence (AI), 14–16, 24, 27, 38, 61, 151–52, 171

Atkins, Kim, 71

attention, 6, 22, 108, 114, 126, 144, 183–87, 192; and contemporary cognitive science, 14, 185; economy, 9; sharing or triangulation, 75. *See also* cognition; memory; mind; perception

attribution, 35, 77, 78, 79, 86, 88

audience, 9, 36, 130n12, 143–44, 158, 178n14, 185

Austerlitz (Sebald), 84

autism, 21, 26, 28n4, 30, 32n7, 34–45, 35n13, 36n14, 152. *See also* Theory of Mind

Baron-Cohen, Simon, 34–36, 43, 77–78, 79 fig. 2.2; *Mindblindness,* 34, 59n24

Barsalou, Lawrence, 8, 10, 27, 50, 55, 117, 117n7, 189; and Leo Dutriaux, and Christoph Scheepers, 69, 177

Barthes, Roland, 66–67, 98n24

Bateman, John, 7

Bell, Charles, 83, 196

Bernstein, D. M., 153

binge read, 23, 183, 184, 189

bodies represented in narrative, 28–30, 38–39, 41, 45–46, 49, 56–58, 60, 70, 72, 84, 85, 95, 99, 102–4, 149, 160, 164, 167, 171–72, 177–78. *See also* embodiment; enactivist; perception

bodily response to art or narrative, 7, 8, 12, 17, 56n22, 103, 114, 117, 120, 123, 124, 129, 133, 134, 136. *See also* embodied cognition; embodiment; perception

Bogost, Ian, 9

Bolter, Jay David, 32

book: altered, 186–95; as archival technology, 23, 146–47, 149, 172, 174, 193; fiction and bookishness, 9, 186; materiality of, 49, 56, 60, 109, 113, 128, 192; as metaphor or metonymy, 149, 166–67, 176–77; as object and media, 6–9, 114, 120, 123, 126, 128, 130, 133–36, 139–42, 166, 184, 185, 194–95. *See also* archive; multimodality

The Book of Portraiture (Tomasula), 65–68, 70, 72–76, 79, 86–89, 92–97, 102–5; mindreading in, 86–89; pictorial modeling of subjectivity in, 65–66, 67–68; predictive processing in, 92–97, 96 fig. 2.4; self-representation in, 68, 72–76, 74 fig. 2.1, 88, 93–94; sensorimotor entanglements in, 102–4; sociality of self in, 68, 70, 72–76, 78–79, 94–97, 102–4, 160

bookwork, 189

Borges, Jorge Luis. *See* "Funes, the Memorious"

Bortolussi, Marisa, 192

Božović, Velibor, 71, 72, 99, 100

Brillenburg Wurth, Kiene, 9, 156, 160, 188, 189

Brockmeier, Jens, 153, 168

Bruner, Jerome, 71

Burke, Michael, 189

Butt, Nadia, 111–12, 121, 144

Cadava, Eduardo, 66n6

Calvino, Italo. See *Invisible Cities*

Caquard, Sébastien, 115–16

Caracciolo, Marco, 3–4, 19, 30, 41, 43, 56n22, 71, 79, 118, 122, 129, 176, 189

Caravà, Marta, 169

Carter, James Bucky, 30, 35, 37

Cartesian Theater, 38, 52. *See also* computationalism and computational theory of mind

cartography, 107, 112, 115–16, 127, 143. *See also* map

causal flow. *See* flow

causal pluralism, 68n7

Chalmers, David, 64, 76, 79n16

Chemero, Anthony, 16, 44, 50, 59n24

Chevaillier, Flore, 66, 88, 104

Ciccoricco, David, 5, 14n10, 20, 27, 108, 154n5

Clark, Andy, 16, 27, 44, 44n15, 45, 59, 64, 69–70, 76, 79, 82, 90n22, 95, 117, 120

Clark, Timothy, 176

Clemmons, Zinzi, 76

climate change, 146, 173, 176–81

cognition: on aesthetic treatments of, 1–5, 10, 16, 20, 25, 181, 196; social, 14, 21, 77, 88, 97; spatial, 18, 22, 108, 110, 111, 114–18, 122–23, 142. *See also* cognitive science; computationalism and computational theory of mind; consciousness; disability; embodied cognition; enactivist; memory; mind

cognitive literary criticism, 1–5, 18–20, 27, 30, 77–79, 79n16, 192–93, 195–96. *See also* cognitive narrative theory/narratology

cognitive map. *See* map

cognitive narrative theory/narratology, 3–5, 3n1, 19–20, 30, 82n19, 117–18. *See also* cognitive literary criticism

cognitive penetrability, 85

cognitive poetics, 12

cognitive schemata/schema, 3, 4, 34, 64

cognitive science, 14–18, 19, 32n9, 68–70, 76–79, 82, 114–17, 145, 150–54, 180, 185, 185n3, 192–93, 196; distinction between first- and second-generation, 14–16, 24–26, 27–28, 32–33, 39, 43–45, 55, 58–59, 59n24, 68–69, 89, 117–18, 126, 146, 148, 153. *See also* embodied cognition; enactivist; extended mind; Theory of Mind

cognitivist, 15, 32, 82, 89, 115, 151

Cohn, Dorrit, 3, 19; "Metalepsis and Mise en Abyme," 52, 52n20; *Transparent Minds*, 18, 53, 61

Cole, Teju, 75, 110, 144; *Blind Spot*, 106, 108

collage, 149, 155–58, 161–62, 166

comics. *See* graphic novel

computationalism and computational theory of mind, 1, 15–17, 18, 24–29, 33–35, 34n11, 38–39, 43–45, 44n15, 50–51, 56–57, 59, 62–63, 67, 82, 84, 116, 151–52, 165, 170n11, 171, 196. *See also* artificial intelligence; computers and the human mind

computers and the human mind, 17, 24–28, 31–34, 38–40, 61–63, 112, 150–51. *See also* artificial intelligence; computationalism and computational theory of mind

connectionism, 44n15

consciousness: atypical, 31–32; representation of, 3–5, 19, 22, 26, 60, 61–63, 93, 109, 172; theoretical positions on, 1, 15, 35, 44, 50, 64, 66, 66n6. *See also* cognition; memory; mind; perception

Cosmides, Leda, 34, 59n24

criminology, 70, 83–84, 87

Crucifix, Benoît, 149

Cuddy-Keane, Melba, 79n15

The Curious Incident of the Dog in the Nighttime (Haddon), 25–46, 61–63; computationalism in, 26, 28, 34–35, 43–44, 45, 170; and computer screen, 38–39, 67; literary criticism on, 30, 32n7, 35, 36n14, 41; mapping in, 110–12, 113; mind-body dualism in, 28–29, 38–39, 42–45; multimodality and typography in, 28–29, 40–45; treatment of autism and disability in, 30, 34–40, 43–45, 152

cybernetics, 14, 24

Danielewski, Mark Z.: *The Familiar*, 31; *House of Leaves*, 7–8, 31, 131n13; *Only Revolutions*, 8, 167

Darwin, Charles, 53n21, 83, 83n20, 87, 196

De Jaegher, Hanne, 45

deixis, 109, 123, 129–30, 129n11, 130n12, 133, 136–37

Dennett, Daniel, 38, 52

Dick, Philip K., 151

Didi-Huberman, Georges, 83

digital (electronic): fiction, 154n5; literature, 9, 20, 108, 131, 195

digital illustration, 130; images and photographs, 67, 72, 73, 74 fig. 2.1, 93. *See also* photography; selfie

digital map and cartography, 109, 111–12, 114, 122, 142–43

digital media ecology, 14, 30n6, 32, 39, 60, 62, 68, 94, 97, 108, 108n2, 142, 184. *See also* computationalism and computational theory of mind; computers and the human mind

digital platform and technologies, 7–8, 9, 10, 14, 33, 40, 61, 63, 109

disability, 36n14, 37, 45. *See also* amnesia; autism; forgetting; memory

disability studies, 30

discourse (narrative), 12, 17, 28, 54, 75n12, 95, 102, 111, 155, 159, 188

Dixon, Peter, 192

Draaisma, Douwe, 1, 66, 148, 150

Driscoll, Kári, 8, 9

Drucker, Johanna, 31

Edelman, Gerald, 15

embodied cognition, 15, 15n12, 34n11, 44–45, 49–50, 61, 69–70, 78, 89, 98n23, 114–18, 120, 121, 129, 133, 150–53, 150n4, 169, 180. *See also* cognition; enactivist; extended mind

embodiment, 98–99, 102–4, 114; and computationalism, 25–26, 38–39, 44, 60; and memory, 147, 148–49, 150–51, 156, 164–65,

167, 171, 176, 181, 189, 193; and reading, 34, 79, 113, 122, 139, 143. *See also* bodies represented in narrative; bodily response to art or narrative

emotion, 17, 20, 36, 76, 77, 78, 90, 99, 103, 134, 137, 158, 163, 169, 171, 176, 184, 196

empathy, 17, 21, 26, 36n14, 40, 41, 87, 98, 98n23

enacting, 75, 75n11, 98, 102, 104–5, 117n7, 118, 149, 163, 168, 171

enactivist: approach to cognition, 16, 17, 45, 50, 69–70, 76–77, 78n14, 79 fig. 2.2, 97, 121, 150n4, 152, 153, 169, 180; approach to narrative, 4, 19, 56n22, 79. *See also* cognition

Erll, Astrid, 184

eugenics, 84

evolutionary theories, 86

exceptionality thesis, 61–62

experientiality, 3, 19, 56, 56n22, 66, 79, 106, 120, 158n6, 193

explanatory pluralism, 18, 26–28, 27n3, 45, 46–50, 59, 63, 65, 79, 145

extended mind, 16–17, 27, 64, 64n1, 76, 79, 90n22, 93, 95, 117, 120, 144, 180

Facebook, 155. *See also* social media

Fauconnier, Gilles, 116–17, 143

Faulkner, William, 32n8

fictional minds. *See* mind

fictional/fictionalized readers, 112, 118, 119, 120, 123, 124, 126, 128, 129, 138, 184

fictional space, 113, 118

Fjellestad, Danuta, 66, 75

Flaubert, Gustave, 139

flow: causal, 69, 73, 79 fig. 2.2, 89–90, 92–93; of information, 34, 40, 94–95; of prediction, 69, 89, 93. *See also* predictive processing

Fludernik, Monika, 3, 3n1, 19, 54–55, 56n22, 158n6

focalization, 160; hypothetical, 161

Fodor, Jerry A., 1, 15, 25, 33, 34, 39, 44n15

Foer, Jonathan Safran, 193, 194; *Everything Is Illuminated*, 146, 193; *Extremely Loud and Incredibly Close*, 31, 37–38, 187, 193; *Tree of Codes*, 8, 185, 186–95, 186n4

folk psychology, 77. *See also* Theory of Mind

Forceville, Charles, 11–12

forgetting, 48, 145–81, 146n1, 183–84, 187, 189; enactive approach to, 169. *See also* amnesia; anti-archival; archive; memory

Fowler, Roger, 42

frame: cognitive, 82, 82n19, 85, 87–89, 117, 176; pictorial and representational, 66, 73, 80–82, 89, 97, 100, 104, 139

Frank, Joseph, 110, 139

Freud, Sigmund, 66n6, 86, 154, 154n5, 187

Fuller, Matthew, 14n10

"Funes, the Memorious" (Borges), 152–53, 154, 188

Gallup, G. G., 67

Gardner, Jared, 146

Garry, Maryanne, 154, 162, 163, 164

Gavins, Joanna, 117

Genette, Gérard, 159, 187

Gerrig, Richard, 117

Ghosh, Amitav, 176

Gibbons, Alison, 12–13, 25, 31, 42, 129, 156, 160, 172, 178n15

Gibbs, Raymond W., 117, 133

Glenberg, Arthur M., 17

Goldman, Alvin, 78

Golonka, Sabrina, 44, 50

González, Christopher, 3n1

Graesser, Arthur C., 17

graphic novel, 12, 146

Gudmundsdottir, Gunnthorunn, 177

Gumbrecht, Hans U., 123, 130, 139

Haddon, Mark. *See The Curious Incident of the Dog in the Nighttime*

Hall, Steven, *See The Raw Shark Texts*

Hallet, Wolfgang, 12

Hansen, Mark B., 150

Harnad, Stevan, 14, 14n11, 34n11

Hayles, N. Katherine, 5, 20, 27, 30, 33, 49, 56, 66, 104, 187, 192

Heise, Ursula, 173, 176

Hemon, Aleksandar. See *The Lazarus Project*

Herbert, Caroline, 122

Herman, David, 4, 4n2, 4n3, 19, 169; on deixis, 129n11; on fictional and actual minds, 61–62; on focalization, 161; on storyworld, 3, 117
hippocampus, 115
Hitchcock, Alfred, 165
homunculus, 38–39
Hustvedt, Siri, 106
Hutchins, Edwin, 59
Hutto, Daniel D., 77, 97, 153

Iacoboni, Marco, 17n13
imagination, 29, 39, 49–50, 54, 153, 154, 156, 177, 178, 193; inflation effect, 162–66
immersion, 56, 130n12, 144, 169; spatial, 122–28
immigrant, 21, 70, 83, 86, 90, 105
intention, 34, 36, 37, 65, 73, 77, 88, 97, 100, 102
interactivity, 9, 120, 185
intersubjectivity, 17. *See also* subjectivity
Invisible Cities (Calvino), 142

Jahn, Manfred, 82n19
James, William, 15, 50–51, 58, 150–51, 150n4
Jameson, Fredric, 110, 144
Jani, Pranav, 112n3
Johnson, Mark, 11–12, 27, 117
Jung, Carl, 77

Kartography (Shamsie), 111–12, 121–23, 126–28, 134–38, 142–44; attitude to mapping in, 111–12, 113–14, 121–22, 138, 142–43; cognitive and artifactual map in, 109, 118, 135 fig. 3.3, 138, 140–41 fig. 3.4, 142–43; deixis in, 134–37; handwriting in, 134–36, 135 fig. 3.3; as postcolonial text, 122, 138, 143–44; spatial immersion in, 126–28; structure of, 109, 115, 121–23
Kellner, Tatana, 147, 164
Keskinen, Mikko, 160
Kim, Sue J., 20, 196
Kittler, Friedrich A., 24
Klein, Stanley B., 153
Kosslyn, Stephen, 67
Kress, Gunther R., 10–12, 11n9

Kukkonen, Karin, 19, 79

Labov, William, 123, 124n9
Lacan, Jacques, 66–67
Lakoff, George, 11–12, 16, 27, 116–17
language comprehension, 16, 21, 29, 34n11, 49, 55; literary vs. other situations, 192–93
Larsen, Reif, 110, 111
The Lazarus Project (Hemon), 65–68, 70–72, 75–86, 87, 89–92, 97–102, 104–5; and Bruno Schulz, 186n5; mindreading in, 80–86; photography in, 67, 71, 75, 80–84, 81 fig. 2.3, 86, 92, 98, 99–102, 101 fig. 2.5; pictorial modeling of subjectivity in, 65–66; predictive processing in, 89–92; self-representation in, 71–72, 90, 99, 184; sensorimotor entanglements in, 97–102; sociality of self in, 68, 70–71, 75–76, 78–79, 90–92, 97–102, 160; spatial thinking in, 111
Lejeune, Philippe, 168
Levi-Strauss, Claude, 178
Linde, Charlotte. 123, 124n9
literary studies and the sciences, 1–5, 195–96. *See also* cognitive literary criticism; cognitive narrative theory/narratology
Ljungberg, Christina, 110
Loftus, Elizabeth, 153–54, 162, 163, 164, 168, 179
Lombroso, Cesare, 83, 88
Lynch, Kevin A., 115–16

Mäkelä, Maria, 3n1, 4, 18
map, 5, 63, 108, 113; artifactual, 40, 109, 110, 111, 123, 124–26, 128, 129, 134–37, 167; cognitive/mental, 109, 112, 114–18, 124, 127, 129, 134, 137, 138; interactive, 112, 122, 142; mapping as action or strategy, 60, 107, 111–12, 120–22, 134, 138, 143; as metaphor, 113, 117, 126, 143; overlay, 108–10, 137–44
Marks, Laura, 164
McCarthy, Tom, 51
McCulloch, Warren S., 15, 15n12
McHale, Brian, 4, 31, 50
media, 1, 5, 8–9, 11, 194; culture, 146, 185. *See also* digital media ecology; digital platform and technologies; social media

memory, 1–2, 6, 14, 29, 50, 59, 84, 92, 111, 138, 145–49; boom, 148; loss of, 26, 30, 51, 54; as process, 153–54; semantic, 150, 192; storage and retrieval model of, 18, 30n6, 150–53, 154. *See also* archive; cognition; forgetting

mental map. *See* map

mental simulation, 10, 45, 78

metacognition, 9, 65, 69, 75, 185, 192, 195

metafiction, 45, 75, 112, 158n6. *See also* self-reflexive narratives

metalepsis, 29, 31, 52–53, 52n19, 52n20, 55–56

metaphors, 1, 2, 16, 37, 61, 66, 67, 84, 113, 116–17, 126, 143, 145, 146, 177; conceptual, 117; and multimodality, 11–12, 42, 43; structural or organizing, 8, 108. *See also* archive; computers and the human mind; map; photography

metonymy, 176

Metzinger, Thomas, 64n3

Mihăilescu, Dana, 66

Miłkowski, Marcin, 59

mind, 1–2, 8–9, 12, 13, 14–18; fictional, 3, 16, 18, 19–20, 23, 28, 61–62, 184; of readers, 3, 6, 23, 183, 187; social, 77–79; shared, 76–77, 79n16. *See also* cognition; computers and the human mind; consciousness; exceptionality thesis; extended mind; Theory of Mind

mindreader, 34–35, 79 fig. 2.2. *See also* mindreading

mindreading, 22, 34, 35, 37, 78, 80–89, 97

mindscreen, 38–39, 41, 44, 50

mindstyle, 37, 40–43, 121

Minsky, Marvin, 82, 82n19

mirror neuron, 17, 17n13, 77–78

Mitchell, William J. T., 66, 150

mode (semiotic), 1–2, 5, 8, 13, 20, 21, 23, 25, 28, 45, 56, 109, 113, 122, 123, 183, 184, 189. *See also* multimodality

Montfort, Nick, 9

multimodality: of literature, 5–10, 11, 12–13, 17, 25, 40, 52, 65, 84, 110, 113–14, 118, 136, 145, 146, 155, 185–86, 193, 196; of mental simulation, 10; of mindstyle, 42; studies and theories of, 10–13, 16, 30

Murray, Stuart, 26, 30, 36n14

Nadel, Lynn, 115

Nagel, Thomas, 35, 137

narrative: account of memory, 153; mimetic, thematic, synthetic components of, 30–31, 158, 158n6, 163; self, 71–73, 90, 99, 121–22, 126–27, 146, 149, 159, 168, 184; unnatural, 31. *See also* cognitive narrative theory/narratology; experientiality; focalization; perspective; storyworld; temporality; voice

narrative theory. *See* cognitive narrative theory/narratology

neural mechanisms, 17, 50, 79 fig. 2.2, 115, 116

neural net, 37, 166

neurocognitive alterations, 14. *See also* plasticity

neuroscience, 27, 65, 152; computational, 70. *See also* cognitive science; mirror neuron

Nietzsche, Friedrich, 24

Nora, Pierre, 148

Nørby, Simon, 179

Nørgaard, Nina, 13, 42, 130

Nünning, Ansgar, 184

O'Keefe, John, 115, 116

Olsen, Lance: on innovative writing, 166; *there's no place like time*, 167n9, 171n12, 172, 172n13. *See also Theories of Forgetting*

Page, Ruth E., 12–13

Palmer, Alan, 19, 77, 79, 79n16

pandemic. *See Theories of Forgetting*

Peirce, Charles S., 11n9

perception: aesthetic treatments of, 2, 21, 28, 41, 43, 45, 49–50, 54–56, 62, 84, 89–97, 152; and phenomenology, 164; and reading, 29, 117, 184; in theories of cognition, 15–17, 25–26, 35, 38–39, 44, 50–51, 66–67, 69, 107, 117n7, 151, 169

perspective: in cognitive science, 17, 45, 65; narrative, 41, 75, 76, 85, 102, 127, 129, 137–38, 159, 161, 168

Phelan, James, 31, 156–58, 158n6

photography, 66–68, 66n6, 72, 75, 75n12, 80, 83–84, 86, 92, 93, 100; language of, 66;

neuropsychiatric, 83, 87, 105. *See also* selfie

picnolepsy, 23, 182–83, 182n1, 184

Pier, John, 52n19

Pinker, Steven, 38, 39, 44n15, 67

Piper, Andrew, 131

Pitts, Walter H., 15

plasticity, 12, 14, 23, 154

Plato, 51, 150

point of view, 124, 130, 137, 161. *See also* focalization; perspective

possible mind, 18

possible world, 18, 29, 29n5, 49, 58, 112

postcolonial, 122, 143–44

posthuman, 30, 66

postmodern, 30, 30n6, 49–50, 144

Poulet, Georges, 6

predictive processing, 44n15, 69–70, 76, 78, 79 fig. 2.2, 79, 82, 89, 97. *See also* flow

Pressman, Jessica, 9, 57

pronoun, 36, 93, 94–95, 130, 168–70

psychoanalysis, 86

psychology. *See* cognitive science

Quian Quiroga, Rodrigo, 152

The Raw Shark Texts (Hall), 45–63; audio book and ebook of, 8; and binge reading, 183; computationalism and mind-body dualism in, 52, 56–61; and computer virus, 58–59; distinction between thought and things in, 50–56; explanatory pluralism in, 26, 48–50, 62–63, 196; and possible worlds, 29–30; and postmodernism, 30–31; and typography, 28, 32, 34, 46, 47 fig. 1.2, 53–56, 58; memory loss in, 26, 51, 146; as metafiction, 45–46, 49, 156; metalepsis and mise-en-abyme in, 29, 31, 52–53, 52n20, 55; nostalgia in, 29, 114; and Rorschach test, 46–48

Rawle, Graham. *See Woman's World*

reader's body. *See* bodily response to art or narrative

reader's mind. *See* mind

repression, 88, 154, 154n5

Rescher, Nicholas, 29

Richardson, Alan, 83

Richardson, Brian, 89

Rochat, Philippe, 97–98, 121

Rosch, Eleanor, 16, 44, 70, 75n11

Rowlands, Mark, 16, 27, 59n24

Ryan, Marie-Laure, 5, 9, 9n8, 20, 29, 29n5; on deixis, 129; on maps and mapping, 113, 118, 137; spatial immersion, 122, 123–24

S. (Abrams and Dorst), 118–21, 122–23, 124–26, 128–34, 137–42, 143–44; artifactual and cognitive maps in, 109, 111, 125 fig. 3.1, 136, 137–39, 142, 143–44; deixis in, 129–30, 133–34; handwriting and marginalia in, 128–34, 131n13, 132 fig. 3.2; reading as mapping in, 112–13, 118, 126; spatial immersion in, 124–26; structure of, 109, 118–21

saccades, 39, 126; definition of, 126n10

Sacks, Oliver, 35

Savarese, Ralph, 30, 36n14

scale, 174–80

Schacter, Daniel L., 151–52, 162, 163, 179

Schulz, Bruno, 186–87, 186n5, 189, 192, 193–95

Searle, John R., 15, 39, 170n11

Sebald, W. G. *See Austerlitz*

self-expression, 87, 154, 155

selfie, 65, 67, 68, 73, 75, 88, 95, 104, 105, 106, 108n2. *See also* photography; self-representation; subjectivity

selfieing, 65, 66, 71, 72, 79, 91, 93, 104. *See also* self-representation; subjectivity

self-narrative. *See* narrative

self-reflexive narratives, 8, 9, 49, 108, 120, 149, 186, 189. *See also* metafiction

self-representation, 18, 21–22, 65, 68, 69; technologies of, 72, 94

semantic: content, 7, 29, 40, 42, 172; memory, 150, 153, 177, 192; networking, 107, 114, 116–18, 124, 129, 138, 143; space, 107, 113, 127

Semino, Elena, 30, 32n7, 35, 117

semiosis, 12, 13

semiotic: channels, 161; systems or resources, 8, 9, 10–13, 23, 50, 93. *See also* mode sensorimotor mechanisms, 25, 34, 34n11, 70, 72, 75, 78, 79 fig. 2.2, 117, 120, 139, 169. *See also* perception

Serpell, C. Namwali, 195

Seth, Anil, 65, 69, 71, 72, 82

Shamsie, Kamila: *Home Fire,* 112n4. See also *Kartography*

share (on social media), 65, 68, 75

shared mind. *See* mind

shared subjectivity. *See* intersubjectivity; subjectivity

Siegel, Susanna, 85

Silverman, Gillian, 7n6, 28n4

simulation. *See* mental simulation

Smith, Zadie, 51

Smithson, Robert, 149, 166, 167, 174–78, 180

social cognition. *See* cognition

social media, 14, 68, 108n2, 112n4, 155. *See also* selfie; selfieing

spatial cognition. *See* cognition

Sperber, Dan, 34

Spiral Jetty. *See* Smithson; *Theories of Forgetting*

Starre, Alexander, 9, 186, 193

Sterne, Laurence. See *Tristram Shandy*

Stewart, Garrett, 189

Stiegler, Bernard, 150–51

Stingelin, Martin, 24

storyworld, 3, 12, 22, 45, 56, 107, 122–26, 185; David Herman's definition of, 117; and deixis, 129–30, 129n11, 138

structuralism, 3, 82n19

subjectivity: aesthetic treatment of, 13, 18, 21–22, 48, 57, 65, 68, 70, 73, 142, 149, 159–60, 162; constituting, 50, 68, 72, 104–5, 108, 119, 120; pictorial modeling of, 21, 66–67, 66n5, 76; scientific and philosophical accounts of, 22, 64–65, 64n2, 71, 76–78, 83; shared, 76, 160. *See also* intersubjectivity; narrative; selfieing; self-representation

temporality: of narratives, 107, 110, 122, 137, 139, 174; of reading, 129n11, 131, 134

Theories of Forgetting (Olsen), 145–49, 154, 166–81, 187; archive and archival metaphor for memory in, 146–49, 154, 166–67, 172, 173–74, 180–81; audiobook and ebook of, 8; and book as archive, 149, 166–67, 176; climate change and problem of scale, 173–80; collage and scrapbooking in, 149, 167, 175 fig. 4.2, 177–78, 179 fig. 4.3; explanatory pluralism in, 171, 196; forgetting in, 146–49, 167–74, 176–80; marginalia in, 149, 171, 172–73, 184; pandemic in, 149, 167, 169, 171–72, 177, 181, 187; self-representation in, 75–76, 168–73; and *Spiral Jetty,* 149, 166–67, 174–78, 175 fig. 4.2

Theory of Mind, 22, 34–36, 35n13, 77–79, 79 fig. 2.2, 79n16, 83, 97, 196. *See also* computationalism and computational theory of mind; folk psychology

Thompson, Evan, 16, 45, 50, 70, 75n11

Tolman, Edward, 114, 115, 116

Tomasula, Steve. See *The Book of Portraiture*

Tooby, John, 34, 59n24

tour (style of narration), 109, 119, 126, 127, 128; definition of, 123–24; reader's enactment of, 129, 139

transparency: mental, 3; of photographs, 84

Transparent Minds (Cohn). *See* Cohn

Tree of Codes (Foer). *See* Foer

Tristram Shandy (Sterne), 6–7; 6n5

Turing, Alan, 1, 14–15, 14n11, 25, 32, 170n11. *See also* Turing test

Turing test, 25, 57, 170

Turner, Mark, 117, 124

Tye, Michael, 67

typography, 6–7, 13, 130; for consciousness representation, 5, 21, 31–34; and *Curious Incident,* 28–29, 40–43; and *Lazarus Project,* 86; and *Raw Shark Texts,* 29, 53–55; and reading, 21, 29, 62, 192–93

unconscious: the collective, 77

universals, 2–3, 3n1, 196

van Leeuwen, Theo, 10–12

Varela, Francisco J., 16, 44, 50, 70, 75n11

Vargha-Khadem, Faraneh, 150

Vega, Manuel, 17

Venkatesh Ghosh, Shoba, 66

Virilio, Paul, 182–83, 182n1

virtual: communities, 112; environments, 9, 185; movement: 110; world: 194

Visual Editions, 7, 194

voice, 53, 149, 156–62, 161n8, 163–64, 165, 166

von Neumann, John, 15

Warde, Beatrice, 6–7

weather, 177. *See also* climate change

Weiner, Sonia, 66, 99

Wildfeuer, Janina, 7

Wilson, Andrew, 44, 50

Wolf, Werner, 82, 130n12

Woman's World (Rawle), 145–49, 154, 155–66, 180–81; archive and archival metaphor for memory in, 146–49, 154–55, 180–81; collage and scrapbooking in, 155–63; imagination inflation in, 162–66; self-representation in, 146, 155, 184; treatment of forgetting in, 146–49, 154, 162, 165–66

Woolf, Virginia, 35n12, 75n12, 110; *Mrs. Dalloway*, 110; *To the Lighthouse*, 51

Yergeau, Melanie, 35–36

Young, James E., 147n3

Zahavi, Dan, 64n3, 65, 70, 70n8, 71, 97–98, 98n23, 121

Zlatev, Jordan, 76–77, 79n16

Zunshine, Lisa, 3, 19, 30, 32n7, 35, 35n13, 43, 77

Zwaan, Rolf A., 192

COGNITIVE APPROACHES TO CULTURE
FREDERICK LUIS ALDAMA, PATRICK COLM HOGAN, LALITA PANDIT HOGAN,
AND SUE J. KIM, SERIES EDITORS

This series takes up cutting edge research in a broad range of cognitive sciences insofar as this research bears on and illuminates cultural phenomena such as literature, film, drama, music, dance, visual art, digital media, and comics, among others. For the purpose of the series, "cognitive science" is construed broadly to encompass work derived from cognitive and social psychology, neuroscience, cognitive and generative linguistics, affective science, and related areas in anthropology, philosophy, computer science, and elsewhere. Though open to all forms of cognitive analysis, the series is particularly interested in works that explore the social and political consequences of cognitive cultural study.

Out of Mind: Mode, Mediation, and Cognition in Twenty-First-Century Narrative
    TORSA GHOSAL

Romanticism's Other Minds: Poetry, Cognition, and the Science of Sociability
    JOHN SAVARESE

Eternalized Fragments: Reclaiming Aesthetics in Contemporary World Fiction
    W. MICHELLE WANG

Capturing Mariposas: Reading Cultural Schema in Gay Chicano Literature
    DOUG P. BUSH

Necessary Nonsense: Aesthetics, History, Neurology, Psychology
    IRVING MASSEY

Shaming into Brown: Somatic Transactions of Race in Latina/o Literature
    STEPHANIE FETTA

Resilient Memories: Amerindian Cognitive Schemas in Latin American Art
    ARIJ OUWENEEL

Permissible Narratives: The Promise of Latino/a Literature
    CHRISTOPHER GONZÁLEZ

Literatures of Liberation: Non-European Universalisms and Democratic Progress
    MUKTI LAKHI MANGHARAM

Affective Ecologies: Empathy, Emotion, and Environmental Narrative
    ALEXA WEIK VON MOSSNER

A Passion for Specificity: Confronting Inner Experience in Literature and Science
    MARCO CARACCIOLO AND RUSSELL T. HURLBURT